MID-AMERICAN
★ FRONTIER ★

This is a volume in the Arno Press collection

MID-AMERICAN
★ FRONTIER ★

Advisory Editor
Jerome O. Steffen

Editorial Board
Richard S. Brownlee
William W. Savage, Jr.

*See last pages of this volume
for a complete list of titles*

A

GUIDE FOR EMIGRANTS

J[ohn] M[ason] Peck

ARNO PRESS
A New York Times Company
New York – 1975

Editorial Supervision: ANDREA HICKS

———◆———

Reprint Edition 1975 by Arno Press Inc.

Reprinted from a copy in The State
 Historical Society of Wisconsin Library

THE MID-AMERICAN FRONTIER
ISBN for complete set: 0-405-06845-X
See last pages of this volume for titles.

Manufactured in the United States of America

Publisher's Note: The foldout map facing
title page has been deleted in this edition.

———◆———

Library of Congress Cataloging in Publication Data

Peck, John Mason, 1789-1858.
 A guide for emigrants.

 (The Mid-American frontier)
 Reprint of the ed. published by Lincoln and Ed-
mands, Boston.
 1. Mississippi Valley--Description and travel--
Guide-books. 2. Northwest, Old--Description and
travel--Guide-books. I. Title. II. Series.
F353.P36 1975   917.7'04'2   75-115
ISBN 0-405-06881-6

A

GUIDE FOR EMIGRANTS,

CONTAINING

SKETCHES

OF

ILLINOIS, MISSOURI,

AND THE ADJACENT PARTS.

BY J. M. PECK,
OF ROCK-SPRING, ILLINOIS.

𝕭𝖔𝖘𝖙𝖔𝖓:
LINCOLN AND EDMANDS.
1831.

DISTRICT OF MASSACHUSETTS, *to wit:*
District Clerk's Office.

BE IT REMEMBERED, That on the twenty-seventh of May, A. D. 1831, Lincoln & Edmands, of the said District, have deposited in this Office the title of a book, the title of which is, in the words following, *to wit:*

"A Guide for Emigrants, containing Sketches of Illinois, Missouri, and the adjacent Parts. By J. M. Peck, of Rock-Spring, Illinois."

The right whereof they claim as Proprietors, in conformity with an act of Congress, entitled, "An act to amend the several acts respecting copy-rights."

JNO. W. DAVIS, *Clerk of the District.*

INTRODUCTION.

Much has been published already about the far-famed West. The Valley of the Mississippi is now known in the annals of the historian, the compilation of the geographer, the sketches of the traveller, and the song of the poet.

No portion of this Valley is so much the subject of inquiry, and excites so particularly the attention of the emigrant, as the States of Indiana, Illinois, Missouri, and the parts adjacent.

Although these new States have come into existence within the last fifteen years, they have been unparalleled in their growth, both in their increase of population, and increase of property: but none have equalled in progress, that of Illinois, within the last five years. This will be seen by a comparison of the census taken in 1825, and in 1830, under the authority of the State government. In 1825, Illinois contained less than 75,000 inhabitants. In September, 1830, they exceeded 161,000.

Introduction.

In 1824, Missouri numbered a fraction over 80,000; in 1828, 112,000; and in June, 1830, 140,000.

Indiana, in 1820, numbered 147,000; in 1830, 341,582.

The population of Arkansas in 1820, was 14,273; in 1830, it amounted to 30,608.

These facts give an importance to these States, not hitherto appreciated; and the following pages will show that, under all the disadvantages we have been placed, the advancement in business and improvements has been equal to the increase of population. The statistics of the counties given in this work, will show that this region of country will continue to advance in the production of property, equal to its progress in numbers.

Amongst the causes which have awakened the attention of the community to these States, and which have enlisted the feelings of the people to emigrate, beyond any former parallel, the following resolution of the American Sunday School Union has had the most extensive influence.

"*Resolved, That the American Sunday School Union, in reliance upon Divine aid, will, within two years, establish Sunday Schools in every destitute place where it is practicable, throughout the Valley of the Mississippi.*"

It was early understood that one of the most serious obstacles to this benevolent project would be found in the want of a supply of superintendents, and teachers, who, from their knowledge and experience in the management of Sunday Schools, are competent to carry the resolution into complete effect. The result has been, that hundreds of families have had their

Introduction. 5

minds directed to these States as a permanent home, with the benevolent intention of aiding in this, and other works of philanthropy. Multitudes of virtuous and industrious emigrants would fix their future residence on our prairies, cultivate our wild lands, aid in building up our towns and cities, and diffuse a healthful, moral and intellectual influence through the mass of our present population, could they feel assured that they can get to the country without great expense and risk, provide for their families to a reasonable extent, and not be swept off by sickness, or overwhelmed by suffering, beyond what is to be expected in a new country.

Within a few months past, the author has received more than one hundred letters, calling for information in detail, on all those subjects about which a man wishes to inform himself before he decides upon a removal, or which may aid him on his journey, and which may enable him successfully to surmount the difficulties of an untried land.

To answer these was impossible. The only feasible method to afford general satisfaction was to write a BOOK. Many valuable works on the western country, or portions of it, have been made already, but none that seemed exactly suited to the present state of things. Besides, what was truth eight or ten years since, is no longer truth. Wide and rapid changes have been made. Extensive tracts of country have been sprinkled over with a population, formed into counties, and begin to show marks of industry and enterprise, which, ten years since, were the hunting grounds of the savage, or only occasionally visited by the white trapper or hunter. What was then frontier,

Introduction.

is now thrown into the middle of States and Territories.

The author is sensible that many imperfections must exist in this work, yet, for the purpose intended, it is believed to be sufficiently accurate.

Of one fact the reader must be apprized. It is impossible to convey entirely correct ideas of this region to one who has never travelled beyond the borders of his native State. The laws and habits of associating ideas in the human mind forbid it. A man raised on the banks of the Hudson, or the Connecticut river, upon first thought, does not conceive of the magnitude of a river four thousand miles in length. He who has been accustomed to associate in his mind the idea of a State with a tract of country seventy miles long and fifty broad, at the first thought, will not form the image of a State of three or four hundred miles in extent. A farmer of Massachusetts associates with the idea of a farm, a number of fields, consisting of meadow, ploughland, woodland, and pasturage, with all the necessary buildings and apparatus for farming. When he thinks of purchasing a farm in Illinois, he forms the same images in his mind. He cannot imagine a farm to consist of one field, of immense extent, and that wholly turned up by the plough, as is the case with many farms in Illinois. Thus it is in relation to almost every subject upon which I have written. Hence statements that are measurably accurate to an inhabitant of Illinois, sometimes convey wrong ideas to a New-Englander. Every thing is contemplated by comparison. The author recollects of travelling in an obscure and sickly place in Missouri, and calling on a family that had emigrated, some time previously, from the low country of South Carolina. Perceiving that nearly all the family were laboring under a paroxysm of the fever and ague, he inquired if they were satisfied with the country, and were not disheartened with sickness. The reply was, " Oh, no ; it is a very healthy country." But are not your family now sick? " No, they have only a little brush of the ague." An emigrant family from the mountainous parts of New-England, would have associated the ideas of sickness and death, in every passing breeze, where this family then lived.

How far the author has succeeded in conveying his ideas so as to produce correct impressions on distant readers, remains to be tested.

The author has derived aid from the labors of Beck, Flint, Darby, Schoolcraft, Atwater, and perhaps some others, from which he has made occasional extracts. His principal sources of information are, his personal observations—having travelled over most of the settled parts of Missouri and Illinois, and a portion of Indiana—together with the aid furnished by intelligent gentlemen residing in various parts of these States. He has availed himself of sketches published in several periodicals. Several valuable papers will be found in the work. The one on the capabilities of Illinois for internal navigation, is the production of Edward Coles, Esq. formerly governor of the State, and contains a valuable body of information on that subject.

He will only add that he has no other interest in inviting emigrants to the West, than that which is common to every wellwisher of his species. Having no connection with the business of land speculation, or town sites, which, without intentional misrepresentation, is apt to color and distort facts, he has aimed to give a plain and unvarnished statement of things.

THE AUTHOR.

Rock-Spring, (Ill.) April 1, 1831.

PART FIRST.

GENERAL, GEOGRAPHICAL AND STATISTICAL VIEW OF THE VALLEY OF THE MISSISSIPPI.

SECTION I.

Boundaries, Extent, Population, Physical Features, &c.

THE Valley of the Mississippi, in its utmost extent, embraces all that tract of country, of which the waters are discharged into the gulf of Mexico, by the "Father of Waters," of which the aboriginal name is Mississippi. The ancient sound and spelling, in French, appears to have been *Meate-Chassippi*.

BOUNDARIES.

IT is bounded on the north by an elevated country, which divides from it the waters that flow into Hudson's bay, and the northern lakes and St. Lawrence; on the east, by the table land which separates the waters that fall into the Atlantic from those that flow to the gulf of Mexico; on the south by this gulf, and on the west by the province of Texas, and the Rocky, or Chippewan Mountains, which separate the waters of the Atlantic from those of the Pacific ocean.

EXTENT.

THIS great Valley is, perhaps, the largest division of the globe, of which its waters pass one estuary.

To suppose the United States and its territory to be divided into three portions, the arrangement would be, the Atlantic slope—the Mississippi basin, or valley—and the Pacific slope.

A glance on any map of North America, will show that this valley includes about two thirds of the territory of the United States. The Atlantic slope contains about 390,000; the Pacific slope, about 300,000; which, combined, are 690,000 square miles: while the Valley of the Mississippi contains at least 1,300,000 square miles, or 833,000,000 acres.

This Valley extends from the 29° to the 49° of N. Latitude, or about 1400 miles from south to north; and from the 3° to the 35° of longitude west from Washington, or about 1470 miles from east to west. From the source of the Alleghany river to the sources of the Missouri, following the meanderings of the streams, is not less than 5000 miles.

Guide for Emigrants. 11

STATES AND TERRITORIES.

The states and territories included, are a small section of New York, western Pennsylvania, western Virginia, Ohio, Indiana, Illinois, Kentucky, Tennessee, Mississippi, Louisiana, Territory of Arkansas, Missouri, the territory lying north of Illinois, and called, by some persons, *Huron*, with the vast regions that lie north and west of Missouri and the Arkansas, now held in reserve for the location of the Indians.

POPULATION.

The following table is made partly from estimation, and partly from the returns of the census of 1830, as published in the newspapers. It is sufficiently accurate for the purposes intended.

Western Pennsylvania, and a section of New York,	Estimated,	330,000
Western Virginia,	Census,	204,175
Ohio,	,,	937,000
Indiana,	,,	341,582
Illinois,	State ,,	161,055
Kentucky,	By estimation,	700,000
Tennessee,	,,	550,000
Mississippi,	,,	120,000
Louisiana,	Census,	214,693
Arkansas Territory,	,,	30,608
Missouri,	,,	140,000
Huron Territory, (not organized)		3,688
	Total,	3,732,801

Guide for Emigrants.

A comparative view of the population of the Valley of the Mississippi, showing the proportional increase of the several states, parts of states, and territories, from 1790 to 1830. A period of 40 years.

States, parts of States, and Territories.	1790.	1800.	1810.	1820.	1830.
Western Pennsylvania, and a fraction of New York,	75,000	130,000	240,000	290,000	330,000
Western Virginia,	90,000	110,000	132,000	147,540	204,175
Ohio,		a 45,000	230,760	581,434	937,000
Indiana,			24,520	147,178	341,582
Illinois,			12,282	55,211	161,055
Kentucky,	73,677	220,959	406,511	564,517	700,000
Tennessee,	35,691	105,602	261,727	422,813	550,000
Mississippi,		b 8,850	40,352	75,448	120,000
Louisiana,			76,556	153,407	214,693
Arkansas Territory,				14,273	30,608
Missouri,			c 20,845	66,586	140,000
Huron Territory, d					3,688
Total,	274,368	620,411	1,445,653	2,518,407	3,732,801

a. Including Indiana, Illinois, and Michigan.
b. Including Alabama.   c. Including Arkansas.
d. Included within Michigan, but will soon form a separate territory.

Probably there is no portion of the globe, of equal extent, that contains as much soil fit for cultivation, and which is capable of sustaining and supplying with all the necessaries and conveniences, and most of the luxuries of life, so dense a population as this great Valley. Deducting one third of its surface for water and desert, which is a very liberal allowance, and there remains 866,667 square miles, or 554,666,880 acres of arable land.

Let it become as populous as Massachusetts, which contains 610,014 inhabitants on an area of 7,800 square miles, or seventy-eight to every 640 acres, and the population of this immense region will amount to 67,600,000. The child is now born which will live to see this result. Suppose its population to become equally dense with England, including Wales, which contains 207 to the square mile, and its numbers will amount to 179,400,000. But let it become equal to Netherlands, the most populous country on the globe, containing 230 to the square mile, and the Valley of the Mississippi teems with a population of 200 millions, a result which may be had in the same time that New England has been gathering its two millions. What reflections ought this view to present to the patriot, the philanthropist, and the Christian!

PHYSICAL FEATURES.

The physical features of this Valley are peculiar.

1. It includes two great inclined planes, one on its eastern, and the other on its western border, terminating with the Mississippi.

2. This river receives all the waters produced on these slopes, which are discharged by its mouths into the gulf of Mexico.

3. Every part of this vast region can be penetrated by steamboats, or other water craft; nor is there a spot in all this wide region, excepting a small district in the vast plains of upper Missouri, that is more than one hundred miles from some navigable water. A boat may take in its lading on the banks of the Chataque lake, in the State of New York; another may receive its cargo in the interior of Virginia; a third may start from the rice lakes at the head of the Mississippi; and a fourth may come laden with furs from the Chippewan mountains, 2,800 miles up the Missouri, and all meet at the mouth of the Ohio, and proceed in company to the ocean.

4. With the exception of its eastern and western borders, there are no mountains. Some portions are level, a large part is gently undulating, or what in the west is called "rolling," and the remainder is made up of abrupt hills, flint and limestone ridges, bluffs, and ravines.

5. It divided into two great portions, the UPPER, and LOWER VALLEY, according to its general features, climate, staple productions, and habits of its population. The parallel of latitude that cuts the mouth of the Ohio river, will designate these portions with sufficient accuracy.

North of this line the seasons are regularly divided into spring, summer, autumn, and winter. In the winter there is usually more or less snow, ice forms and frequently blocks up the rivers, navigation is obstructed, and cotton is not produced in sufficient quantity or quality to make it a staple for exportation. It is the region of furs, minerals, tobacco, hemp, live stock, and every description of grain and fruit that grows in New England. Its white population are mostly accustomed to labor.

South of this line, cotton, tobacco, indigo, and sugar are staples. It has little winter, snow seldom covers the earth, ice never obstructs the rivers, and most of the labor is done by slaves.

SECTION II.

Rivers.

THE rivers are, the Mississippi and its tributaries, or more correctly, the Missouri and its tributaries. No river on earth can compare with this for the length of its course, the number and extent of its tributaries, the vast country they drain, and their capabilities for navigation. Its tributaries generally issue either from the eastern or western mountains, and flow over this immense region, diffusing not only fertility to the soil, but affording facilities for commerce a great part of the year.

MISSOURI RIVER.

The Missouri is unquestionably the main stream, for it is not only longer and discharges a larger volume of water than the Mississippi above its mouth, but it has branches, which, for the extent of country they drain, their length, and the volume of water they discharge, far exceed the upper Mississippi.

The characteristics of these two rivers are each distinctly marked. The Missouri is turbid, violent in its motions, changing its currents, its navigation is interrupted or made difficult by snags, sawyers, and planters, and it has many islands and sand-bars. Such is the character of the Mississippi below its mouth. But above the mouth of the Missouri, its waters are clear, its current gentle, while it is comparatively free from snags and sand-bars.

The Missouri, which we have shown to be the principal stream, rises in the Chippewan mountains in latitude 44° north, and longitude about 35° west from Washington city. It runs a northeast course till after it receives the Yellow Stone, when it reaches past the 48° of latitude, thence an east, then a south, and finally a southeastern course, until it meets the current of the Mississippi, 20 miles above St. Louis, and in latitude 38° 45′ north. Besides numerous smaller streams, the Missouri receives the Yellow Stone and Platte, which, of themselves, in any other part of the world, would be called large rivers, together with the Sioux, Kansas, Grand, Chariton, Osage, and Gasconade, all large and navigable rivers.

Its length, according to Darby,* upon an entire comparative course, is 1870 miles, and upon a particular course, about 3000 miles. Lewis and Clark make the distance from the Mississippi to the great falls, 2580 miles.

There are several things in some respects peculiar to this river, which deserve notice.

1. Its current is very rapid, usually at the rate of four or five miles an hour, when at its height, and it requires a strong wind to propel a boat with a sail against it. Steam overcomes its force, for boats ply regularly from St. Louis to the towns and landings on its banks within the borders of the state, and return with the produce of the country.

* Article *Mississippi*, in the American edition of the New Edinburgh Encyclopœdia.

Owing to the shifting of its current, and its snags and sand-bars, its navigation is less safe and pleasant than any other western river, but these difficulties are every year lessened by genius and enterprise.

2. Its water is always turbid, being of a muddy, ash color, though more so at its periodical rise than at other times. This is caused by extremely fine sand, received from the neighborhood of the Yellow Stone, of which there are immense ridges, that at a distance resemble hills of snow. This is held in solution in large quantities. During the summer flood, a tumbler of water taken from the Missouri, and precipitated, will produce about one fourth of its bulk in sediment.

This sediment does not prevent its habitual use by hundreds who live on its banks, or move in boats over its surface. Some wait for it to settle, or apply some substance to it, as a little meal, but many more drink it, and use it for culinary purposes, in its natural state.

When entirely filtrated, it is the most limpid and agreeable river water I ever saw. Its specific gravity then, is about equal to rain water; but in its turbid state, it is much heavier than ordinary river water, for a boat will draw three or four inches less in it than in other rivers, with the same lading, and the human body will swim in it with but very little effort.

It has some peculiar properties, and some people suppose it is medicinal. While residing in St. Charles, in 1819, I put a small quantity into an open cask, and placed it in the hot sun for three weeks without any signs of putrefaction. It appeared as fresh as when first taken from the river. Others have made the same experiments with similar results. In hot weather, a bucket of water from the Missouri will become quite cool and palatable by standing ten or twelve hours. Eruptions on the skin, and old ulcerous sores are cured by wading or frequent bathings in its water. It usually has a cathartic effect upon those unaccustomed to its use.

The width of the Missouri at St. Charles, 20 miles from its juncture with the Mississippi, was measured by the author in 1819, and found to be 520 yards. By the washing of the right bank, it has become much wider since. At its lowest stage of water, the same season, it was but five and a half feet deep in the main channel. It has been forded at Belle Fountaine, four miles above its mouth, by a soldier passing across, and supporting himself against the current by means of a canoe. Doubtless these statements will surprise some readers.

In the fall of 1820, and when, from the unusual drought which prevailed that season, streams everywhere were low, the *surface* of the Missouri was from three to four feet *lower* than on the preceding year, and yet in the middle of the channel, and at the same place where the depth was five and a half feet, in 1819, it was then 15 feet deep. From these facts, it will be seen that the Missouri runs upon a bed of sand, which is continually shifting its position; now, excavating a broad and deep channel, and the next year, perhaps, exhibiting a sand-bar in its place. Hence, in navigating the river, the pilot must be guided to the channel by the appearance of the surface, and by continually throwing the lead.

From the moveable character of its bed, there is a singular phenomenon constantly appearing on its surface in different places. An undulatory motion, like the whirling of an eddy, or the boiling of a pot, is seen in various directions. After a few moments, these subside, and others commence in other places. There is scarcely a ferry from its mouth to the western boundary of Missouri, but what I have passed, and I have never crossed without witnessing this commotion of its waters. The boatmen often speak of its bottom falling through. These whirls or boilings are not of sufficient force to change the direction of the skiff or canoe. They are caused by the shifting of the sand in the bed of the river.

The fact can easily be made to appear, that the bed of the river, at different places and seasons, is elevated or depressed, and that the height of its surface is no certain data from which the volume of water can be measured that passes any place in a given season.

It often happens that keel boats ascending or descending the Missouri, strike on a sand bar, apparently but a few inches under water. The hands jump on the bar to shove off the boat. Sometimes they feel the bar suddenly giving away under them, spring into the boat, and find the water ten or twelve feet deep in a moment.

Another circumstance of this river, which I do not recollect of having seen noticed by any writer, is the vast disproportion of its length, and the size of its tributaries, to the volume of water it actually discharges into the Mississippi. I have already mentioned that its width at St. Charles is less than half a mile, and that in one season it had less than six feet of water in the deepest place. At the Mandan villages, 1600 miles from the Mississippi, it is said to be nearly as wide and deep at any period as at St. Charles. And yet between these points it receives the Platte, an immense river of itself, and a number of large tributaries. What then produces this apparent diminution of its waters? First, evaporation consumes large quantities. Secondly, the absorption of its bottoms consumes much more. The bottom lands on this river through the State of Missouri, are from three to four miles in width, including the river itself, which is from one half to three fourths of a mile wide, or about one sixth of its valley. The bottom is a porous soil of sand and loam, entirely alluvial, which absorbs vast quantities of the river water.

In digging wells on this soil, it is necessary to descend as low as the surface of the river at its lowest stage, and the water in the well will rise and sink invariably with the changes of the river. Even volumes of sand frequently will come into the well, as the river rises. These facts show that the whole width of the bottom is saturated with the water of the Missouri, and that only a small proportion received from its tributaries is ever seen passing down its channel. The water in wells on these bottoms, in flowing through the earth, changes its quality, and becomes of a sulphurous or brackish taste. Hence there are but few good wells on the bottoms of the Missouri, or the Mississippi below its mouth.

Its periodical rise is another fact that must be noticed. Ordinarily this river has three periods of rising and falling. Its first rise is usually upon breaking up of winter, the latter part of February, or first of March, when the Gasconade, Osage, Kanzas, and smaller branches of the Missouri, together with the Illinois and Mississippi, pour down their floods. Its second rise is ordinary in April, when the Platte and other streams break up and discharge their surplus waters. But the rise that more especially attracts attention from its uniformity, occurs between the

10th and 25th of June, and is caused by the melting of the snows on the Chippewan mountains. This flood is scarcely ever less than five, nor more than sixteen feet at St. Louis, and is attended invariably with a spell of wet weather. In 1820, the season of the greatest drought ever known in this region, it amounted only to a few slight showers. In 1824, the wettest season we have had, it was one continual pouring out of the clouds. For the period of fourteen years, I have never known it to fail, but that this annual rise of the Missouri was attended with more or less rain. So uniform is this in the country of the Upper Missouri, the region beyond the State, that the seasons are uniformly divided into *wet* and *dry*. The wet season commences about the first of June, and continues till the river subsides, when the dry season commences, and continues till late in autumn.

Pumice stones, and other volcanic productions, occasionally float down its waters. The author has specimens which he gathered from its surface in 1819, which are unquestionably of volcanic origin.

MISSISSIPPI RIVER.

The Mississippi Proper takes its rise in Cedar lake, in latitude 47° north. From this to the falls of St. Anthony, a distance of about five hundred miles, it runs a devious course, first southeast—then, southwest—and, finally, southeast again; which last it continues without much deviation, till it reaches the Missouri, the waters of which strike it at right angles, and throw the current of the Mississippi wholly upon the eastern shore. When at a moderate, or low stage, the waters of the two rivers do not mingle till they have passed St. Louis, but when high, the current of the Missouri entirely overwhelms that of the Mississippi, and the "Father of Waters" is swallowed up in the "Mother of Floods."*

The prominent branch of the Upper Mississippi, in the St. Peters, which rises in the great Prairies in the northwest, and enters the parent stream a little below the falls of St. Anthony. Towards the sources of this river the quarries exist from which are made the red stone pipes of the Indians. This is sacred ground. Hostile tribes meet here, and part unmolested.

Rock river drains the waters from the northern part of Illinois, and enters the parent stream at 41° 30′ north latitude. In latitude 39° comes in the Illinois, signifying the "River of Men;" and eighteen miles below this, it unites with, and is lost in the Missouri.

I expect that custom has fixed unalterably the name *Mississippi*, to this united body of waters, that rolls its turbid waves towards the Mexican

---

* Said to be the aboriginal meaning of Missouri.

gulf; though, as has been intimated, it is but a continuation of the Missouri.

Sixty miles below St. Louis, the Kaskaskia joins it, after a course of 200 miles. In $36\frac{1}{2}°$ north latitude, the Ohio pours in its tribute, called by the early French explorers, " La Belle Riviere," the beautiful river. A little below 34°, the White river enters after a course of more than 1,000 miles. Thirty miles below that, the Arkansas, bringing its tribute from the confines of Mexico, pours in its waters. Above Natches, the Yazoo from the east, and eighty miles below, the Red river from the west, unite their waters with the Mississippi. Red River takes its rise in the Mexican dominions, and runs a course of more than 2,000 miles.

Hitherto the waters in the wide regions of the west have been congregating to one point. The "Father of Waters," is now upwards of a mile in width, and several fathoms deep. During its annual floods, it overflows its banks below the mouth of the Ohio, and penetrates the numerous bayous, lakes, and swamps, and especially on its western side. In many instances these floods extend thirty or forty miles into the interior. But after it receives the Red river, it begins to throw off its surplus waters, which flow in separate channels to the gulf, and never again unite with the parent stream. Several of these communications are held with the ocean at different and distant points.

C

OHIO RIVER.

The Ohio river is formed by the junction of the Alleghany and Monongahela, at Pittsburg. The Alleghany river rises not far from the head of the western branch of the Susquehannah, in the highlands of McKean county, Pennsylvania. It runs north till it penetrates Cataraugus county, New York, then turns west, then southwest, and finally takes a southern course to Pittsburg. It receives a branch from the Chatauque lake, Chatauque county, New York. The Monongahela rises near the sources of the Kenhawa, in western Virginia, and runs north till it meets the Alleghany.

The general course of the Ohio is southwest. Its current is gentle, and it receives a number of tributaries, which are noticed in the following letter, taken from a series published in the *Sunday School Journal*. With a few trifling inaccuracies, it is a correct description of this region; and besides what I have said on this river, presents much additional information.

"The Valley of the Mississippi has been divided by Mr. Darby, into four great subdivisions.*

---

* These subdivisions do not embrace the vallies of the rivers which run to the gulf of Mexico, eastward of the Mississippi, in Mississippi State, Alabama, and West Florida.

Guide for Emigrants. 27

1. The *Ohio Valley*, length 750 miles, and mean width 261; containing 196,000 square miles.

2. *Mississippi Valley*, above Ohio, including the minor valley of Illinois, but exclusive of Missouri, 650 miles long, and 277 mean width, and containing 180,000 square miles.

3. *Lower Valley of the Mississippi*, including White, Arkansas, and Red river vallies, 1,000 miles long, and 200 wide, containing 200,000 square miles.

4. *Missouri proper*, including Osage, Kansas, Platte rivers, &c. 1,200 miles long, and 437 wide, containing 523,000 square miles.

"The *Valley of the Ohio* is better known than any of the others; has much fertile land, and much that is steril, or unfit for cultivation, on account of its unevenness. It is divided into two unequal portions, by the Ohio river; leaving on the right or northwest side 80,000, and on the left or southeast side, 116,000 square miles. The eastern part of this valley is hilly, and rapidly acclivous towards the Appalachian mountains. Indeed its high hills, as you approach these mountains, are of a strongly marked mountainous character. Of course the rivers which flow into the Ohio—the Monongahela, Kenhawa, Licking, Sandy, Kentucky, Green, Cumberland, and Tennessee—are rapid, and abounding in cataracts and falls, which, towards their sources, greatly impede navigation. The western side of this Valley is, also, hilly fo a considerable distance from the Ohio, but towards its western limit, it subsides to a remarkably level region. So that whilst the eastern line of this Valley lies along the high table land, on which the Appalachian mountains rest, and where the rivers of the eastern section of this Valley rise, which is at least 2000 miles generally above the ocean level; the western line has not an elevation of much more than half of that amount on the north, and which greatly subsides towards the Kaskaskia. The rivers of the western section are Beaver, Muskingum, Hockhocking, Scioto, Miami, and Wabash. Along the Ohio, on each side, are high hills, often intersected with deep ravines, and sometimes openings of considerable extent, and well known by the appellation of "Ohio hills." Towards the mouth of the Ohio, these hills almost wholly disappear, and extensive level bottoms, covered with heavy forests of oak, sycamore, elm, poplar, and cotton wood, stretch along each side of the river. On the lower section of the river, the water, at the time of the spring floods, often overflows these bottoms to a great extent. This fine Valley embraces a population exceeding 2,500,000, which is considerably more than one half of the whole population of the entire Valley of the West. The western parts of Pennsylvania and Virginia, the entire states of Ohio, Indiana, and Kentucky, the larger part of Tennes-

Guide for Emigrants. 29

see, and a smaller part of Illinois, are in the Valley of the Ohio.

"*The Upper Mississippi Valley*, (lying above the Missouri,) has been imperfectly explored.* It possesses a surface far less diversified than the Valley of the Ohio. According to Mr. Schoolcraft, the sources of the Mississippi river have an elevation of 1330 feet above the ocean level. This is about the elevation of the level marshy table land, which extends from Lake Superior to the Missouri at the Mandan villages. Throughout the whole of the Upper Valley of the Mississippi, of which we are speaking, there is nothing which deserves the name of a *mountain*. There is not probably on earth an equal extent of territory, which is of so level and monotonous a character. The highest sources of the Mississippi river originate in the numerous small lakes which lie between the sources of the Assiniboin and Lake Superior. On the western side, it receives, as you descend from its sources, the Leech-lake river, Vermillion, Pine, Crow, Elk, Jac, St. Peters, Upper Iowa, Little Maquaquetois, Galena, Great Maquaquetois, Lower Iowa, and Lemoine. From the eastern side, the Thornberry, Round-lake, Turtle, Portage, Chevreuill, Prairie, Trout, Sandy-lake, St. Francis, Rum river, St. Croise, Chippeway, Black, Le Crosse, Ouisconsin, Sissinawa, Riviere au Fevre, (Fever

---

* It is well known below the Falls of St. Anthony. *P.*

river,) Rock, Henderson, and Illinois, pour in their several streams. It will be readily perceived that this Valley has great advantages for internal navigation and commerce.

"The Upper Mississippi Valley is very dissimilar to the Valley of the Ohio. The former is remarkably level and uniform, the latter broken, hilly, even approaching to mountainous. The one abounds in lakes and marshes, the other is wholly destitute of them. The former is covered with *prairies*, that is, extensive districts, destitute of trees, and covered with high grass and wild flowers, and low shrubs; the latter is covered, in its natural state, with interminable *forests*, which are only here and there, even now, interrupted by the cultivated field. In the Upper Valley of the Mississippi, clumps of trees may be seen along the rivers and water courses, whilst the far greater proportion of it is open prairie, either elevated and dry, or low and marshy, possessing generally great fertility of soil, (although there are many strong exceptions,) and greatly destitute of timber. It will be the great region of pastoral wealth, abounding in pasture for innumerable herds and flocks. In latitude 45°, are the Falls of St. Anthony, where the river Mississippi is precipitated over rocks of sixteen or seventeen feet of elevation. The Valley of the Ohio has a similar, but not equal, impediment to its navigation, in the rapids at Louisville, Ky. where the Ohio has a fall of several feet, in the distance of two or three miles. We may add that there are millions of acres, in the Valley of the Mississippi, of marsh and lake, which are covered with wild rice, zizania aquatica, which feed innumerable flocks of water fowls, and which will probably be an article of food to a large population, as it now, occasionally, affords to the famished hunter and Indian the means of satisfying their hunger. Upon the whole, the Valley of the Upper Mississippi is greatly inferior to the Valley of Ohio.

"The *Lower Valley of the Mississippi*, has a length of 1,200 miles, from northwest to southeast, having the source of the Arkansas, and the mouth of the Mississippi river as extreme points; reaching from north latitude 29° to 42°, and without estimating mountain, ridges, or peaks, differing in relative elevation at least 500 feet. And as an elevation of 500 feet is believed to be equal, as it regards temperature, to one degree of latitude northward on the level ocean shore, if we add the actual difference of latitude, 13°, to an allowance of 10° for relative elevation, the climate at the northwest extreme must differ from that of the Delta, (or Islands, in the mouth of the Mississippi,) 23° in temperature, and render the seasons at the head of the Arkansas, as severe as those in north latitude 52° on the Atlantic coast of Labrador.*

---

* Not quite correct.

"From the influx of the Missouri, to that of the Ohio, the volume of the Mississippi rolls by a general S. S. E. course of 190 miles by its windings; but on receiving the Ohio, it inflects to a course of S. S. W. 380 miles, to the entrance of the White and Arkansas rivers; it then turns to a very little west of south, crosses three degrees of latitude, or about 360 miles, by its sinuosities to the influx of the Red river, and $1\frac{1}{2}$ miles below the outlet of Atchafalaya. From this point the Mississippi inflects its general course, and bends to the southeast, which it pursues to its final discharge into the gulf of Mexico, a distance by the river of 335 miles. So that from the mouth of the Missouri, the length of the Mississippi, by all its windings, is 1265 miles, but by a direct line, only 820 miles.

"Into the Mississippi, as a recipient, are poured from the east, below the mouth of the Ohio, the Obion, Forked Deer, Big Hatche, Coosahatchie, Yazoo, Big Black, and Homochitto; and from the west, or northwest, the St. Francis, White, Arkansas, and Red rivers, with other streams of lesser note.

"It is a most remarkable circumstance that there is such a prodigious inequality between the two opposing planes, down which are poured the confluents of the Mississippi, below the mouth of the Ohio. The western inclined plane, falling from the Chippewan mountains, sweeps over 800 or 1000 miles, whilst the eastern, slop ing from the States of Tennessee and Mississippi, does not average a width of 100 miles. And whilst the White river flows down 1200 miles, the Arkansas near 2500, and the Red river from 1500 to 2000, there is no river on the eastern plane whose whole course exceeds 200 miles. The Arkansas and Red rivers are immense streams, and as they approach the Mississippi river, have many branches which, after leaving the parent river, run parallel to it, and finally unite with it again. Near the mouth of the former, some of these bayous on the south side, in high water, never return to the parent stream, but run directly to the Red river; and some of those which break from Red river, make their way to the Atchafalaya, and find an outlet for their waters many leagues westward of the Mississippi.

"The Arkansas rises near north latitude 42°, and longitude 34° west, and falls into the Mississippi at 33° 56', passing over eight degrees of latitude. Red river rises in the mountains of Santa Fe, in north latitude 32°—35°, and west longitude 25°—28°, from Washington, and falls into the Mississippi in latitude 31°. They are both remarkable rivers for their extent, the number of their branches, the volume of their waters, the quantity of the alluvion which they carry down to the parent stream, and the color of their waters. They doubtless cause the Mississippi to infringe so often upon the bluffs which are so conspicuous on its eastern bank. Impregnated by saline particles, and colored by ochreous earth, the waters of these two rivers are at once brackish and nauseous to the taste, particularly near their mouths; that of Red river is so much so, that at Natchitoches at low water, it cannot be used even for culinary purposes.

"At a short distance below the mouth of the Red river, a large bayou, (as it is called,) or outlet, breaks from the Mississippi on the west, by which, it is believed, that as large a volume of water as Red river brings to the parent river, is drained off, and runs to the gulf of Mexico, fifty miles from the mouth of the Mississippi. The name of this bayou is Atchafalaya, or as it is commonly called, *Chaffalio.* Below this bayou, another of large dimensions, breaks forth on the same side, and finally falls into the Atchafalaya. This is the Placquemine. Still lower, at Donaldsonville, ninety miles above New Orleans, on the same side, the Lafourche bayou breaks out, and pursues a course parallel to the Mississippi, fifty miles west of the mouth of that river. On the east side, the Ibberville bayou drains off a portion of the waters of the Mississippi, into lake Maurepas, Ponchartrain, Borgnes, and the gulf of Mexico, and thus forms the long and narrow island of Orleans.

"In the lower Valley of the Mississippi there is a great extent of land of the very richest kind. There is also much that is almost always overflown with waters, and is a perpetual swamp. There are extensive prairies in this Valley, and towards the Rocky mountains, on the upper waters of the Arkansas and Red rivers, there are vast barren steppes or plains of sand, dreary and barren, like the central steppes of Asia. On the east of the Mississippi, are extensive regions of the densest forests, which form a striking contrast with the prairies which stretch on the west of that great river.

" *The Valley of the Missouri* extends 1200 miles in length, and 700 in width, and embraces 253,000 square miles. The Missouri river rises in the Chippewan mountains, through eight degrees, or nearly 600 miles. The Yellow Stone is its longest branch. The course of the Missouri, after leaving the Rocky mountains, is generally southeast, until it unites with the Mississippi. The principal branches flow from the southwest. They are the Osage, Kansas, Platte, &c. The three most striking features of this Valley are, 1st. The turbid character of its waters. 2d. The very unequal volumes of the right and left confluents. 3d. The immense predominance of the open prairies, over the forests which line the rivers. The western part of this Valley rises to an elevation towards the Chippewan mountains, equal to ten degrees of temperature. Ascending from the lower verge of this widely extended plain, wood becomes more and more scarce, until one naked surface spreads on all sides.

Even the ridges and chains of the Chippewan, partake of these traits of desolation. The traveller, who has read the descriptions of central Asia, by Tooke or Pallas, will feel on the higher branches of the Missouri, a resemblance, at once striking and appalling; and he will acknowledge if near to the Chippewan mountains in winter, that the utmost intensity of frost over Siberia and Mongolia, has its full counterpart in North America, on similar, if not on lower latitudes. There is much fertile land in the Valley of the Missouri, though much of it must be forever the abode of the buffalo and the elk, the wolf and the deer."

In addition to the foregoing description, I will suggest an idea in relation to Ohio, Indiana, and Illinois, which I do not recollect to have seen in any author.

The whole district of country embraced within these states, excepting a strip on the lakes, was once a plane with an inclination of a few degrees towards the mouth of the Ohio.

Supposing the rivers that drain this tract, which fall into the Ohio and the Mississippi, to have once run on the surface of this plane, and in process of time to have excavated the vallies, ravines, and channels through which they now run, the appearance of the surface would have been what it now is.

The attention of the author was arrested with this idea, while travelling through the extent of Ohio, from its northeastern to its southwestern corner, and from thence through Indiana, in 1826. The summit level of Ohio, which is within a few miles of lake Erie, appeared to him to be but a few feet higher than the bluffs that overhang the Ohio river, and in conversation with an intelligent gentleman, in Cincinnati, who had accompanied the engineer in levelling for the Ohio canal, the same observation was made.

This subject is well worth the attention of the geologist. This district furnishes abundant evidences of a diluvial formation, and on the supposition that upon the waters subsiding, the rivers sought and excavated their own channels, and in process of time scooped out the deep vallies through which they now run, and by annual depositions formed their alluvial bottoms, the appearance of the surface of this country is explained on simple and probable principles.

CLIMATE.

The following observations on this head, are taken from the Sunday School Journal of March 10, to which I have added several remarks by way of correction.

"We may number four distinct climates between the sources and the outlet of the Mississippi. The first commencing at its sources and terminating at Prairie du Cheins, in latitude 43°

corresponds pretty accurately to the climate between Montreal and Boston ; with this difference, that the amount of snow falling in the former, is much less than in the latter region. Five months in the year may be said to belong to the dominion of winter. The Irish potato, wheat, and the cultivated grains, succeed well in this climate ; but the apple, peach, pear, and the species of corn, called *gourd seed*, require a more southern climate to bring them to perfection.

The next climate includes the belt of country between 41° and 37°. In this climate lie Missouri, Illinois, Indiana, Ohio, Western Pennsylvania and Virginia, and the larger part of Kentucky. The severity of winter commences with January, and ends with the second week of February. Wheat is at home in this climate. The Irish potato flourishes well in the northern, and the sweet potato in the southern part of this climate. It is the favored region of the apple, the pear, and the peach tree. The persimon is found throughout, and the pawpaw with its luscious fruit, is found in the southern part of this climate.

The next climate extends from 37° to 31°. Below 35°, in the rich alluvial soil, the apple tree begins to fail in bringing its fruit to perfection, Between 37° and 33°, cotton is raised for home consumption, but is not a very certain crop ; but below 33°, is the proper climate for its cultivation, and there it becomes the staple articles

Wheat is not seen in the lower part of this climate, as an article of cultivation. The fig tree brings, in the lower part of this belt, its fruit to full maturity.

Below 31°, to the Gulf of Mexico, is the region of the sugar cane and the sweet orange tree. It would be, if it were cultivated, the region of the olive. Snow is not seen here, and the streams are never frozen. Winter is only marked by nights of white frost, and days of north-west winds, and these do not last longer than three days at once, and are succeeded by south winds and warm days. Cotton and corn are planted from March to July. The trees are generally in leaf by the middle of February, and always by the first of March. Early in March the forests are in blossom. Fire flies are seen by the middle of February. In these regions the summers are uniformly hot, although there are days when the mercury rises as high in New England as in Louisiana. The heat, however, is here more uniform and sustained, commences earlier, and continues later. From February to September, thunder storms are common, accompanied sometimes with gales and tornadoes of tremendous violence.

The climate of the Valley of the Mississippi corresponds, it is believed, more exactly with the latitude, than that of the Atlantic States does; this is owing to the uniformity of the Valley, and its freedom from mountains and other natural causes affecting climate. The elevation of the northern part, and especially that of the extreme eastern and western parts of its great plains, gives a colder climate than the same parallels on the level shores of the Atlantic ocean. In some places this elevation is sufficient to make a difference of from three to five degrees in the temperature.

"In the southern and middle regions of this valley, the wide, level, and heavy timbered alluvions, are intrinsically more or less unhealthy. In these situations the new resident is subject to bilious complaints, to remitting fevers, and especially to fever and ague, the general scourge of the valley. The slopes of the Alleghanies, interior of Ohio and Kentucky, Tennessee and Indiana, where the forest is cleared away, and stagnant waters, if any, drained, the high grounds of Illinois and Missouri, and the open country towards the Chippewayan, are as salubrious as any other region."

Remarks. The climate north of Prairie du Cheins does not bear resemblance to that between Montreal and Boston in all respects. Its winters are not as severe, and its summers are more equal in temperature. Abundance of wild rice grows in the numerous lakes at the head of the Mississippi, and constitutes an important item of the food of the natives. The Indians run their canoes amongst it, and with much dexterity strike the heads with their paddles, so as to thresh it on to mats in the canoe. Spring opens late in this region, owing to the vast body of frozen water still further to the north; but the mild and elastic air of autumn is continued much longer than in the same parallel on the Atlantic. A small species of maize called the Mandan corn, and produced by the Mandan and other Indians on the Upper Missouri, flourishes in this latitude.

The climate between Prairie du Cheins and the mouth of Ohio is tolerably well described, excepting that winter usually commences as early as the 20th of December, and continues till the middle of February. Illinois stretches nearly through this climate, and of course there is considerable difference between the northern and southern parts of the State in the severity of its winters. Cotton is produced for home consumption throughout more than half its extent.

Between 37° and 33° cotton is a pretty certain crop, and much is raised for exportation. Tennessee, the northern portion of Alabama, the lower corner of Missouri, and the Arkansas territory, all north of 33°, produce vast quantities of cotton, and in some parts it is a staple production. Experiments have tested that cotton and even the sugar cane can be produced to tolerable perfection in a much higher latitude than formerly supposed.

D

PRODUCTIONS.

A few general remarks will be exhibited respecting the productions of the *lower* valley, and I shall dismiss that portion, and confine my observations to the upper district, or the country north of the mouth of the Ohio.

Minerals. But few mines exist in this region. Nitrate of potash is found in great abundance in caves in Kentucky and Tennessee, from which large quantities of saltpetre are manufactured. Sulphate of magnesia is found in Warren county, Ky. and probably in other places.

Coal exists in immense quantities in the Cumberland mountains, and other parts of Tennessee. Muriate of soda (common salt) exists in inexhaustible quantities among the uplands.

In Kentucky and Tennessee numerous salt springs are worked, and furnish a considerable portion of the supply for consumption. Near the northern sources of the Arkansas river, this salt forms incrustations of considerable thickness and solidity. It is usually formed in the depressed parts of the surface of the immense plains and prairies in that region, which in the wet season are covered with brine, and which is evaporated by the sun, and leaves a salt crust. I have seen a block ten or twelve inches square, hewn out and brought to St. Louis, from this region. Thousands of bushels may be gathered here in a little time.

Jefferson lake, near the Arkansas river, has its water saturated with salt, and is of a bright red color, from the red clay that comes from the Canadian. East of this lake are three mountains in a range, in the crevices of which are beds of muriate of soda, from which large blocks of rock salt may be cut. Potter's clay is found in Alabama, and the Chickasaw bluffs, Mississippi.

Various species of iron ore are found in Kentucky, Tennessee, and Arkansas. Red oxide of iron is found on Elk river, Tennessee. Sulphate of iron, in its native pure state, together with native plumous alum, is found in a cave in the Cumberland mountains.

The only minerals of Mississippi State are, amethyst, of which but one crystal has yet been found; potter's clay, at the Chickasaw bluffs, and near Natchez; sulphuret of lead, in small quantities, about Gibsonport; and sulphate of iron. In 1800, an extraordinary drought laid bare the bottom of the Mississippi opposite Natchez, for one hundred yards from the shore, and exhibited to view immense trunks of trees in a petrified state, besides thousands of other bodies of various shapes and sizes, all petrified.

Louisiana, being chiefly alluvion, furnishes only two specimens of minerals, but it is conjectured the pine barrens of Natchitoches, if explored, would add to the number. They are sulphuret of antimony, and meteoric iron ore.

Of the last named mineral, a mass weighing upwards of three thousand pounds was found near the Red River, four hundred miles above Natchitoches, and presented to the museum of the Literary and Philosophical Society of New York.*

A large proportion of the lower valley, being alluvion, it is not rich in mineral productions. Arkansas Territory has the greatest variety, and the most in quantity. In many parts of this district, the uplands are either flint knobs, bare hills, or shrubby plains. Mount Prairie, in Hempstead county, a rich and populous settlement, is a circular eminence of table land, about sixteen miles in diameter, and rising considerably above the circumjacent country. The soil is a texture of marl and clay, very black, and during the dry season inclined to bake, and open in fissures. Through this extraordinary stratum of earth the people dig for water, one hundred feet. Here are found large marine shells, bleached perfectly white, and in great abundance, five hundred miles from the Mexican gulf. They are found on the surface of the earth, and through each stratum to the bottom of the wells. Mr. Flint, whose authority in part we rely upon for these facts, supposes this once to have been the bed of a lake. We add to the idea the suggestion that it was thrown up by an earthquake.

* Comstock.

The Cove of Washita is a curiosity. It is formed by a circular mountain shaped like a horse shoe, and located in Clark county, towards the head of the Washita river, fifteen miles below the hot springs. The cove encloses an area of nine miles. The mountain contains sparry iron stone, and heavy spar. In its neighborhood is found the native magnet, or magnetic oxide of iron, possessing strong magnetic powers. Iron ores are very abundant, and the loadstone is represented to be found in great quantities. Mica, or slate, is common in the transition rocks of this region. Sulphate of copper, sulphuret of zinc, alum, and aluminous slate, exist in the neighborhood. Buhr stone is in the hills around this cove, and pronounced by good judges to be of a superior quality. In this cove are all kinds of earth of the best quality for furnaces and crucibles, used in glass manufactories and iron foundries, amongst which is kaolin, for making porcelain, and abundance of materials for glass. In a cave on one of the branches of White river is alabaster, in masses sufficiently large to be employed in the arts. This cavern contains stalactites in enormous columns. Sulphate of lime, various species of quartz, sulphuret of lead, talc, agate, and several other mineral productions, are found in this Territory north of the Arkansas river.

The hot springs are interesting on account of the minerals around them, the heat of their waters, and as furnishing a place of retreat to valetudinarians, from the sickly regions of the south. They are situated on a branch of the Washita, (French Ouachitta, and commonly pronounced Washitaw,) a large stream which empties into Red river. They are six miles west of the road from Cadron, to Mount Prairie. They are about thirty in number, and issue from a bed of fibrous heavy spar. The heat of the water is 192° of Farenheit. Common quartz, limped quartz, mica, and novaculite, are the minerals that abound in the vicinity of the springs.

Vegetable Productions. Many of the tropical fruits grow to maturity in the lower section of this valley. Oranges are an article of exportation. The apple does not flourish well south of latitude 33°. The magnolia is a native of this region. It is a beautiful tree, producing a large white blossom. The cypress is a chief timber tree from the mouth of the Ohio to New Orleans. Across lake Pontchartrain, in Florida, and up the Red river above Natchitoches, the timber is all pine—the longleaf pine—covered with festoons of long moss. On the uplands the varieties of timber common to the Middle States are found.

The sugar cane flourishes about New Orleans, and towards the gulf. A visitor there estimates that about 100,000 hogsheads of sugar, and 500,000 gallons of molasses, were made or exportation the past year.

The china-tree, catalpa, fig, pomegranate, banana, and orange, with their beauty and fragrance, charm the eye of the beholder.

In opposition to the notion that has prevailed that the whole state of Louisiana is composed of alluvion, swamp, and their productions, Mr. Flint estimates that two thirds of the state is covered with pine woods. He observes, "These woods have their millions of pine trees, and the soil is covered with grass. They are finely undulated with hill and dale, and in the vallies burst out innumerable springs. The streams that water them have clear, transparent water, that runs over white sand, and are alive with trout and other fish.

"The soil is comparatively poor. The bottoms are only second rate land. They will bring three or four crops of corn without manure, and are admirable for the sweet potato. The people who live in the pine woods, generally support themselves by raising cattle, which they number by hundreds. The planters in Attakapas and Opelousas, have in some instances four or five thousand cattle. Nothing can be easier than subsistence in the pine woods."*

And yet the inhabitants are not rich, except in the article of cattle. They labor little, and are content with indolence, health, and poverty.

* Ten Years' Recollections, by Rev. T. Flint.

ANIMALS.

THE immense herds of cattle that live in the pine woods on the western side of Louisiana, and adjoining the province of Texas, have been noticed already. No part of the world for the raising of stock is equal to the country west and north west of New Orleans, and extending into the Mexican dominions. Mules and horses are brought from the Spanish country to the Louisiana market. The *alligator* is found in all the lakes and bayous, and the *moccasin snake*, in the swamps and thickets. The alligator is a huge, clumsy reptile, resembling, at a distance, a log of wood floating on the water. It is amphibious, and frequently comes out of the water, and carries off the pigs and poultry of the settlers. Sometimes children are its prey. Other animals common to the middle and southern states are found in the lower Valley of the Mississippi, Deer abound in the pine barrens, and hunting is the favorite amusement with the planters. Mr. Flint gives the following animated description of what is called the "Fire hunt," of which he was a party.

"The dogs are leashed together. One dog carries a bell. Two or three black boys carry over their shoulders fire pans, being a grating of iron hoops, appended to a long handle, and filled with blazing torches of the splinters of the fat pine. The light is brilliant and dazzling.

A group of gentlemen, clad in their hunting frocks, mounted on fine horses, the joyous cry of the attending dogs, the blacks with their fire pans, the whole cavalcade as seen at a distance by the flickering light among the foliage of the trees, furnishes altogether a striking spectacle. They scour the woods. The deer is tracked. The hound that carries the bell is unleashed. The other dogs know his note, and chime in on his key. The bell indicates where he is. The deer, dazzled and appalled by the noise, arouses from sleep, and gazes in stupid surprise. The eyes are discovered shining like balls of fire. The hunter aims his rifle between the eyes, and the poor animal is sure to fall. Such is the most common mode. They calculate upon success with so much certainty, that I have often been promised for the next day a haunch of venison from a deer yet running in the wild woods. I seldom failed to receive my promised present."

Of the insect tribes, the moscheto and gallinipper will the soonest attract the notice of the stranger. Every person must sleep under the protection of the *moscheto bar*, if he would enjoy a moment's rest or peace. The moscheto bar is made of coarse muslin gauze, sufficiently porous to admit the free circulation of the air, without letting in the insect. This is drawn around the bed or mattrass like a curtain, and affords a tolerable protection. Innumerable dragon flies are brought by southwest winds from La Fourche and bayou Atchafalaya, towards New Orleans. Flies and bugs of every description are far more prolific in a southern than a northern latitude.

Of the feathered tribe, I have not sufficient information to afford satisfaction. The pelican, with its pouch holding several quarts, is about the rivers, and the paroquette, with its fine plumage, annoys the orchards and gardens. Geese, ducks, swans, and other water fowl, retire from the northern lakes, to the lower Valley for winter, and return in the spring to the rice lakes of the upper Mississippi for procreation.

GENERAL OBSERVATIONS ON THE LOWER VALLEY.

THE Mississippi is one of the most important outlets for the produce of a large proportion of the great Western Valley; and probably there is now no river on the globe that throws off as much of the production of the soil for exportation. What then must be its importance in a commercial point of view, when this valley shall teem with the population to which it is ultimately destined. Consequently, New Orleans must become, at least the second city in our Union. Viewing it either in relation to its *moral, religious,* or *national* importance, it deserves something more than a passing notice. But as an introduction to this great emporium of the west, we will make a hasty survey of that portion of the lower Valley which borders on the Mississippi.

Starting from the mouth of the Ohio, we notice on our right hand there is not a solitary bluff, unless we except an eminence near the mouth of the St. Francis. For fifty miles back, the country is wholly alluvion, and considerable portions are dead swamps. Most of it is heavily timbered with all the varieties common to this country, and in addition, the *tulipifera liriodendron*, or yellow poplar, one of the finest and loftiest trees of the forest. The new species of trees, and the new classes of creeping vines, all show that you have passed to another and more southern climate. Big Prairie, Little Prairie, and a few other spots, are exceptions to our remarks on timber. After passing the county of New Madrid, you come to the region of inundation. At the periodical rise of the Mississippi, the country on the west is covered with water, eight or ten feet deep, with the exception of occasional eminences, like islands in a vast lake. The cypress, poplar, sweet gum, and other timber trees, resist this flood, and continue to grow.

On the left hand you meet with alternate bluffs, bottoms, and bayous. The yellow banks, the Iron banks, and Chickasaw bluffs, are well known.

The Mississippi is noted for its short bends and curves. One of these was cut through, the past winter, and the distance shortened thirty miles. With the exception of Point Chico, on the west side, for two hundred miles below the mouth of the Arkansas, the country is one unbroken and inundated wilderness. At Point Chico commences that singular drapery of the forest, the long moss. Here, too, commences the palmetto, a beautiful evergreen, betwixt a shrub and an herb. On the eastern shore, above Natches, several towns are springing up, the most considerable of which is Memphis, in the southwestern corner of Tennessee.

Below the mouth of the Yazoo, are the Walnut hills. They are beautiful eminences, rising above the surrounding country, and covered with the trees whose name they bear.

Here the stranger begins to notice indications of the wealthy southern planter, surrounded with a cluster of negro houses. From the Walnut hills to Baton Rouge, between two and three hundred miles, the bluffs either touch the river, or approach very near its eastern shore. They are of every form, and covered with beach and hickory trees. Here you begin to discover the ever verdant laurel magnolia, with its beautiful foliage, of the thickness and feeling of leather. The holly and a variety of evergreens are among the trees. On the opposite shore, you still have the sombre and inundated forest, deep covered with its drapery of moss, and here and there indented with its plantation.*

NATCHES is situated on the east bank, some distance below the mouth of the Yazoo. It has two divisions, the town *on* the hill, and the town *under* the hill. The river business is transacted at the latter place. Here all that are vile, from the upper and lower country congregate. Here is the place for Kentucky boatmen to lose their money, credit, health, and souls. Dancing, drinking, fiddling, and *rows*, that often end in murder, are the order of the day, or rather the night.

The upper town is situated on the summit of a bluff, three hundred feet in height, from whence there is a beautiful prospect of the surrounding country. On the opposite shore, in Louisiana, you look over the cultivated strip of Concordia, to the boundless and level tops of the cypress swamps beyond. On the right and left you trace the windings of the river among the bluffs, while on the east you behold a rolling, rich, and beautiful country. The town is neat, the streets broad and comfortable, and some of the public buildings handsome. Its staple of trade is cotton. With all its advantages in point of health, it has been visited severely and repeatedly with the yellow fever.

---

* Flint's Recollections.

About one hundred and fifty miles above New Orleans, the leveé commences. This is an artificial mound of earth, raised from six to ten feet above the natural surface, to prevent the inundation of the river. It is on both sides of the river, and continues below New Orleans, as far as plantations have been made. To form a just conception of the surface of that country, the reader must keep in mind an important fact, that pertains to all our western rivers, where they run through an alluvial tract of country, but which in the country of the lower Mississippi, is more strongly marked than elsewhere. *The immediate banks of all our streams are more elevated than the surface of the earth at a little distance.* This elevation is so great on the borders of the lower Mississippi, as to give it the appearance of running on a ridge. Consequently, the moment its waters break over its banks, they pass off into the low grounds in the interior. But this natural elevation of its banks is insufficient to prevent its waters from deluging the surrounding country. Hence an artificial ridge, called a *leveé*, in French, is constructed, and kept up by the planters, on the same principles that roads and bridges are made, only each land holder, through whose land it passes, has to bear his due proportion of the construction and repairs of the leveé. Innumerable mill seats are formed by this means, which afford sufficient fall and an abundant supply of water during the rise of the river. It requires only the cutting of a sluice through the leveé at any place, and securing the earth from the action of the water, to form a mill seat; and the water, when it has turned the mill, passes off into the swamps.

Only a narrow strip of land on the river is cultivated, forming one tier of plantations. Back of this are swamps and alligators. At Point Coupeé, you begin to see the beautiful orange groves, and the live oak. All the plantation houses are surrounded with rich and beautiful groves of orange and other trees.

Baton Rouge is a beautiful village on the eastern bank of the Mississippi, and one hundred and fifty miles above New Orleans. Here terminates the bluffs of the eastern shore, and below this, the banks of the river become uniform.

The cultivation of sugar cane and rice now becomes regular. For the whole distance to New Orleans, plantation touches plantation. The extensive plantation houses, the massive sugar houses, and the immense groups of negro huts succeed each other, and form a singular and striking appearance. The dwelling houses of the planters are neat, some are splendid, and are all seated amidst groves of oranges and jessamine, and surrounded with the multiflora rose and other shrubs. This is probably the richest agricultural district in the United States, and presents a beautiful and delicious scenery, beyond any thing of which a stranger can conceive. But all this beauty, and richness, and grandeur, with all its animating power, brings a heart sickening feeling over the contemplative mind. All this is the work of *slaves*. It is the price of tears, and groans, and blood. And let it be registered on high, and graven on the heart of every American, the State of Louisiana has forbidden, under the most severe penalties, the miserable slaves the poor boon of being *taught to read even the Scriptures!!* Now let not my New England readers exult in the thought that their favoured land is free from such enormities, and their Louisianian brethren are in a semi-barbarous state; lest I point to their incarcerated *debtors*, and tell them that slavery with all its horrors, is not a greater violation of human rights, than the odious practice of imprisonment for debt!

One hundred and five miles from the mouth of the Mississippi, and something over one thousand from the mouth of the Ohio, stands the CITY OF NEW ORLEANS, the great commercial city of the Valley of the Mississippi.

Introductory to a very few remarks of my own, I lay before the reader the following letter to the editors of the New York Observer, written immediately after the great Sunday School meeting at New Orleans, gotten up by Messrs. Baird and Welch, agents of the American Sunday School Union.

"*New Orleans, Feb.* 14, 1831.

"GENTLEMEN,—This letter, as you perceive, is dated at the most remarkable city, in some respects, of our country. It is the great commercial mart of the valley of the Mississippi, situated 105 miles from the mouth of the father of western rivers, and on the first favorable site for a city, receiving from above the productions that grow along a hundred noble streams, which pour their waters into the grand recipient upon whose bank it stands—and from below, the productions of every clime, wafted to it by every wind that blows,—it increases rapidly in wealth and population, and is destined to be the *second*, if not the *first*, city of this Union. Where on earth can another city be found, whose situation is so favorable, in regard to the extent of country, whose productions, as it were, naturally tend to one great centre of trade; almost like the material substances on the earth's surface to the centre of gravitation? Above it are more than 1,200,000 square miles of the most fertile country, taken as a whole, that earth affords in equal extent; a country which will one day, and that not very distant, contain a population of 100,000,000 immortal beings, blest with intelligence and virtue, and happy under a delightful and just government, established and maintained by a virtuous people; or else rent into factions, distracted into opposing communities, suffering all the evils that anarchy and irreligion can bring upon a people.

New Orleans was founded in 1719, by Bienville, who succeeded his brothers, Ibberville and Sanvolle, in the government of the French colony of *Louisiana*—a name which was then applied to the whole region which is now called the Valley of the Mississippi. This name was given to it, in honor of Louis XIV, by La Salle, or rather by Father Hennepin, I believe, about the year 1671 or 1672.

The country on both sides of the Mississippi is very low and perfectly level, or rather declines gradually from the river. On each side, the bank is cultivated along the margin to the distance back of about a mile. Beyond this narrow but amazingly fertile strip of land, there is nothing but swampy land, covered with live oak, cypress, &c. A levee eight or ten feet in height, and about thirty wide, extending many miles above and below the city, protects it from the overflowing of the Mississippi in the months of June and July, the season of its periodical rising.

"The city stands on the northern bank of the river. There is here, however, one of those remarkable bends of the river which makes it difficult to say, as it regards the points of the compass, on which bank the city stands. For just above the city it runs almost due south, then it turns to the east, in a short distance almost due north, then east, and finally south. So that the city, which stretches along the river quite three or four miles, in the upper part, faces the east ; in the centre it faces the south ; and in the lower part it inclines to the west or southwest. Those streets which may be said to run along the river, or parallel to it, are somewhat in the shape of an Indian's bow, except that the extremes form large angles, instead of curves, at the junction of their central parts. Those streets which run out from the city towards the woods or swamps in the rear of the city, may be said to be at right angles with that section, (1 was going to say, *segment*,) of the river from which they commence. Of course there are some queer *squares*—not indeed, like that which an Irishman found in the lower part of Philadelphia, that is, a *round* one, but somewhat in the shape of a *wedge*.

The streets are narrow, and many of them not yet paved. Yet it ought to be said that the city authorities are making very great efforts to improve the convenience, and the health too, of the city, by paving it as fast as it can be done—a work which is attended with much expense, as all the stone must be brought from the north. The houses are low framed houses, particularly those built by the French and Spanish. Those which have been built by the Americans, are, many of them, of two or three stories, and built of brick. Many of them have several feet of ground around them, or at least on each side, where you may see the beautiful China-tree, the ornamental tree of this region—the fig-tree, the olive, banana vegetable, the pomegranate, the orange, with much beautiful shrubbery, such for beauty and splendor and fragrance, the *Northerners* have never seen, and of course would not have a conception of, if I should attempt to describe it.

"The population has increased rapidly. In 1810, it was 17,242; in 1820, it was 27,156; and in 1830, about 50,000. This is the stationary or fixed population. In the season of business, that is, the winter, you may add 20 or 25,000 more. As to the trade, you may have some idea of it from the fact that this year about 100,000 hogsheads of sugar, probably 5,000,000 gallons of molasses, 40,000 hogsheads of tobacco, and 400,000 bales of cotton will be exported; besides immense quantities of flour, &c.

"This is one of the most wonderful places in the world. Take a little turn with me on the levee; and first survey the river. As far as you can see, almost up and down, the margin is lined with flat-bottomed boats, come from above, from every point almost in the valley of the Mississippi. Some are laden with flour, others with corn, others with meat of various kinds, others with live stock, cattle, hogs, horses, or mules. Some have travelling stores; occasionally some are to be found which are full of negroes; and some full of what is infinitely worse, "Old Monongahela" whiskey. Along the lower part, you will see a forest of masts; higher up, you may see 20 or 30 steamboats, with their bows up against the levee, or else projecting over an "up country" flat-bottomed boat. Every day some come from above and others depart, on *short* excursions of trade of a thousand or two miles, to St. Louis, or Louisville, or Nashville, or Pittsburg, or hundreds of other places. For distance is no longer thought of in this region—it is almost annihilated by steam! And if you cast your eye down the river, you may see a whole fleet, sometimes, coming up without a sail stretched, or an oar manned—all carried along, and that not a slow rate, by a steam tow-boat, of tremendous power. I was perfectly amazed the first time I saw this spectacle. It was the Grampus, or Porpoise, or Shark tow-boat, marching up, having two large ships grappled to her sides, two or three brigs at a cable's length behind, and still further in the rear, one or two schooners and two or three sloops! all moving along very reluctantly, and not unlike lazy urchins following a rigid master to the task; they went because they could not help it.

And if you turn your back to the river, you will see wonderful "sights," as our friends in Pennsylvania would say. In one place you will see the busy and anxious looking merchant, receiving from the steam-boat, or putting on board his ship, his cotton, his sugar, his molasses, tobacco, coffee, boxes of goods, &c. which cover the levee far and wide. Along the whole line are the owners of the flat bottomed boats trading with the citizen shop-keeper. Whole rows of English and Americans are to be seen peddling those valuable little stores which one can move about in a hand-barrow, or carry in a basket. And then such crowds (especially along that part of the levee which is opposite the market-house) of *Negresses* and Quatre-unes, (written *Quadroons* by those who don't understand French,) carrying on their *bandanaed* heads, and with solemn pace, a whole *table*, or platform as large as a table, covered with goodies, such as cakes, and apples, and oranges, and figs, and bananas or plantains, and pine-apples, and cocoa-nuts, &c. which it would be too tedious for me fully to enumerate.

"And then if you go through the city, you may look at the steam saw mills, steam cotton compressing machines, the market-house, the state-house, of ancient appearance, the hotels, the theatres if you like, the cathedral, the calaboos, (calaboosa, I suppose) or jail, the charitable hospital, and last, as the terminating point to us all, the place where repose, in the stillness of the tomb, those who once inhabited this city now so full of life, activity and mirth. There is nothing in New Orleans more interesting to a reflecting man, than the Catholic and Protestant grave yards, which seem to be covered with beautiful white mausoleums, some of several feet in height, some standing solitary, and others crowded together. It was with mingled emotions that I stood by that of the eloquent and youthful *Larned*, bearing as the most fit epitaph, the simple name of him whose ashes are resting there. And there too rests *De Fernex*, cut down at a time, when, so far as human eye can see, his usefulness was commencing. But good is the will of the Lord!

"The population of this place is exceedingly various. A large portion speak the French language; some, but the number is not great, the Spanish; and the remainder, the English or American. Those that speak the French, are generally Catholics, and are through all their conditions and complexions, a polite, agreeable, and interesting people; honest, frugal, and inoffensive. Too many of the Americans who reside here, and more especially those who make but a transient stay, are devoted to the exclusive business of acquiring wealth, and are so immersed in business as to neglect, it is to be feared, generally the interests of the immortal spirit.

"Still there is progress made in the diffusion of evangelical religion, and an increase of its practice. There is a small Baptist church without a pastor, an Episcopal church, of which the

Rev. Mr. Hull is pastor; a considerable Methodist society, which has a pastor, whose name escapes me at this moment—but a very worthy man; the Rev. Mr. Clapp's congregation is large, and highly respectable; and a second Presbyterian church, to which the Rev. Mr. Aikman had begun to minister with good prospects, when he was laid aside, for a while at least, by the mysterious but still righteous providence of God. The Rev. Mr. Winslow is laboring among the mariners. It is a pity that their building is not yet completed. Could not a few thousand dollars be raised among your wealthy and liberal men in New York for this purpose? I am persuaded that if they were here a week, they would see the importance of doing so. The brethren here are few in number, not generally wealthy, truly liberal, but have much to do, and support heavy burdens.

"The tract cause prospers; and with prudence it will do so. The agent is a worthy young man. Sunday Schools too are making progress. There are five in number, which embrace about four or five hundred scholars, all white: the colored people are not, as you know, allowed to be taught in schools. There is nothing needed, with the blessing of God, but for the American Sunday School Union to keep an agent here continually, an able, agreeable, and devoted man, who shall confine his labors principally to this city for a year or two. If this course were pursued, the number of schools would soon be doubled and trebled. There will be some difficulty in finding teachers, but they could be found by a suitable man stationed at this great political *heart* of the Valley of the Mississippi. I am glad that the American Sunday School Union is directing its attention to this region. Yesterday we had a large meeting at Mr. Clapp's church, to consider and act upon the recent resolution of the Society to establish Sunday schools throughout this Valley. The way had been prepared by the labors of the society's agents, Rev. Mr. Baird and Rev. Mr. Welch, who had been here some days. The meeting was opened by appointing the Hon. J. A. Smith, President of the Senate of the State, and the Hon. Mr. Ker, a member of the same body, as Chairman and Secretary of the meeting. After prayer, by Rev. Mr. Clapp, the Rev. Mr. Baird addressed the meeting, and gave a very interesting history of this undertaking. When he was done, Mr. Duncan, Dr. M'Connell, Mr. Conrad, A. Hennen, Esq. and J. A. Maybin, Esq. presented resolutions, which were unanimously adapted, approving of Sabbath schools, and of the noble resolution of the Society. Whilst the last gentleman was speaking, the subscription and collection went round, and you will rejoice that about *one thousand* dollars were subscribed for this object, which is an evidence of the interest felt in this cause by the people of this city. The influence of the meeting will be long felt, it is believed. The Hon. Judge Harper, of the U. S. District Court, a man of fine talents, was prevented from speaking only by the want of time.

"Upon the whole, whilst there is much to be done in this city, there are some things encouraging. It has its wickedness, as has every city. Of the permanent population much might be said of an interesting character. There is much intelligence among them. Here are five daily papers, three of which are partly in French and partly in English, and all are conducted with ability. The French are an amiable people, very sober in their habits, and inoffensive, good citizens. There is but little drunkenness among them, be it said to their honor. And the most of the intemperance to be found here, (for it is not a *drunken* city, far from it—it is better in this respect than New York,) is to be found among the half horse, half alligator characters that come down the river; and even they are greatly reformed—yes, reformed by *steam!* I have not time now to tell you how—but it is a fact, as you shall know.

"I ought to add that at Natches, near eight hundred or one thousand dollars have been raised for the promotion of Sabbath schools in the State of Mississippi.

Yours, &c.   PHILANDER.

To the foregoing is added a letter addressed to the author, by an old friend and fellow-laborer, soon after a meeting was held at New Orleans, on behalf of the Sunday school project, for the Valley of the Mississippi, dated

"*New Orleans, Feb.* 15, 1831.

"DEAR SIR,—Knowing the interest you have long felt in the rising prospects of the west, I have no doubt you will feel pleased to hear that a public meeting has been lately held in this place upon the subject of Sabbath schools, and more particularly to devise means to aid the American Sunday School Union in accomplishing their noble resolution, which was passed at their last anniversary, to establish Sabbath schools throughout the Valley of the Mississippi. A subscription was obtained, amounting to $1030, most of which has been actually paid. This is said to have been the largest amount ever collected in this State, on any one occasion for any benevolent object.

"A division has lately taken place in the Presbyterian church here, and a second church has been formed. The Methodists have a meeting-house, society, and stationed preacher. The Baptists have a good meeting-house, built and owned by a brother C—— P——g, but they have no regularly organized church, although at present they have occasional preaching. There are, perhaps, fifty individuals of the Baptist denomination in the city, and many of them possessed of talents and wealth ; and yet they have hitherto, in a great measure, stood aloof from each other—have neither sought, nor enjoyed much intercourse, are comparatively strangers to each other, and are without a settled preacher. Is there no man of talents and self-denial, who can be found, willing to come into this, the most extensive field in the United States, gather up these scattered sheep, and give efficiency and direction to the talents and wealth that are here abundantly sufficient for a flourishing Baptist church? It is to be hoped that the Baptist Missionary Society of Massachusetts will have regard to this field as soon as possible. Present circumstances are unusually favorable, and I hope the crisis will not be permitted to pass unimproved.

Sincerely yours,   J. E. W."

It is to the spiritual state and wants of this important city I design more particularly to draw the attention of the philanthropic and pious reader. Capitalists, merchants, seamen, and all descriptions of worldly-minded men, will never hesitate where their interest calls them. They need no urging to hazardous points. But the "children of light," need urging, coaxing, and goading; and then, with pale faces, they will start back, and with palpitating hearts, cry,

"Is it a sickly place? Do you think I shall enjoy health? Can I get a comfortable support?"

Speaking of the immense advantages of New Orleans as a commercial depot, Mr. Flint, who resided there some time, observes: "It has one dreary drawback—the insalubrity of its situation. Could the immense swamps between it and the bluffs be drained, and the improvements commenced in the city be completed; in short, could its atmosphere ever become a dry one, it would soon leave the great cities of the Union behind.

"The police of the city have been at great expense in erecting steam works to supply the city with water. That of the Mississippi, when filtrated, is admirable. The streets are also washed, and the sewers cleansed, by water from the river. When these works are carried into complete operation, no city in the Union will be more amply supplied with better water than this place."

MANNERS AND CUSTOMS.

The same writer observes, "In respect to the manners of the people, those of the French citizens partake of their general national character. They have here their characteristic politeness and urbanity; and it may be remarked, that ladies of the highest standing will show courtesies that would not comport with the ideas of dignity at the north. In their convivial meetings, there is apparently a great deal of cheerful familiarity, tempered however, with the most scrupulous observances, and the most punctilious decorum. They are the same gay, dancing, spectacle-loving race, that they are everywhere else. It is well known that the Catholic religion does not forbid amusements on the Sabbath. They fortify themselves in defending the custom of going to balls and the theatre on the Sabbath, by arguing that religion ought to inspire cheerfulness, and that cheerfulness is associated with religion.*

"Much is said about the profligacy of manners and morals here; and this place has more than once been called the modern Sodom. Amidst such a multitude, composed in a great measure of the low people from all nations, there must of course be much debauchery and low vice. Where it appears in this form, it is so disgusting, and the tippling houses and other resorts of vice, have such an aspect of beastliness and degradation, as to render them utterly *unbearable*. Perhaps the tenants of these houses, without intending it, do a good office to the inhabitants in general, acting as the Helotes to the Spartan children, rendering these exhibitions of vice and degradation more odious and disgusting. Society here is very much assorted. Each man has an elective attraction to men of his own standing and order.

---

* In this particular they appear to coincide with a class of religionists in New-England. *P.*

"It is a questionable point, and has excited discussion here, whether it is not disgraceful to the city, to license gambling, and other houses of ill fame. Much is said in defence of this practice; that since vice will exist, they had better have a few houses filled, than all spoiled; they had better bring vice as much together as possible, and compel it to act under the trammels of law and order; and that by devoting the great funds that arise from this license, to the charity hospital, and other benevolent purposes, they compel, in the phrase of the country, 'the devil' to pay tribute to virtue. I have never, of course, seen the interior of the 'temple of fortune.' But I have often heard it described. Everything that can tempt avarice or the passions is here. Here is the 'roulette,' the wheel of fortune, every facility for gambling, and in all quarters piles of dollars, and doubloons, as nest eggs, to make new gulls lay to them. Here is everything to tempt the eye, and inflame the blood. Here the raw cullies from the upper country come, lose all, and either hang themselves, or get drunk, and perish in the streets. A spacious block of buildings was shown me, which was said to have been built by a gambler from the avails of his success. One night he lost everything, and the next morning suspended himself from the roof of an upper apartment."

The foregoing portraiture of the gaming houses of New Orleans is, no doubt, graphically true. If I recollect right, there are six large establishments that regularly pay license, and produce a revenue of many thousand dollars annually.

The following extract from Mr. Flint's Recollections, glances at another subject which, I am sorry to add, is too frequently the cause of animadversion in slave-holding States, and amongst a mixed population. And not only as it respects *yellow* complexions, but faces many shades darker! A stranger in visiting any of our southwestern towns and cities, is struck with the occular demonstration that *color* rather invites, than constructs a barrier against, illicit intercourse. The number of mulattoes seen in every direction, is a melancholy proof of the irregularities that prevail.

In relation to New Orleans, Mr. Flint observes: "Much has been said about certain connections that are winked at with the yellow women of this city. I know not whether this be truth, or idle gossiping. The yellow women are often remarkable for the perfect symmetry of their forms, and for their fine expressions of eye. They are universally admitted to have a fidelity and cleverness as nurses for the sick, beyond all other women. When a stranger is brought up by the prevailing fever, the first object is to consign him to the care of one of these faithful nurses, and then he has all the chance for life that the disorder admits.

"On the whole, I judge from an observation at different times of thirty weeks, that this city, as it respects people who have any self-estimation, is about on a footing with the other cities of the Union in point of morals. There are many excellent people here, many people who mourn over the prevailing degeneracy."*

It is a painful reflection in the mind of a serious Protestant, that so large a proportion of the population of this city, and indeed of the State, are Roman Catholics. Even whole districts are found in which hardly the forms of christian worship exist. In the settlements along the river from St. Francisville to New Orleans, the Catholics have churches, or houses for worship, at intervals of eight or ten miles. The spire surmounted by the Holy Cross, is to be seen through the clumps of the trees. The cathedral in New Orleans, is described as a noble pile of buildings. The walls are very thick and massive. Beneath and around it, the dead sleep.

Viewed by themselves, the Roman Catholics in Louisiania, Missouri, &c. are increasing, partly from emigration, which is chiefly from Ireland, and partly from the influence their schools, seminaries, and nunneries have on the young mind. But view them in relation to other denomination, and they *decrease.*

---

* Ten years Recollections.

The proportion of Protestant emigrants is greater than that of the Roman Catholics. But were Protestants to make no particular efforts to sustain what they believe to be the principles of the Bible, and especially to preserve the rising generation from the captivating influence of the numerous seminaries and nunneries, all places of resort to male and female youth, the Catholics would soon advance upon them with accelerated steps. I have merely adverted to the subject here, intending in a more appropriate place to pursue it more in detail.

A college has been founded in New Orleans, upon which large funds have been expended, but its usefulness to literature may be doubted. The Ursuline nuns have a convent, and, as at all these institutions in the west, receive boarders and day-scholars. The Female Orphan Asylum is spoken of in meritorious terms, as a valuable institution for charity. It was founded by a benevolent French gentleman by the name of Poydras.

The Protestants have several benevolent societies and charitable institutions. A mariners' church has been erected, and means provided for the religious instruction of the numerous seamen that visit this place; but a heavy debt hangs over the building. The Louisiana Bible Society has done much to disseminate the word of God, and supply the destitute in the State. I have no data to show whether all the State has been explored and supplied.

A Tract depository has been established there, and an agent employed, by the American Tract Society. The impulse given to Sunday schools at the late meeting, already noticed, it is hoped will result in the establishment of Sunday schools wherever it is practicable.

What I do not hesitate to call the barbarous, wicked, and foolish laws of that State, *which prohibit the slaves from being taught to read*, are a serious impediment to the moral and religious instruction of that numerous and unfortunate class. Such laws display on the part of the law makers, little knowledge of human nature and the real tendency of things. To keep *slaves* entirely ignorant of the rights of man, in this spirit-stirring age, is utterly impossible. Seek out the remotest and darkest corner of Louisiana, and plant every guard that is possible around the negro quarters, and the light of truth will penetrate. Slaves will find out, for they already know it, that they possess rights as men. And here is the fatal mistake now committed in the southern slaveholding States—legislating against the instruction of their slaves—to keep them from knowing their rights. They will obtain some loose, vague, and undefined notion of the doctrine of human rights, and the unrighteousness of oppression in ,this republican country. Keeping from them all the moral and religious instruction which Sabbath schools, the Bible, and other good books are calculated to impart, and with those undefined notions of liberty, and without any moral principle, they are prepared to enter into the first insurrectionary movement proposed by some artful and talented leader. The same notion prevailed in the West Indies half a century since, and many of the planters resisted and persecuted the benevolent Moravians, who went there to instruct the blacks in the principles and duties of religion. A few of the planters reasoned justly. They invited these benevolent men on their plantations, and gave them full liberty on the Sabbath, and at other suitable seasons, to instruct their slaves. The happiest effects followed. On these plantations, where riot, misrule, and threatened insurrections, had once spread a panic through the colony, order, quietness and submission followed. Such would be the effects if the southern planter would invite the minister of the gospel and the Sunday school teacher to visit his plantation, allow his slaves to be instructed to read, and each to be furnished with a copy of the Scriptures. The southern planter hourly lives under the most terrific apprehensions. It is in vain to disguise the fact. As Mr. Randolph once significantly said in congress, "*when the night bell rings, the mother hugs her infant closer to her breast.*" Slavery, under any circumstances, is a bitter draught—equally bitter to him who tenders the cup, and to him who drinks it. But in all the northern slaveholding States, it is comparatively mild. Its condition would be much alleviated, and the planter might sleep securely if he would abolish his barbarous laws, more congenial with Asiatic despotism, than American republicanism, and provide for his slaves the benefits of wholesome instruction. Philanthropy and interest unite in their demands upon every southern planter to provide Sunday school instruction for his slaves.

Americans come to New Orleans, from all parts of the Union, with a single object in view, that of accumulating wealth, and spending it somewhere else. But death — which they scarcely take into the account—arrests them before their scheme is accomplished. "They have, as might be expected of an assemblage from different regions, mutual jealousies, and mutual dispositions to figure in each other's eyes; of course, the New Orleans people are gay, gaudy in their dress, houses, furniture, and equipage, and rather fine than in the best taste."*

New Orleans is certainly a place of great business and commerce. Fifty steam-boats, and from one thousand to fifteen hundred flat boats and keels, are frequently lying in the harbor; while a forest of masts of the ships of the ocean, is seen as far as the eye can reach. More cot-

---

* FLINT.

ton is shipped from this port than any other in the world. Immense piles fill the streets and crowd the levee, when it is coming in from the interior plantations. Sugar begins to be a staple article of trade, and as to the produce from the upper country, no limits can be set to its amount or probable increase.

Almost every variety of costume and language is seen and heard here. Specimens of almost every nation of Europe, Mexican and South American, Spaniards, Creoles, intermixtures of Negro and Indian blood, samples from every Atlantic and Western State, with the Kentucky "half horse and half alligator" boatmen, a race that the genius of Fulton is every day lessening, are to be found in this city.

Below New Orleans, the same unbroken line of plantations extends along the banks of the river, as was noticed above the city, until the land becomes too low, and has been too recently reclaimed from the ocean to admit of cultivation.

Southwest of the city, and towards the gulf, is an extensive region, well adapted to the sugar making business. Along the bayou of Atchafalaya, Teche, and La Fourche, plantations are already made, and the sugar-houses resemble the large cotton factory buildings of the north. These plantations extend along the coast, and on some islands near the shore. To commence this business profitably, an immense capital is required. Some plantations with the stock and slaves have cost from two to three hundred thousand dollars. The process of making sugar is extremely simple. The cane is planted the latter part of autumn, in slips, and when full grown, resembles in some respects, a field of Indian corn. The stalk is about the size of that of southern corn, which is full of a rich and luscious juice. The stalks are ground in a mill, the liquor extracted and converted into sugar by boiling and evaporation. With a reasonable protection on this article, in a few years enough may be made for the consumption of the whole United States; and when the plantations are once made, and the planters relieved from the heavy debts they incur in commencing a new business, that requires an extensive capital, competition alone will reduce the price of sugar as low as will be desirable, and thus every part of the nation receive a share of the benefit. Already the Louisiana sugar business, is, indirectly, a source of profit to the Illinois and Missouri farmer. Pork, beef, corn, and corn meal, in large quantities, go to supply these plantations. In laying in their stores, the sugar planters calculate upon supplying at the rate of one barrel of second or third rate beef or pork per annum, to each laboring hand. Large quantities of provisions, put up in the States of Illinois and Missouri, are taken to these sugar plantations. Large drafts for sugar mills, engines, and boilers, are made upon the Cincinnati and Pittsburgh iron foundries, and vast numbers of mules and horses, brought by the Missouri traders from the Mexican dominions, go to furnish these plantations.

In exhibiting these sketches, imperfect as they appear, it is not beyond my province to present such facts as go to prove the propriety of the great principle of national protection to every branch of home industry, and the bearing that a reasonable protection will have upon those parts of the country not apparently benefitted. I say *not apparently*, because I do not believe that reasonable protection afforded to the business of one section of the Union, does oppress another section, but that every part, indirectly receives benefit.

With the political agitations of this subject, the writer has nothing to do, and cares as little for the good or ill opinions of any party in politics. On subjects of national importance, as that of the protective system, he sometimes takes the liberty of examining facts, and judging for himself.

Probably no ultimate disadvantage—perhaps some benefit—may result from the recent modification of the tariff on sugar, though it may check, somewhat, the proportionate increase of that branch of national industry. But were protection to the sugar making business to be wholly abandoned, in its present state, the result would be more disastrous to the south and west, than the influx of foreign goods was to the infant manufactures of the north, and to the prosperity of the whole country, in 1816—and produce greater calamities on the south and west, than was felt from that cause in the stagnation of business, and the prostration of enterprise, in 1818, '19, and '20.

"Protection to the cultivation of the cane in Louisiana, is, of itself, worth more to the southern States, than the whole amount of taxes they pay to the general government, in the advanced value of their lands and slaves, which that protection causes. Destroy the sugar plantations of Louisiana, and the lands and slaves of the cotton growing states will have a diminished value of more than two hundred millions of dollars."*

The "Times," of Columbia, S. C. with all its opposition to the tariff, has told the truth in an article of the 12th of February last, which I copy from Niles' Register, for April 2d, 1831.

"Our friends in Congress are at this moment preparing a blow for us, and nobly sacrificing our interests to our principles: We are encouraging them in it, which will be speedily and

---

* The interest on a capital of two hundred millions at six per cent, is twelve millions—being almost *twice as much* as the planting states pay in taxes to the national government......NILES.

severely felt throughout the south. One of the reasons that the wretched policy of the national government has not been more palpably oppressive, is, that the duty which it has placed upon sugar, has created an immense diversion of the planting interest from the cultivation of cotton into that channel. Let the duties be taken off from sugar, and the consequence will be *not only total ruin to nine tenths of the sugar planters*, but it will, by rendering it no longer a profitable crop, turn from fifty to a hundred thousand laborers, and countless acres of land, the best adapted, perhaps, in the world, to such a purpose, back again to the cultivation of cotton."

The above is not only strictly true, in respect to the effects of a repeal of the sugar protecting tariff on the interests of the south, but it would destroy one of the best markets for the produce of the Upper Valley of the Mississippi.

Rice and indigo were formerly cultivated in Louisiana to a greater extent than at present. Mr. Flint thinks the rice of this country has a whiteness and fairness that render it more valuable than that of Georgia, and the indigo that was formerly made on Red river, is said to have been not much inferior to Spanish float.

With the following extract from Mr. Flint's "Recollections," I shall close my sketch of the Lower Valley.

"This state [Louisiana] being almost uniformly level, and extending from 30° to 33° has a climate which might be naturally inferred from its position.

"The summer is temperate, the thermometer seldom indicating so much heat as there often is at the same time at the north. But the heat is uniform and unremitting, and this is what renders the summer oppressive. The days are seldom fanned with the northwestern breeze. The autumn becomes cool, almost as early as at the north. It is dry, and the atmosphere of that mild and delightful blue, peculiar to a southern sky. This season, so delightful elsewhere, is here continued three months. The leaves are long in acquiring their mingled hues of red, yellow, and purple. Frost sometimes occurs in November, but not often before December. Then the leaves yield to the wind, and drop into the pool, and we have that season that invites to 'solemn thought and heavenly musing.'

"January is chilly, with frosty nights, but never sufficiently severe to freeze tender vegetables in the house. A few flakes of snow sometimes fall, though I have seen none during my residence in the country.* Even in this month there are delightful days, when we sit with comfort at the open window. The daffodil and mul-

---

* Snow fell in New Orleans and throughout Louisiana, in considerable quantities the last winter, and it is thought the orange trees have suffered severely......*P.*

tiflora rose are in full blossom through the winter. The turnip patches are yellow with flowers, and the clover has a vigorous growth, and a delightful green. I have eaten green peas in January, and many garden vegetables are brought to market. In February, the rainy season commences, and spring begins to return. The night brings thunder clouds and copious rain, often with loud thunder. In March, spring is in her gayest attire. Planting commences with the first of the month, and continues until July. In the first of the summer, there are thunder showers, attended with vivid lightning, and terrible peals of thunder.

"The latter part of the summer is generally dry. The diseases, except the New Orleans epidemic, differ but little from those of the upper country. The bowel complaint is more common and fatal. The bilious disorders commence earlier in the season, and run more rapidly to their crisis."

PART SECOND.

GENERAL AND PARTICULAR VIEWS OF THE STATES OF ILLINOIS, MISSOURI, INDIANA, AND THE ADJACENT PARTS.

SECTION I.

BOUNDARIES, &c.

We are now prepared to enter upon an extensive and very important section of the Upper Valley of the Mississippi. This section is within the following boundaries: Beginning at the mouth of the Ohio, following up that river to the mouth of the Miami; thence north, to the northwest corner of Ohio; thence along the line between the State of Ohio and Michigan Territory, to Lake Michigan; thence north, through the lake, to its most northern boundary; thence west to the Mississippi, and down that river, south, to the Rapids of Des Moines; thence westward to the northwestern corner of Missouri; thence south, along the western line of Missouri, till it intersects the northern line of the Territory of Arkansas; thence along the southern boundary of Missouri till it reaches the Mississippi; and thence up that river to the place of beginning.

These boundaries include the States of Indiana, Illinois, and Missouri, and the *Wisconsin* territory lying west of Lake Michigan, and north of Illinois, put down on the map as the Northwestern territory.

Probably there is not a tract of country in all America, that in all respects offers as many advantages and as few inconveniences to the emigrant, as that now under consideration. It contains about 200,000 square miles. With a few exceptions of flintstone ridges in Missouri, and steril bluffs, and lakes, north of the Wisconsin river, it is all literally arable land; and much of it superior in quality to the richest land of New England or New York. Here are no steril plains, few rocky or precipitous ridges, (and those rather add to, than lessen the value of the country,) with scarcely a swamp on its surface. Nearly every portion of its soil possesses extraordinary fertility, and is well adapted to the perfect growth of all the grains, grasses, fruits, and roots common to the temperate zone.

Not one half of this wide region, in a state of nature, is covered with timber; and yet there is not a square mile of land but what may be cultivated and furnished with timber at less cost than clearing the same amount of timbered land. In our largest prairies, there are few places more than five miles distant from some point of forest, and I am persuaded the whole country will be studded with farms, and thousands of smiling villages, as soon as the increase of population will require it. There is an abundance of timber in the country for all necessary purposes, and it is distributed in a manner so nearly equal, as to present far less inconvenience to the future occupant of the soil, than is generally supposed. This is a reflection that experience has taught me, contrary to my first impressions in travelling over these extensive prairies. Those who have been habituated to associate the idea of interminable forests with new countries, upon their first arrival in this country, naturally enough conclude there is a great destitution of timber. That this is not the fact, will be shown in another place.

Most of this region is of diluvial formation, and rests upon secondary limestone rock. In many places this approaches within a few feet of the surface, and frequently shows itself in the points of our bluffs, and on the margin of our rivers, and their bottoms. This foundation has never been penetrated, although in boring for salt water, in many places, the augur has been down to the depth of five or six hundred feet.

No country on earth possesses such an agricultural capacity, where "every rood may support its man," and at the same time is so abundant in mineral riches.

Bituminous coal is found in nearly all this region, of a pure quality, and which costs less to quarry it, than to chop an equal quantity of wood.

Iron ore is found in many parts of Indiana and Illinois; but in Missouri alone there is enough, probably of the first quality, to supply the United States with iron for an hundred thousand years to come. I have often seen it in masses on the surface of the ground, through the hilly country south of the Missouri river. In Washington county there is the *iron mountain,* five miles in extent, and four or five hundred feet in height, which yields from 75 to 80 per cent of fine malleable iron.

The lead districts of Missouri, Illinois, and Wisconsin, would cover over more than two hundred square miles. They seem inexhaustible, and the richest region of lead on earth.

Copper exists in large quantities in the northern parts of Illinois, and the adjoining territory.

Salt water is found over the whole extent of this region, yielding from one eighth to one twelfth its weight in pure salt. In many places this water breaks out in the form of fountains or springs; but more frequently it is obtained by boring, which is oftentimes done to the depth of from three to six hundred feet, and when the vein is struck, it generally rises to the surface.

Gypsum abounds in many places, and saltpetre is obtained from the caves in the limestone rock in great abundance. Red and yellow ochre, chalk, alum, copperas, and most of the clays and earths used in the arts, may be found here. All these facts will appear more in detail, when we enter upon a more particular description of each section.

SECTION II.

ILLINOIS.

SITUATION, BOUNDARIES, AND EXTENT.

This State is situated between 37° and 42° 30′ north latitude, and 10° 20′ and 14° 20′ west longitude. It is bounded on the north by Wisconsin Territory, on the east by Lake Michigan, which separates it from Michigan Territory, and the State of Indiana; southeast and south by Kentucky, and west by the State and Territory of Missouri. Its medium length is about 350 miles, and its medium breadth is about 160; the area being about 56,000 square miles, or 35,840,000 acres.

The act of Congress permitting the people of Illinois to form a State government, and the Convention in framing the constitution, described the following as the boundaries of the State. "Beginning at the mouth of the Wabash river, thence up the middle of said river, to the point where a line due north from Vincennes last crosses that stream; thence due north to the middle of Lake Michigan, and along the middle of said lake to 42° 30′ north latitude; thence due west to the Mississippi river; thence down the middle of the main channel thereof, to the mouth of the Ohio river; thence up the latter stream, along its northern or right shore to the place of beginning."

FACE OF THE COUNTRY, AND QUALITIES OF SOIL.

" This State is not traversed by any ranges of hills or mountains; the surface in general is level, but in a few instances uneven, and approaching to hilly. It may be arranged under three general heads. 1. The alluvions of rivers, which are from one to eight miles in width, in some places elevated, and in others low, and subject to inundation. They consist of an intermixture of woods and prairie. The soil is almost invariably fertile—such are the bottoms on the banks of the Mississippi, Wabash, Illinois, Kaskaskia, &c. 2. After leaving the alluvions, and rising to the 'bluffs' which bound them, is a tract of level land, elevated from fifty to one hundred feet, and which is sometimes called 'table land.' The greater proportion of this is prairie, which in some places is dry, and in others wet and marshy, depending upon the convexity or concavity of the surface. The soil is less fertile than that of the alluvions, but is generally preferred by emigrants. The tract of country between the Mississippi and Kaskaskia rivers belongs to this class. 3. In the interior and towards the northern part of the State, the country becomes rough and uneven. It consists of an intermixture of woods and prairies, diversified with gentle or abrupt slopes, sometimes attaining the elevation of hills, and irrigated with a number of streams. The soil is in many places steril."

The above general description, which I have copied from Beck's Gazetteer, is tolerably accurate, except the last division in the northern part of the State. Ten years since, when Dr. Beck wrote his Gazetteer of Missouri and Illinois, the northern portion of this State, was but little known, excepting on the banks of the navigable streams, where its rough, uneven, and steril character appeared. It is now well known that this region contains a soil as fertile and arable as other portions of the State.

But to afford the information now called for, it is necessary to particularize in describing the *face of the country*, and *qualities of soil*. Under these general heads, we shall divide the surface of the State into the following particulars.

 1. Inundated Lands.
 2. River and Creek Bottoms.
 3. Level Prairies.
 4. Rolling Prairies.

5. Barrens.
6. Timbered Uplands.
7. Knobs, Bluffs, Ravines, and Sink-holes.
8. Stony Ground.

INUNDATED LANDS.

We apply this term to all those portions, which, for some part of the year, are under water. These include portions of the river bottoms, and portions of the interior of large prairies, with the lakes and ponds which, for half the year or more, are without water. The term "bottom," is used throughout the west to denote the alluvial soil on the margins of rivers, usually called "intervals," in New England. Portions of this description of land are overflowed for a longer or shorter period, when the rivers are full. I have already noticed this fact in describing the lower valley bordering on the Mississippi. Probably one sixth of our bottom lands are of this description; for though the water may not stand for any length of time, it wholly prevents settlement and cultivation, though it does not interrupt the growth of timber and vegetation. These tracts are on the bottoms of the Wabash, Ohio, Mississippi, Illinois, and all the interior rivers.

When the rivers rise above their ordinary height, the waters of the smaller streams, which are backed up by the freshets of the former, break over their banks, and cover all the low grounds. Here it stands for a few days, or for many weeks, especially towards the bluffs; for it is a striking fact in the geology of the western country, that all the river bottoms are higher on the margins of the streams than some distance back. Consequently, when the superfluous waters break out of their channels, lakes and ponds are immediately formed towards the bluffs, and the waters being unable to return to the channels of the streams, they remain to be taken up by evaporation, or absorbed by the soil. I have estimated the portion of land thus inundated, and rendered useless for present settlement and cultivation, as one sixth part of the river bottoms. But whenever increase of population shall create a demand for this species of soil, the most of it can be reclaimed at comparatively small expense. Its fertility will be inexhaustible, and if the waters from the rivers could be shut out by dykes or levees, or turned into their natural channels as the rivers subside, the soil would be perfectly dry. Most of the small lakes on the American bottom disappear in the summer, and leave a deposit of vegetable matter undergoing decomposition, or a luxuriant coat of weeds and grass.

As our prairies mostly lie between the streams that drain the country, the interior of the large ones are usually level, or a few inches lower than the elevated parts of their borders. Here are formed ponds and lakes after the winter and spring rains, which remain to be drawn off by evaporation, or absorbed by an adhesive soil. Hence the middle of our large level prairies are uniformly wet, and for several weeks portions of them are covered with water. To remedy this inconvenience completely, and render all this portion of soil dry and productive, only requires a ditch or drain of two or three feet deep to be cut into the nearest ravine. In many instances a single furrow with the plough, would drain many acres. At present, this species of inundated land offers no inconvenience to the people, except in the production of miasmata, and even that, perhaps, becomes too much diluted with the atmosphere to produce mischief before it reaches the settlements on the borders of the prairie. Hence the inference is correct that our inundated lands present fewer obstacles to the settlement and growth of the country, and can be reclaimed at much less expense than the swamps and salt marshes of the Atlantic states.

What is known in New England by the name of *swamp* can scarcely be found in Illinois, and a quagmire is of still rarer occurrence.

It may be well to note here, that of the inundated bottoms described, considerable portions exist on the bottoms of both the Illinois and Mississippi rivers, in that section of the State usually known by the name of the *military tract*. Much of the bottom land in the counties of Pike,

Guide for Emigrants. 95

Calhoun, Schuyler, and Fulton, is overflowed in the spring.

RIVER AND CREEK BOTTOMS.

EVEN the surface of our alluvial bottoms is not entirely level. In some places it resembles alternate waves of the ocean, and looks as though the waters had left their deposit in ridges, and retired.

The portion of bottom land capable of present cultivation, and on which the waters never stand, if, at an extreme freshet, they are covered, resemble, in external appearance, the rich intervals and meadows on the Connecticut river, but possessing a soil of exhaustless fertility; a soil that for ages past has been gradually deposited by the annual floods. Its average depth, on the Missouri and Mississippi, is from 20 to 25 feet. Logs of wood, and other indications of the surface are found at that depth. The soil dug from the bottom of wells on these bottoms, produce luxuriantly the first year, when brought to the surface.

AMERICAN BOTTOM. The most extensive and fertile tract, of this description of soil, in this state, is the *American Bottom*, a name it received when it constituted the western boundary of the United States, and which it has retained ever since. It commences at the mouth of the Kaskaskia river, five miles below the town of Kaskaskia, [see the map] and extends northwardly along the Mississippi to the bluffs at Alton, a distance of ninety miles; and extending back to a chain of bluffs and precipices at the distance of from four to eight miles from the river. Its average width is five miles, and it contains about 450 square miles, or 288,000 acres. Opposite St. Louis, in St. Clair county, the bluffs are seven miles from the river, and filled with inexhaustible beds of coal. The soil of this bottom is an argillaceous or a siliceous loam, accordingly as clay or sand happens to predominate in its formation.

On the margin of the river, and of some of its lakes, is a strip of heavy timber, with a thick undergrowth, which extends from half a mile to two miles in width, but from thence to the bluffs, it is principally prairie. It is interspersed with sloughs, lakes and ponds, the most of which become dry in the fall season. From one sixth to one eighth of its surface is inundated land. The rest is dry and arable at all seasons.

In a few instances, the waters of the Mississippi, at its annual rise, break out of its banks, and inundate the low grounds of the bottom. The old French village of Cahokia, five miles below St. Louis, and a little back from the river, on the border of the prairie, is protected from such casualties by a dyke or levee, kept up at the common expense of the village.

In 1784, after a winter of extraordinary snows, the river rose many feet above its usual height, overflowed a large portion of this bottom, drove the Cahokians from their village to the bluffs, covered the town of Kaskaskia to the depth of two or three feet, and furnished navigation for boats from Kaskaskia to St. Louis, over the prairies. The preceding winter, the snow lay from two to three feet deep in St. Louis, and proportionably deeper at the heads of the Missouri.

The soil of the American bottom is as rich as land can be made, and that to the average depth of twenty-five feet. About the French towns it has been cultivated, and produced corn in succession, without manuring, for more than a century, without exhausting its fertilizing powers. It is evident, however, that such an injudicious method as has been pursued by farmers in this country, renders the soil more adhesive or clammy, and exposes it to bake in the sun.

There is much valuable timber and prairie on this bottom that can be purchased. Many of the titles are held by grants made to the early French settlers, but are thought to be valid. It would cost from two to five dollars per acre. Considerable tracts are still owned by government, and can be had at $1,25 per acre. The only objection that can be offered to this tract is its unhealthy character. This, however, has diminished considerably within eight or ten years. The geological feature noticed in the last article—that all our bottoms are higher on the margin of the stream than towards the bluffs, presents the cause why so much standing water is on the bottom land, which, during summer, stagnates and throws off noxious effluvia. These lakes are usually full of vegetable matter undergoing decomposition, and which produces large quantities of miasma. Some of the lakes are clear and of a sandy bottom, but the most are of a different character. The French settled near a lake or a river, apparently in the most unhealthy places, and yet their constitutions are little affected, and they usually enjoy good health, though dwarfish and shrivelled in form and features.

"The villages of Kaskaskia, Prairie du Rocher, and Cahokia, were built up by their industry in places where Americans would have perished. Cultivation has, no doubt, rendered this tract more salubrious than formerly; and an increase of it, together with the construction of drains and canals, will make it one of the most eligible in the States. The old inhabitants advise the emigrants not to plant corn in the immediate vicinity of their dwellings, as its rich and massy foliage prevents the sun from dispelling the deleterious vapours."*

These lakes and ponds could be drained at a small expense, and the soil would be susceptible

---

* Beck.

of cultivation. The early settlements of the Americans were either on this bottom, or the contiguous bluffs, and they suffered much from sickness. This circumstance alone, probably gave the character of a sickly region to Illinois, and produced an impression abroad prejudicial to the character of the country, from which it has not yet entirely recovered. Multitudes in the old States, but without evidence, associate in their minds the idea that Illinois is not as well calculated for health as other portions of the west. It will appear in its proper place that this idea is wholly incorrect.

Origin of the American Bottom.—Many speculations have been made as to the geological formation of this bottom. In the south part of St. Clair, in Monroe, and in the north part of Randolph counties, the bluffs on its eastern border terminate in abrupt precipices of limestone rock, from fifty to two hundred feet in height. On these rocks, at considerable elevation, are evident marks of water friction. Opposite, and on the Missouri side, they are still more elevated, and overhang the river. About Herculaneum they are used for shot towers in the manufacture of shot. The hypothesis of some is, that in former times the Mississippi laved the eastern bluffs, and the bottom land lay on its western side; that by gradual encroachments of the river it was all washed away, islands and sand-bars were formed in its former channel, and by annual deposits from the Missouri, the whole American bottom was formed. This hypothesis is specious and plausible; but unfortunately for the antiquary and geologist, we have no official documents to prove it. Objections may be raised to it. Not to mention the water marks already alluded to, far above the present reach of the waters,—on this bottom are an immense number of *mounds*, and other marks of antiquity, of which some are immensely large. In the distance of seven miles from the ferry opposite St. Louis, and within sight of the road to Edwardsville, I have counted seventy-three mounds of all forms and sizes, from sixty or seventy feet high, to a small elevation above the plain. These are *supposed* to have been formed by the labor of man. They must all have been formed since the river retired to its present channel, and the bottom attained its present elevation.

Others conjecture this bottom must have been carved out by the universal deluge, when the whole valley of the Mississippi received its present geological structure; but wherever it has been penetrated for water, it gives unquestionable proof of a later origin.

With a third class of system makers, it was once a lake studded with small islands—that at some distance below the mouth of the Kaskaskia river, where a singular rock rears its rugged head far above the surface of the river, and a chain of rocks now extend across the whole channel, there was once a tremendous barrier forming the grand cataract of the Father of Waters, as famous in the days of yore for the safe passage of the Indian's canoe, as were the falls of Niagara when Goldsmith wrote his graphical sketch. Here are really indications on both the east and west side of the Mississippi, to sustain the plausibility of an immense chain of rock extending across the river from bluff to bluff. On the Missouri side the precipices that overhang the water, and which frowned down upon the boatman toiling at the cordelle, as he slowly tugged his keel along, and at a height far above the possible reach of the river in its extreme floods, are the distinctive marks of water friction. Towards the eastern shore is the *Grand Tower,* a circular column of sand rock, with its sides nearly perpendicular, and corresponds in its appearances and stratification, with the banks of the Mississippi. The top is flat, and supports a stratum of soil on which grow a clump of trees and shrubs. East of this, and towards the bluffs, is a slough, through which a portion of the river passes at its flood. A chain of rocks extend from the Grand Tower quite across the bed of the river, immense masses of which may be seen at low water. All these appearances lead to the conclusion that here was once a complete barrier to the waters of the Mississippi, which rushed down stupendous falls, greater even than those of Niagara. From this point, which is only a few miles above the mouth of the Big Muddy river, in Jackson county, to the mouth of the Kaskaskia, there is no bottom, except that of Bois Brule, on the Missouri side. The bluffs line the river, and exhibit appearances of being worn through by water, or broken down by some convulsion. Admit the existence of these falls, and the geological formation of the American bottom is decided. It was once a lake through which the Mississippi passed, and in which the Missouri, Illinois, Kaskaskia, and several smaller streams discharged their waters. It extended from the present mouth of the Kaskaskia, to the mouth of the Illinois, and approached to the foot of the Mamelles, within three miles of St. Charles.

By the ordinary wear of the waters, as is the case at Niagara, or the more probable convulsion of an earthquake, a rupture was made in the dam below, the Mississippi rushed through and sought its present level, the lake disappeared, and the annual deposits from the Missouri, with the washing down of the adjacent bluffs, soon produced the present bottom. That this bottom is, in the strictest sense, alluvion, is abundantly evident. The single fact of striking upon trees, vegetable mould, leaves, and petrifactions, prove it. In another place, a thought will be suggested in respect to the mounds, especially the larger ones.

The following streams, or in the language of the country, creeks, pass through portions of the American bottom:

In Monroe county, Fountain and L'Aigle creeks unite in the bottom, and empty into the Mississippi, one mile below Harrisonville. Prairie du Pont rises in the bluffs of St. Clair county, southwest from Belleville, and passes through the bottom a short distance below the village of Cahokia.

Cahokia creek rises in the borders of Maquapin county, passes near Edwardsville, enters the bottom four miles west of that place, passes down the bottom nearly parallel with the Mississippi, and discharges its waters one and a half miles below St. Louis ferry. On this stream are several mills, both in the bottom and on the high ground.

Canteen creek is a small stream that rises in the south part of Madison county, passes near Collinsville, and enters the Cahokia in the bottom. Indian creek is another branch of Cahokia, above Edwardsville. Wood river rises in the north part of Madison county, crosses the north part of the American bottom, and enters the Mississippi nearly opposite the mouth of the Missouri. Some of these creeks would be navigable to the bluffs, for light boats, if the drift wood and other obstructions were removed.

Other particulars of this bottom will be found under the sketches of Madison, St. Clair, Monroe, and Randolph counties.

Besides the American bottom, there are others that resemble it in its general characters, but not in extent. In Union county there is an extensive bottom on the borders of the Mississippi. Above the mouth of the Illinois, and along the borders of the counties of Calhoun, Pike, and Adams, there are a series of bottoms, with much good and elevated land, but the inundated grounds around, present objections to a dense population at present.

The bottoms of Illinois, where not inundated, are equal in fertility, and the soil is less adhesive than most parts of the American bottom. This is likewise the character of the bottoms in the northern parts of the state.

The bottoms of the Kaskaskia are generally covered with a heavy growth of timber, and in many places inundated when the river is at its highest floods.

The extensive prairies adjoining will create a demand for all this timber. The bottom lands on the Wabash are of various qualities. Near the mouth, much of it is inundated. Higher up, it overflows in high freshets. Opposite Vincennes, sand plains begin, mostly prairie, and extend through Crawford and Clark counties, with alternate sand ridges.

These bottoms, especially the American, are the best regions in the United States for raising stock, particularly horses, cattle, and swine. Seventy-five bushels of corn to the acre is an ordinary crop. The roots and worms of the soil, the acorns and other fruits from the trees, and the fish of the lakes, accelerate the growth of swine. Horses and cattle find exhaustless supplies of grass in the prairies; and pea vines, buffalo grass, wild oats, and other herbage in the timber, for summer range; and often throughout most of the winter. In all the rush bottoms, they fatten during the severe weather on rushes. The bottom soil is not so well adapted to the production of small grain, as of maize or Indian corn, on account of its rank growth, and being more subject to blast, or fall down before harvest, than on the uplands. The upper part of the American bottom is somewhat subject to a disease in cattle called the *milk-sickness*, described under the head of diseases.

On the whole, I cannot recommend emigrants from the northern states to place their families on the bottom lands, if they seek for healthy locations, though doubtless in many places in the open prairie, and remote from stagnant ponds, a reasonable degree of health may be had on many bottoms.

LEVEL PRAIRIES.

Under this head I mean all prairie land not included in the term "inundated ground," and yet not sufficiently undulating to carry off the water with facility. This description of soil in some seasons, and especially in a time of drought, is the most deceptive land of any in the state. Strangers to the country have been taken in repeatedly, by locations on wet prairies, and they possess this character merely from being level. The water does not run off freely, but is absorbed by the soil, until it becomes saturated, or remains in this state till relieved by evaporation. In the spring season, the labor of the farmer will be impeded by the wetness of the soil; water will stand in his furrows, and the soil is heavy and compact. In the dry season the moisture becomes exhausted, the surface bakes and cracks on exposure to the sun, and the crop is injured by the drought. Crawfish throw up their hillocks in this soil. The emigrant may mistake in the dry season, and fancy he has a rich, level, and dry farm in prospect, but the next spring will undeceive him. The greatest proportion of this species of land is found in the interior of the large prairies, but there are many smaller portions near the timber. To a man of some experience in the country, wet prairie is readily known, even in a dry time. The stranger, by close observation, may soon learn to detect that soil which will not suit him. To a careless observer, and especially one accustomed to a hilly surface, all our prairies will seem level; but a little attention will enable one to distinguish between a sloping surface, and one entirely level, or a little concave. It is a very common notion amongst the people of the Atlantic states, that a prairie is necessarily wet. Nothing is more inaccurate. *Prairie* is a French word signifying *meadow*, and means any description of surface, covered with grass, and entirely void of timber and brush wood.

Wet, dry, level, and rolling, are circumstances merely, and apply to prairies in the same sense as they do to timbered lands.

ROLLING PRAIRIES.

Under this head I include all our prairie land, which is undulating, or sloping sufficiently to drain off the water, and which is susceptible of immediate cultivation. It should be the first object of the reader to form clear and distinct ideas of a prairie. I have intimated already that very incorrect ideas prevail abroad. Many suppose a prairie necessarily to be a swampy, wet soil, hardly fit for cultivation. Others imagine it to be a sandy and shrubby plain. The reader has only to imagine a tract of country, neither an entire plain, nor broken with hills, but undulating—with occasional bluffs and ravines near the streams and water courses, entirely destitute of timber and shrubs, and clothed in summer with grass and flowers. An extensive meadow will give a correct idea. Nor must the reader figure to himself a boundless tract for many miles in extent, and no timber to break the unvaried prospect. Who has not heard of the grand prairie in Illinois, and what traveller has not reported it to be twenty-four miles across? And yet near the grand prairie are large bodies of timber on the right and left of the road from four to six miles distant.

In some instances, especially south of the great road that leads from Vincennes to St. Louis, the prairies are small, in many instances from one to three miles in circumference, and surrounded with heavy timber. As we go northward they widen, and extend on the more elevated ground between the water courses to a vast distance, and are frequently from six to twelve miles in width. Their borders are by no means uniform. Long points of timber project into the prairies, and line the banks of the streams, and points of prairie project into the timber between these streams. In many instances are copses and groves of timber, from one hundred to two thousand acres, in the midst of prairies, like islands in the ocean. This is a common feature in the country between the Sangamon river and lake Michigan, and in the northern parts of the State. The lead mine region, both in this State and the Wisconsin territory, abounds with these groves.

Origin.—Various conjectures and theories have been formed as to the origin of these prairies. Their continuance is easily solved. Every season the fires sweep over them, burn up the growth of summer, blacken the surface, and leave a deposit of ashes to enrich the soil. Wherever settlements are formed around the smaller prairies, the fires are stopped, and in a few years a growth of timber is produced. I am acquainted with portions in St. Clair county, where thirty-five years since, the first American settlers mowed their hay, that are now covered with a forest of young timber large enough for small buildings.

The following graphical description is copied from the Illinois Monthly Magazine, conducted by James Hall, Esq. a gentleman well known abroad as a fine writer. It is from the pen of the editor, under the head of Notes on Illinois, vol. i. pp. 60—64.

"The most of the country which lies south of a line drawn from the mouth of the Wabash to the mouth of the Kaskaskia, is covered with timber. A very few prairies, and those inconsiderable in point of size, may be found immediately south of this line. Crossing that line, the timber is found to decrease in quantity, and the prairies to expand; yet the latter are still comparatively small, wholly unconnected with each other, and their outlines distinctly marked by the thick forests which surround and separate them. Advancing to the north, the prairie surface begins to predominate; the prairies now become large, and communicate with each other like a chain of lakes, by means of numerous avenues or vistas; still, however, the traveller is surrounded by timber; his eye never loses sight of the deep green outline, throwing out its capes and headlands; though he sees no more than dense forests and large trees, whose deep shade almost appalled him in the south.

"Travelling on from the centre of the State to its northern limit, we find ourselves surrounded by one vast prairie. In the country over which we have passed, the *forest* is interspersed with these interesting plains; *here,* the *prairie* is studded with groves and copses, and the streams fringed with strips of woodland. The eye sometimes wanders over immense plains covered with grass, discovering no other object on which to rest, and finding no limit to its vision but the distant horizon; while more frequently it wanders from grove to grove, and from one point of woodland to another, charmed and refreshed by an endless variety of scenic beauty.

"The prairies afford a subject of curious inquiry to every traveller who visits these States. That these vast and fertile plains should be totally destitute of trees, seems to be an anomaly in the economy of nature. Upon the mind of an American, especially, accustomed to see new lands clothed with timber, and to associate the idea of damp and silent forests with that of a new country, the appearance of sunny plains, and a diversified landscape, untenanted by man, and unimproved by art, is singular and striking. Perhaps if our imaginations were divested of those associations, the subject would present less difficulty; and if we could reason abstractly, it might be as easy to account for the existence of a prairie as of a forest.*

"It is natural to suppose that the first covering of the earth would be composed of such plants as arrived at maturity in the shortest time. Annual plants would ripen, and scatter their seeds many times, before trees and shrubs would

---

* This idea has long dwelt upon my mind. Probably more than one half of the land surface of the earth, in a state of nature, was prairie and desert. Much of it, like our western prairies, is covered with a luxuriant coat of grass and herbage. The *Steppes* of Tartary, the *Pampas* of South America, the *Savannas* of the southern, and the *Prairies* of the western States, are but different names for the same description of country. Had the pilgrim fathers of New England sailed up the Mississippi, and first peopled the prairies of the west, as their posterity approached the interminable forests that once covered all the country east of the Alleghany ridge, they would have found as much difficulty in solving the question how the earth came wholly covered with timber, as we now do in accounting for the origin of prairies. Where did the Patriarchs of the Old Testament feed their flocks? Undoubtedly on the prairies of Syria, Mesopotamia, Judea, and Arabia. *P.*

acquire the power of reproducing their own species. In the mean time, the propagation of the latter would be liable to be retarded by a variety of accidents,—the frosts would nip their tender stems in the winter—fire would consume, or the blast would shatter them—and the wild grazing animals would bite them off, or tread them under foot; while many of their seeds, particularly such as assume the form of nuts or fruits, would be devoured by animals. The grasses, which are propagated both by the root and by seed, are exempt from the operation of almost all these casualities. Providence has, with unerring wisdom, fitted every production of nature to sustain itself against the accidents to which it is most exposed, and has given to those plants which constitute the food of animals, a remarkable tenacity of life; so that although bitten off, and trodden, and even burned, they still retain the vital principle. That trees have a similar power of self-protection, if we may so express it, is evident from their present existence in a state of nature. We only assume that in the earliest state of being, the grasses would have the advantage over plants less hardy, and of slower growth; and that when both are struggling together for the possession of the soil, the former would at first gain the ascendancy; although the latter, in consequence of their superior size and strength, would finally, if they should ever get possession of any portion of the soil, entirely overshadow and destroy their humble rivals.

"We have no means of determining at what period the fires began to sweep over these plains, because we know not when they began to be inhabited. It is quite possible they might have been occasionally fired by lightning, previous to the introduction of that element by human agency. At all events it is very evident that as soon as fire began to be used in this country by its inhabitants, the annual burning of the prairies must have commenced. One of the peculiarities of this climate is the dryness of its summers and autumns. A drought often commences in August, which, with the exception of a few showers towards the close of that month, continues throughout the season. The autumnal months are almost invariably clear, warm, and dry. The immense mass of vegetation with which this fertile soil loads itself during summer, is suddenly withered, and the whole surface of the earth is covered with combustible materials. This is especially true of the prairies where the grass grows to the height of from six to ten feet,* and being entirely exposed to the sun and wind, dries with great rapidity. A

---

* This is true of the spires that run up to seed. The leaves or body of the grass usually is from two to three feet high. *P.*

single spark of fire, falling anywhere upon these plains, at such a time, would instantly kindle a blaze, which would spread on every side, and continue its destructive course as long as it should find fuel. Travellers have described these fires as sweeping with a rapidity which renders it hazardous to fly before them. Such is not the case; or it is true only of a few rare instances. The flames often extend across a wide prairie, and advance in a long line. No sight can be more sublime than to behold in the night, a stream of fire of several miles in breadth, advancing across these wide plains, leaving behind it a black cloud of smoke, and throwing before it a vivid glare which lights up the whole landscape with the brilliancy of noon-day. A roaring and cracking sound is heard like the rushing of a hurricane. The flame, which in general rises to the height of about twenty feet, is seen sinking and darting upwards in spires, precisely as the waves dash against each other, and as the spray flies up into the air; and the whole appearance is often that of a boiling and flaming sea, violently agitated. The progress of the fire is so slow, and the heat so great, that every combustible object in its course is consumed. Wo to the farmer whose ripe cornfields extend into the prairie, and who suffers the tall grass to grow in contact with his fences! The whole labor of the year is swept away in a few hours. But such accidents are comparatively unfrequent, as the preventive is simple, and easily applied.

"It will be readily seen, that as soon as these fires commenced, all the young timber within their range must have been destroyed. The whole state of Illinois, being one vast plain, the fires kindled in different places, would sweep over the whole surface, with a few exceptions, of which we are now to speak. In the bottom lands, and along the margins of streams, the grass and herbage remain green until late in the autumn, owing to the moisture of the soil. Here the fire would stop for want of fuel, and the shrubs would thus escape from year to year, and the outer bark acquire sufficient hardness to protect the inner and more vital parts of the tree. The margins of the streams would thus become fringed with thickets, which, by shading the ground, would destroy the grass, while it would prevent the moisture of the soil from being rapidly evaporated, so that even the fallen leaves would never become so thoroughly dry as the grass of the prairies, and the fire here would find comparatively little fuel. These thickets grow up into strips of forests, which continue to extend until they reach the high table land of the prairie; and so true is this, in fact, that we see the timber now, not only covering all the bottom lands and hill sides, skirting the streams, but wherever a ravine or hollow extends from the low grounds up into the plain, these are filled with young timber of more recent growth. But the moment we leave the level plane of the country, we see the evidences of a continual struggle between the forest and the prairie. At one place, where the fire has on some occasion burned with greater fierceness than usual, it has successfully assailed the edges of the forest, and made deep inroads; at another, the forest has pushed out long points or capes into the prairie.

"It has been suggested that the prairies were caused by hurricanes, which had blown down the timber, and left it in a condition to be consumed by fire, after it was dried by laying on the ground. A single glance at the immense region in which the prairie surface predominates, must refute this idea. Hurricanes are quite limited in their sphere of action. Although they sometimes extend for miles in length, their track is always narrow, and often but a few hundred yards in breadth. It is a well known fact, that wherever the timber has been thus prostrated, a dense and tangled thicket shoots up immediately, and, protected by the fallen trees, grows with uncommon vigor.

"Some have imagined that our prairies have been lakes; but this hypothesis is not tenable. If the whole state of Illinois is imagined to have been one lake, it ought to be shown that it has a general concavity of surface. But so far from this being true, the contrary is the fact; the highest parts of the state are in its centre. If we suppose, as some assert, that each prairie was once a lake, we are met by the same objection; as a general rule, the prairies are highest in the middle,* and have a gradual declivity towards the sides; and when we reach the timber, instead of finding banks corresponding with the shores of a lake, we almost invariably find vallies, ravines, and water-courses depressed considerably below the general level of the plain.

"Wherever hills are found rising above the common plane of the country, they are clothed with timber; and the same fact is true of all broken lands. This fact affords additional evidence in support of our theory. Most of the land in such situations is poor; [?] the grass would be short, and if burned at all, would occasion but little heat. In other spots, the progress of the fire would be checked by rocks and ravines; and in no case would there be that accumulation of dry material which is found on the fertile plain, nor that broad, unbroken surface, and free exposure, which are necessary to afford full scope to the devouring element.

"By those who have never seen this region, a very tolerable idea may be formed of the man-

---

* I think the writer is mistaken here. Most of our large prairies are so nearly level, or slightly concave *in the centre*, as to render many places wet, and others inundated......P.

ner in which the prairie and forest alternate, by drawing a colored line of irregular thickness, along the edges of all the water-courses laid down on the map. This border would generally vary from one to five or six miles, and often extend to twelve. As the streams approach each other, these borders would approach or come in contact; and all the intermediate spaces not thus colored would be prairie. It would be seen that in the point formed by the junction of the Ohio and Mississippi, the forest would cover all the ground; and that as these rivers diverge, and their tributaries spread out, the prairies would predominate."

BARRENS.

This term is used extensively in the west, to designate a species of land which combines some of the features of timber and prairie. It by no means indicates *poor* land, but rather that of a second quality.

The timber is generally scattering, of a rough and stunted appearance, interspersed with patches of hazle and brushwood, and where the contest betwixt the fire and timber is kept up, each striving for the mastery.

In the early settlements of Kentucky, much of the country below and south of Green river, presented a dwarfish and stunted growth of timber, scattered over the surface, or collected in clumps, with hazle and shrubbery intermixed.

This appearance led the first explorers to the inference that the soil itself must necessarily be poor, to produce so scanty a growth of timber, and they gave the name of *barrens* to the whole tract of country. Long since it has been ascertained that this description of land is amongst the most productive soil in the state. The term barren has since received a very extensive application throughout the west. Like all other tracts of country, the barrens present a considerable diversity of soil. In general, however, the surface is more uneven or rolling than the prairies, and sooner degenerates into ravines and sink-holes. Wherever timber barely sufficient for present purposes can be found, a person need not hesitate to settle in the barrens. These tracts are almost invariably healthy; they possess a greater abundance of pure springs of water, and the soil is better adapted for all kinds of produce, and all descriptions of seasons, wet and dry, than the deeper and richer mould of the bottoms and prairies. The writer selected a location in a tract of this description, in preference to others, in 1821, after having explored the country on both sides of the Mississippi to a great extent, and learned, by experience and observation, the various qualities of soil and situation.

When the fires are stopped, these barrens produce timber, at a rate of which no northern emigrant can have any just conception. Dwarfish shrubs and small trees of oak and hickory are scattered over the surface, where for years they have contended with the fires for a precarious existence, while a mass of roots, sufficient for the support of large trees, have accumulated in the earth. Soon as they are protected from the ravages of the annual fires, the more thrifty sprouts shoot forth, and in ten years are large enough for corn-cribs and stables. My eyes now rest upon a clump of oaks, that, in the spring of 1822, were carefully preserved from being trampled upon by the teams while hauling logs for a cabin I was then erecting for a home. These insignificant and dwarfish shrubs, then spared with the hope they might become shade trees some years hence, are now respectable trees, and measure from eighteen inches to two feet in circumference.

As the fires on the prairies become stopped by the surrounding settlements, and the wild grass is eaten out, and trodden down by the stock, they begin to assume the character of barrens; first hazle and other shrubs, and finally a thicket of young timber, covers the surface.

TIMBER, AND TIMBERED UPLANDS.

We have already noticed the appearance of the timber on the bottoms, and margins of the streams, and glanced at the groves and points in the larger prairies. A few general remarks on the timber of the country will suffice.

The reader is already acquainted with the fact, that the apparent scarcity of timber, is not so great an obstacle to the settlement of the country, as has been generally supposed;—that in most parts an abundant supply can be had for the present generation;—that for many of the purposes for which timber is ordinarily used, substitutes are conveniently found, and in great abundance;—and that in another generation, timber will be more abundant in Illinois, than at the present time. The rapidity with which the young growth pushes itself forward, without a single effort on the part of man, to accelerate its growth but merely stopping the fires, and the readiness with which the clear prairie becomes converted, first into thickets, and then into a forest of young timber, all sustain me in the position assumed. I again repeat it, and challenge investigation on the subject, that the prospects for timber in Illinois half a century hence, is far superior to the present condition, and future prospects of New England and New York. Extensive tracts of country in those States, that were once overspread with dense and gloomy forests of hemlock, beech, maple, and other timber, and which required many years of severe labor to exterminate, will not reproduce their former growth. The want of wood and timber in many large districts is now more severely felt by the population, than it ever can possibly be in Illinois.

Kinds of timber.—The growth of the bottom lands consists of black walnut, ash of several species, hackberry, elm, (white, red, and slippery,) sugar-maple, honey-locust, buck-eye, catalpa, sycamore, cottonwood, pecan, hickory, mulberry, several oaks—as, over cup, bur oak, swamp or water oak, white, red or Spanish oak; and of the shrubbery are red-bud, papaw, grape vine, dogwood, spice bush, hazle, greenbrier, &c. Along the margin of the streams, the sycamore and cottonwood often predominate, and attain to an amazing size. The cottonwood is of rapid growth, a light, white wood, sometimes used for rails, shingles, and scantlings, not lasting, but of no great value. Its dry, light wood is much used in steam-boats. It forms the chief proportion of the drift wood that floats down our rivers, and is frequently converted into planters, snags, and sawyers. The sycamore is the button wood of New England, is frequently hollow, and in that state procured by the farmers, cut at suitable lengths, cleaned out, and used as depositories for grain. They answer the purpose of large casks. The size of the cavity of some of these trees appears incredible in the ears of a stranger to the luxuriant growth of the west. To say that twenty or thirty men could be comfortably lodged in one, would seem a monstrous fiction to a New Englander, but to those accustomed to this species of tree on our bottoms, it is nothing marvellous.

The uplands are covered with various species of oak, amongst which is the post oak, a valuable and lasting timber for posts; white oak, black oak of several varieties, and the black jack, a dwarfish, knarled looking tree, good for nothing but fuel, for which it is equal to any tree we have. Of hickory, we have both the shagbark, and smooth bark, black walnut, in some parts, white walnut, or butter nut, Lynn, (the basswood of New England,) cherry, and many of the species produced in the bottoms. The black walnut is much used for building materials, and cabinet work, and sustains a fine polish. The different species of oaks, walnuts, hackberry, and occasionally hickory, are used for fencing.

In some parts of the State, the white and yellow poplar prevails. Beginning at the Mississippi a few miles above the mouth of the Muddy river, on the map appended to this work, and extending a line across the State to the mouth of the Little Wabash, leaves the poplar range south, interspersed with occasional clumps of beach. Near the Ohio, on the low creek bottoms, the cypress is found. No poplar exists on the eastern borders of the State, till you arrive at or near Palestine, while on the opposite shore of the Wabash, in Indiana, the poplar and beach predominate. Near Palestine in Crawford county, the poplar again commences, entermixed with beach, and all the varieties of timber, and extends northward further than I have explored. A spur of it puts into the interior of the State on the Little Wabash, above Maysville. It is reported that in some of the northern portions of the State, same chestnut timber is found. I have never seen a tree in its natural growth, west of the middle of Indiana. Occasional clumps of stunted cedar are to be seen on the clifts that overhang the bottoms, but no pine, unless it exists in the wild regions west of Lake Michigan.

Timber not only grows much more rapid in this country than in the northern States, but it decays sooner when put in buildings, fences, or in any way exposed to the weather. It is more porous, and will shrink and expand as the weather is wet or dry, to a much greater extent than the timber of New England. This may be owing partly to the atmosphere, but it is unquestionably owing in part to the quality of the timber. I have brought two waggons, or carriages, to this country, which were made in Litchfield, Connecticut, and they have lasted much longer than those made from the timber of Illinois. Our fences require to be new laid, and one third of the rails provided anew, in a period of from seven to ten years. A shingled roof requires replacing in about twelve years. This, however, may not be a fair estimate, because most of our timber is prepared hastily, and in a green state. Doubtless with proper care in the seasoning, and in the preservation, it would last much longer. Timber is ordinarily required for *four* purposes; fencing, building, fuel, and mechanical operations. I have already shown that rails is almost the only article used for fencing. In making a plantation in this mode, requires a great waste of timber. Nor will a man, with a moderate capital, and with the burden of an increasing family, stop to make experiments. He must have fields enclosed, and takes the quickest and cheapest method, by cutting down the most convenient timber and making rails. Ditching has been attempted in but a few instances, and without success. In the dry season, the turf withers on the embankment, the dry earth crumbles down, and the ditch offers no obstacle to the inroads of cattle, horses, and swine, and these must run in droves over the prairies.

Some feeble attempts have been made to substitute a live hedge of crab apple, and of honey locust, without success. So long as such extensive portions of the country lie uncultivated and waste, as a great common field for cattle, horses, swine, and all other stock, it is not an easy matter to produce a hedge that will be impervious to these animals. The white thorn has not yet been tried within my knowledge. It may succeed, especially if set within an enclosure, for a few years, till its growth is matured.

A farm is about to be enclosed within a few miles from my residence, with plank, or as a New Englander would say, *boards*, sawed at the mill, the cost of which will not exceed seventy-five cents per rod. But a great saving in fencing is made, by making large fields, from forty to 150 acres. I have no doubt but time will bring forth substitutes for fencing, and which will be a great saving of timber.

The first buildings put up are of logs, slightly hewn on two sides, and the corners notched together. The roof is made of clap boards split like staves, four feet in length, and six or eight inches in width. Two layers of these are so adjusted as to cover the cracks, and on the whole are laid heavy poles to bind down and hold the roof. This description of building is called a "*Cabin.*" These are made single, or double, with a space between, according to the enterprise, force, or taste, of the owner. Around it are usually put up a meat or smoke house, a kitchen or cook house, a stable and corn crib, and perhaps a spring house to keep milk cool in summer, all built in the same manner as the dwelling. Floors are usually made of timber split into slabs, called "*puncheons,*" with the upper surface hewn level. The next step in advance for a dwelling is a *log house*. This is made of logs hewn on two sides to an equal thickness, the ends notched together, apertures cut through for doors and windows, a framed and shingled roof, and a brick or stone chimney. The chimney of the cabin is invariably built of sticks of wood, the largest at the bottom, and the smallest at the top, and laid up with a supply of mud or clay mortar. The interstices between the logs of both the cabin and log house are chinked with strips of wood, and daubed with the same species of mortar, both outside and in, unless the convenience of lime is added.

It is perfectly obvious that this mode of building sweeps off vast quantities of timber, that by a more judicious and economical plan, would be saved for other purposes. In a few years, brick, and in some instances stone, will take the place of these rude and misshapen piles of timber. This begins to take effect in those counties where the people have obtained the means—for brick and framed houses are fast erecting. The sub-stratum of the soil, in any place, is excellent for brick, and in many of the bluffs inexhaustible quarries of lime stone exist. The waste of timber for buildings then will be greatly lessened as the country advances in improvement, population and wealth.

As in all countries where the population have been accustomed to burn excessive quantities of wood before they emigrate, and where they live in cold and open cabins, there is a great waste of timber for fuel. This will be remedied as the people obtain close and comfortable dwellings, and make use of proper economy in this article. In almost every direction through the country, there are inexhaustible stores of stone coal near the surface of the earth. Here is fuel for domestic purposes, and for steam-engines without limits.

For mechanical purposes there is timber enough, and will continue to be.

On the whole, it will be perceived that Illinois does not labor under as great inconveniences for timber, as many have supposed. If provision is made for the first fifty years, future supplies will be abundant. I have said nothing about the artificial production of timber. This may be effected with little trouble or expense, and to an indefinite extent. The black locust, a native growth of Ohio and Kentucky, may be raised from the seed, with far less labor than a nursery of apple-trees ; and as it is of very rapid growth, and a valuable and lasting timber for fencing, buildings, and boats, it must claim the attention of our farmers. Already it forms one of our cleanliest and most beautiful shades, and when in blossom, presents a rich prospect, and a most delicious fragrance.

KNOBS, BLUFFS, RAVINES, AND SINK-HOLES.

Under these heads, I shall include considerable tracts of broken country in various parts of Illinois, and other western States.

Knobs are ridges of earth, or more commonly

of flintstone, intermingled and covered with earth, and elevated from one to three hundred feet above the neighboring bottoms. This species of land is of little value for cultivation, but in many instances, as in Missouri, it contains minerals. It is usually thinly covered with dwarfish and stunted timber, like the barrens. In some parts of Missouri, I have travelled on these ridges for miles where the soil was too scanty to admit the plough or hoe. In these tracts of country are usually strips of bottom lands on the streams and in the vallies of exceeding fertility. The Gasconade hills, improperly called the Ozark mountains, are of this description. Considerable strips of the country on the Merrimac and St. Francois rivers in Missouri, and on the White river and its branches in Arkansas, are made up of knobs. In Illinois they are not frequent. A portion of Indiana, bordering on the Ohio, contains knobs.

The steep hills and natural mounds that border on the large bottoms have obtained the name of *bluffs*. Some are long parallel ridges, others resemble artificial mounds. Some take the form of the sugar loaf, others that of the pyramid. In some places precipices of rock, composed of layers of limestone, and in other places, embankments of earth form these bluffs. They are from fifty to two or three hundred feet high, with sides either perpendicular, or too steep to admit of cultivation with any convenience.

Ravines are the depressions made amongst the bluffs, and near the borders of the prairies, by the washing down of the soil.

Sink-holes are circular depressions in the surface resembling a basin or bowl. I have seen them of various sizes, from ten to fifty feet deep, with steep acclivities, and from ten to fifty yards in diameter at the surface of the ground. They usually are found near the bluffs, and in most cases contain an outlet at the bottom for the water received by the rains to descend into the earth, and find a subterraneous passage amongst the rocks below. Trees and grass are found growing within these cavities.

In all countries where the sub-stratum is of secondary limestone, caverns and subterranean passages exist. By the action of the water the soil above these passages becomes loosened, and is gradually undermined till a *sinking* of the surface takes place. I have seen these sink-holes in all stages of existence, from that where the earth had just fallen in, to those which were partially filled up by the annual deposits, and sustaining large trees on the bottom and sides.

STONY GROUND.

It has been intimated before that loose stones imbedded in the soil, to be turned up by the plough, as is common throughout New England, is not a common feature in our soil. With the exception of a ridge in Jackson county, I have not seen any portion of such land in Illinois, and but few instances in Missouri. The plough can pass over millions of acres without a stone or a pebble to interrupt its course. Towards the northern parts of Illinois such soil is found, and there are tracts in the interior of Indiana, at the heads of Blue river.

Rock is by no means as scarce in Illinois as a stranger would imagine from the appearance of the surface. Quarries of stone, of good quality for building purposes, are usually found in the bluffs, and are distributed throughout the State. This article can be obtained in most places within the distance of a few miles, for walling cellars, walls, &c. In some places it will be the cheapest article for buildings.

Having given a particular description of the face of the country and qualities of soil, I shall arrange under the next head, its

PRODUCTIONS.

These are naturally classed into *minerals, animals,* and *vegetables.*

Minerals. The northern portion of Illinois is inexhaustibly rich in mineral productions, while coal, secondary limestone, and sandstone, are found in every part.

Iron ore is found in the southern parts of the State, and is said to exist in considerable quantities near the rapids of Illinois.

Native copper in small quantities has been found on Muddy river, in Jackson county, and back of Harrisonville, in the bluffs of Monroe county. One mass weighing seven pounds was found detached at the latter place. A shaft was sunk forty feet deep in 1817, in search of this metal, but without success. Red oxide of iron, and oxide of copper were dug out. Crystalized gypsum has been found in small quantities in St. Clair county. Quartz crystals exist in Gallatin county.

Silver is supposed to exist in St. Clair county, two miles from Rock-Spring, from whence Silver creek derives its name. In the early settlements by the French, a shaft was sunk here, and tradition tells of large quantities of the precious metal being obtained. In 1828, many persons in this vicinity commenced digging, and began to dream of immense fortunes, which however vanished during the following winter. They dug up considerable quantities of *horne blende*, the shining specula of which were mistaken for silver.

Lead is found in vast quantities in the northern part of Illinois, and the adjacent territory. Here are the richest lead mines hitherto discovered on the globe. This portion of country lies principally north of Rock river and south of the Wisconsin. Dubuque's, and other rich mines, are west of the Mississippi.

Native copper, in large quantities, exists in this region, especially at the mouth of Plum creek, and on the Peekatonokee. Plum creek is the second small creek, marked on the map, above Rock river, which puts into the Mississippi. Peekatonokee is a branch of Rock river.

The following is a list of the principal diggings in that portion of the lead mine region that lies between Rock river and the Wisconsin, embracing portions of Illinois state, and Wisconsin territory.

Labaume & St. Vrain on Apple Creek,
GALENA and vicinity,
Cave Diggings,
Buncombe,
Natches,
Hardscrabble,
New Diggings,
Gratiot's Grove,
Spulburg,
W. S. Hamilton's,
Cottle's,
McNutt's,
Menomonee Creek,
Plattsville,
CASSVILLE and vicinity,
Madden's,
Mineral Point,
Dodgeville,
Worke's Diggings,
Brisbos,
Blue Mound,
Prairie Springs,
Hammett & Campbell's,
Morrison's.

AMOUNT OF LEAD MANUFACTURED.

For many years the Indians, and some of the French hunters and traders, have been accustomed to dig lead in these regions. They never penetrated much below the surface, but obtained considerable quantities of the ore, which they sold to the traders.

In 1823, the late Col. James Johnson, of Great Crossings, Ky. and brother to the Hon. R. M. Johnson, obtained a lease of the United States Government, and made arrangements to prosecute the business of smelting, with considerable force, which he did the following season. This attracted the attention of enterprising men in Illinois, Missouri, and other States. Some went on in 1826, more followed in 1827, and in 1828 the country was almost literally filled with miners, smelters, merchants, speculators, gamblers, and every description of character. Intelligence, enterprise, and virtue, were thrown in the midst of dissipation, gaming, and every species of vice. Such was the crowd of adventurers in 1829, to this hitherto almost unknown and desolate region, that the lead business was greatly overdone, and the market for awhile nearly destroyed. Fortunes were made almost upon a turn of the spade, and lost with equal facility. The business is now reviving, and probably will be prosecuted in future more in proportion to the demand for lead. Exhaustless quantities of mineral exist here, over a tract of country two hundred miles in extent.

The following table shows the amount of lead made annually at these diggings, from 1821, to Sept. 30, 1830.

Pounds of lead made from 1821, to

		Sept. 30, 1823,	335,130
Do. for year ending Sept. 30, 1824,	175,220
Do.	do.	do.	1825,	664,530
Do.	do.	do.	1826,	958,842
Do.	do.	do.	1827,	5,182,180
Do.	do.	do.	1828,	11,105,810
Do.	do.	do.	1829,	13,343,150
Do.	do.	do.	1830,	8,323,998

Total, 40,088,860 lbs.

The government formerly received ten per cent, in lead, for rent. It is now reduced to six per cent. These lands will soon be surveyed, and probably sold, which will add greatly to the stability and prosperity of the mining business.

Coal. I have already mentioned that stone coal abounds in Illinois. It may be seen frequently in the ravines and gullies, and in the points of bluffs. Exhaustless beds of this article exist in the bluffs of St. Clair county, bordering on the American bottom, of which large quantities are transported to St. Louis for fuel. It sells in St. Louis from ten to twelve and a half cents per bushel. From twelve to fifteen large ox waggons are employed most of the year in hauling it to market, the distance of seven miles across the American bottom. There is scarcely a county in the State, but what can furnish coal in reasonable quantities. Large beds are said to exist near the junction of Fox river with the

Illinois, and in the vicinity of the rapids of the latter.

Agatized Wood. A petrified tree, of black walnut, was found in the bed of the river Des Plaines, about forty rods above its junction with the Kankakee, imbedded in a horizontal position, in a stratum of sandstone. There is fifty-one and a half feet of the trunk visible—eighteen inches in diameter at its smallest end, and probably three feet at the other end.

Muriate of Soda, or common salt. This is found in various parts of the State, held in solution in the springs. The manufacture of salt by boiling and evaporation is carried on in Gallatin county, twelve miles W. N. W. from Shawneetown; in Jackson county, near Brownsville; and in Vermillion county, near Danville. The springs and land are owned by the State, and the works leased. A more specific description will be given under the head of these counties.

A coarse marble, much used in building, is dug from quarries near Alton, on the Mississippi, where large bodies exist.

Scattered over the surface of our prairies, are large masses of rock, of granitic formation, roundish in form, usually called by the people *lost rocks.* They will weigh from one thousand to ten or twelve thousand pounds, and are entirely detached, and frequently are found several miles distant from any quarry. Nor has there ever been a quarry of granite discovered in the

State. These stones are denominated *boulders* in mineralogy. That they exist in various parts of Illinois is an undoubted truth; and that they are of a species of granite is equally true, as I have specimens to show. They usually lie on the surface, or are partially imbedded in the soil of our prairies, which is unquestionably of diluvial formation.

It is a curious question, and one which has elicited some attention among thinking men, how came they here, of the shape, and in the position, in which they are found? Without pretensions to much geological science, or as having investigated the subject to any extent, I will offer a mere conjecture. Were not these stones transported in some former period, from the Chippewan, or rocky mountains? Hunters and traders and some men of intelligence and observation, have informed me that these rocks, and the cliffs and rocks of those mountains towards the northern parts, as high as the fiftieth degree of latitude, exactly resemble each other; that as the traveller approaches those mountains, similar rocks of various forms and sizes are strewed over the surface. Did not the flood of Noah spread over this region? Would the season of the year, and the coldness of the climate admit of the formation of vast bodies of ice in those regions? Would these rocks crumble off from the adjacent cliffs, and lodge on the ice, which, upon breaking up, and being put in motion, would be wafted by northwestern winds to a milder region, dissolve, and as the waters subsided, the rocks remain upon the surface of the vast bed of mud and sand that was deposited in this country? This notion is strengthened by the fact that in the small lakes in the Wisconsin territory, which freeze at a considerable depth in winter, a similar occurrence, on a small scale, actually takes place in the spring. In the severity of winter, the rocky cliffs that overhang the northern shores of these lakes crumble off, and fall in considerable masses upon the ice, which upon breaking up in the spring, transports them frequently to the opposite shore in ridges. This fact was stated to me by an intelligent gentleman, now a resident in that Territory.

Vegetable Productions. The principal trees and shrubs of Illinois have been noticed under the heads of timbered lands and bottoms.

In most parts of the state, grape vines, indigenous to the country, are abundant, which yield grapes which might advantageously be made into excellent wine. Foreign vines are susceptible of easy cultivation. These are cultivated to a considerable extent at Vevay, Switzerland county, Indiana, and at New Harmony, on the Wabash. The indigenous vines are prolific, and produce excellent fruit. They are found in every variety of soil; interwoven in every thicket in the prairies and barrens; and climbing to the tops of the very highest trees on the bottoms. The French in early times made so much wine as to export some to France; upon which, the proper authorities prohibited the introduction of wine from Illinois, lest it might injure the sale of that staple article of the kingdom. I have not the document at hand that will attest this fact, but of its truth there is no doubt, and I think the act was passed by the board of trade, in 1774.

The editor of the Illinois Magazine remarks, "We know one gentleman who made twenty-seven barrels of wine in a single season, from the grapes gathered with but little labor, in his immediate neighbourhood."

I have frequently drank of this domestic beverage. Almost any family, if they choose, can make a barrel or two for their use.

The wild plum is found in every part of the state; but in most instances the fruit is too sour, for use, unless for preserves. Crab apples are equally prolific, and make fine preserves with about double their bulk of sugar. Wild cherries are equally productive. The percimmon is a delicious fruit, after the frost has destroyed its astringent properties. The black mulberry grows in most parts, and is used for the feeding of silk worms with success. They appear to thrive and spin as well as on the Italian mulberry. The gooseberry, strawberry and blackberry grow wild and in great profusion. Of our nuts, the hickory, black walnut, and pecan deserve notice. The last is an oblong, thin shelled, delicious nut, that grows on a large tree, a species of the hickory, (The *Carya olivæ formis* of Nuttall.) The papaw grows in the bottoms, and rich timbered uplands, and produces a large pulpy and luscious fruit. Of domestic fruits, the apple and peach are chiefly cultivated. Pears are tolerably plenty in the French settlements, and quinces are cultivated with success by some Americans. Apples are easily cultivated, and are very productive. I have seen a tree in Missouri, which bore apples the third year from the seed. They can be made to bear fruit to considerable advantage in seven years from the seed. Many varieties are of fine flavour, and grow to a large size. I have measured apples, the growth of St. Clair county, that exceeded thirteen inches in circumference. Some of the early American settlers provided orchards. They now reap the advantages. But a large proportion of the population of the frontiers are content without this indispensable article in the comforts of a yankee farmer. Cider is made in small quantities in the old settlements. In a few years a supply of this beverage can be had in most parts of Illinois.

Peach trees grow with great rapidity, and decay proportionably soon. From ten to fifteen years may be considered the life of this tree. Our peaches are delicious, but they sometimes fail, by being destroyed in the germ by winter frosts. The bud swells prematurely. In the severity of the past winter, most of the young buds, and in some instances the limbs of the tree have been destroyed.

Garden Vegetables can be produced here in vast profusion, and of excellent quality. I must beg leave to dissent entirely from the opinion of Mr. Flint, although an accurate observer in general, that "under this powerful sun, all the roots and vegetables are more tasteless than those of the north. It is instantly perceived that the onion is more mild, and the blood beet less deeply colored; and this thing holds good, as far as my experience goes, in the whole vegetable creation. Take every thing into consideration, this is not so good a country for gardens. Cabbage and peas, owing to the burning heat of the sun, and the dryness of the season, are inferior in quality and abundance."*

That we have few of the elegant and well-dressed gardens of gentlemen in the old states, is admitted; which is not owing to climate, or soil, but to the want of leisure and means. It is impossible to conceive by what process of reasoning Mr. Flint came to the conclusion that "this country is not good for gardens." I have heard the question frequently propounded to eastern gentlemen, in the country, and at the tables of boarding houses in St. Louis, with a distinct reference to this opinion, and the uni-

* Ten Years' Recollection, pp. 246—7

form answer has been, that most of our vegetables are more abundant and of a finer flavor than in New England. Observation was particularly made by the writer, while in New England, in 1826, and immediately upon reading this passage in Mr. Flint's book for the first time, on the quantity and quality of the vegetables from the best cultivated gardens, but with conclusions directly the reverse from those of this distinguished author. Our Irish potatoes, pumpkins, and squashes are inferior, but not our cabbages, peas, beets, onions, or radishes. It is true that onions have less of the rank flavor, and radishes are more mild, but this is a superior, and not an inferior quality.

The following remarks from the Illinois Magazine, and from the pen of the editor, will furnish all necessary information on this subject.

"Soil and climate are the most important agents in rearing fine vegetables; but these luxuries are, after all, mainly produced by the wealth, the labor, and the ingenuity of man. In new countries, therefore, they are not to be expected. Few persons here, we might say none, have money and leisure to expend on matters of taste and luxury. Farmers, especially, are apt to commit this department to the females of their household, whose other cares allow them to devote to it but little care. We plead guilty, then, as a general fact of having bad gardens. But we by no means admit that our vegetables are deficient, either in abundance or quality, when proper care is paid to their culture. We know that the contrary is true. The simple fact is, that our country teems with the bounties of nature in such rich profusion, that people not being obliged to labor to supply their tables, are apt to grow careless. They put their seed in the ground, and trust to Providence to give the increase. Their garden grounds are not only badly prepared, and as badly attended, but the seeds are selected without any care. The reason, therefore, why, as a general fact, the art of horticulture has been brought to but little perfection at the west, is evident.

"But when it is said that the vegetables of this country are inferior in quality, we come to another question, to decide which, it is proper to refer to the cases in which they have been subjected to a sufficient degree of culture. Almost every farmer here raises cabbages, and we are sure that we have never seen larger or better. A hundred heads are sold at Vandalia for a dollar and fifty cents. The parsnips and carrots of this country are remarkable for their size, sweetness, and flavor; the former, especially, have a richness which we have never noticed elsewhere. Our beets are as delicate and sweet as possible; and we only forbear stating a fact, with regard to their size, which has come to our knowledge, from the fear of startling the credulity of our readers. Peas are excellent, and very prolific.

We had a radish on our table, a few days ago, [November,] which was three inches in thickness, and perfectly solid, mild, and crisp. Our lettuce, if well dressed, (there is a great deal in that,) is capital. The tomato is common all through this country. It is only necessary to plant it once, after which, it comes up every year spontaneously, and bears abundantly from the middle of the summer, till nipped by the frost. Thousands of bushels of onions have been raised with no other labor than sowing the seed broadcast, in new ground; and as to their quality, it would do the heart of a Wethersfield lady good to look at them. That goodly town of Connecticut would be depopulated, if its worthy inhabitants could see the onion fields of Morgan county and the Military tract. We might enumerate other articles; but it is enough to say that, in general, the vegetables suited to our climate, are produced in their greatest perfection. It would, indeed, be an anomaly in the economy of nature, if garden plants did not flourish vigorously in a soil of unrivalled depth, fertility, and freshness.

"While we are on the subject of gardening," continues Judge Hall, "it may not be amiss to publish some memorandums, which we made last spring, [1830,] and which will give some idea of the forwardness of our seasons.

April 1. Peach trees in bloom.
      2. Asparagus fit for the table.
      3. Peas, beans, and onions planted.

April 6. Heart's ease and violets in bloom.
     7. Beets, carrots, parsnips, and other roots planted.
    10. Spring had completely opened; and the prairies were green. Gooseberry and currant bushes in bloom.
    15. Cabbage-plants transplanted.
    18. Lilac and strawberries in bloom.
    19. A great variety of wild flowers in full bloom.
    20. Nearly all our garden seeds had been planted.
    25. Raspberries in bloom.
    27. Lettuce, radishes, and pepper-grass fit for use.
    30. Roses and honey-suckles in full bloom.
None of the above articles were injured by frost."

In corroboration of the foregoing facts, the following are submitted. A gentleman of veracity, who belonged to the army, stated to the writer, that in 1815, at Fort Osage, near the western border of Missouri, he measured a cabbage in his garden, without expanding the leaves, that was seventeen feet six inches in circumference, around the head. The Western Observer, published at Jacksonville, Ill. of Nov. 13, 1830, states, "A gentleman of this town, whose veracity may be depended upon, informed us that he saw a cabbage, which was raised on the farm of Major

Simms, Diamond Grove, that measured thirteen feet and three inches in circumference." A cabbage head three feet in diameter, or nine feet in circumference, is no novelty in this soil. Beets often grow to the size of sixteen or eighteen inches in circumference. Parsnips will penetrate our light, porous soil, to the depth of thirty inches. Turnips sown the 10th of September, will grow to an enormous size before winter. These things are so well known in Illinois, as to excite no curiosity. I am well aware a man hazards his reputation for veracity by narrating such things to a New Englander. It reminds one of the story of the Dutch ambassadors when sent to propose a treaty of amity and commerce with the king of Siam. His Siamese majesty not quite relishing the appearance of the strangers, appointed some of his ministers to catechise them in private about their country, its habits, customs, &c. During the interview, it became necessary for the Dutchmen to describe the climate of their country, and its difference of seasons. Amongst other strange, and to the Siamese, unnatural prodigies, they stated that in Europe, at a certain season of the year, the water became so hard as that men and horses could walk upon it. When the result of the conference was reported to the king, who had never seen ice, he exclaimed with great indignation, "Send these men back. Do they think I will believe their tales about hard water."

Our New England friends must not put down every statement about this country as romance, because its vegetable productions so far exceed the scanty growth of the granite regions of the north.

The *cultivated vegetable productions in the field*, are maize or Indian corn, wheat, oats, barley, buck-wheat, Irish potatoes, sweet potatoes, turnips, rye for horse feed and distilleries, tobacco, cotton, hemp, flax, and every other production common to the middle states.

Maize is the staple production. No farmer can live without it, and thousands raise little else. This is chiefly owing to the ease with which it is cultivated. Its average yield is fifty bushels to the acre. We have oftentimes seen it produce seventy-five bushels to the acre, and in a few instances, exceed one hundred.

Wheat produces a good and sure crop, especially in Morgan, Sangamon, and other counties north. I have weighed the growth of St. Clair county repeatedly, and its average weight per bushel exceeded sixty pounds. A gentleman of this county harvested a field of thirty acres, in 1820. He gave a friend one measured acre, which he reaped, threshed it out on the ground, (a usual mode,) and cleaned up thirty-five bushels and eight quarts. Some, of course, was wasted. I purchased my wheat, in 1821, of this farmer, from the same field, and weighed several bushels, which averaged sixty-six pounds to the bushel.

A gentleman, and a large wheat grower, emigrated from the interior of New York the same season, with whom I had several pleasant disputes about the quality of Illinois wheat; he constantly affirming it could never equal the wheat of the lake country of New York. I took him to a yard in the vicinity, where were twelve or fifteen large stacks of wheat. He pulled out a number of handfuls from different stacks, examined them carefully, and his opinion yielded in a moment. Flour from the Illinois river, and from the Boon's lick country, in Missouri, now has preference in the New Orleans market, before Ohio and Kentucky flour. A commission house in St. Louis showed me letters from New Orleans, substantiating that fact. In 1821, '22, and '23, the wheat was poor in this region. Since that time, our wheat crops have been good.

The weavel has been injurious to wheat in many parts of the south and west. This is a greyish winged insect, the egg of which is deposited in the berry when first formed, and which hatches some time after the wheat has lain in the stack or the granary. If it be kept above or below a certain temperature, the insect will not be produced, and no injury results. The weavel made its appearance in Illinois, near St. Louis, in September, 1825, and destroyed much of the wheat before it was threshed. Wheat was damaged by this insect the following season. In 1827, the wheat harvest was good, and in most cases, escaped the weavel.

The writer had a large harvest that season, the most of which lay in his barn unthreshed, till the close of the following winter, without receiving damage. It has been ascertained that by threshing out the wheat soon after harvest, before the egg, which is scarcely visible to the naked eye, is hatched in the grain, and packing it away in the chaff in the granary, it may be preserved in safety This insect is far more destructive in some parts of Ohio and Kentucky, than in Illinois. It has not yet made its appearance as far north as Morgan county.

A very common, but bad practice amongst our farmers, is to sow wheat in the cornfields, amongst the standing corn, in September, and plough it in by running a few furrows between the rows. The dry stalks are cut down in the spring, and left on the ground. Even by this imperfect and slovenly mode, fifteen or twenty bushels of wheat to the acre are produced. But where the ground is duly prepared by fallowing, and the seed put in at the proper time, a good wheat crop, averaging from thirty to thirty-five bushels to the acre, rarely fails. The ordinary price of wheat is fifty cents per bushel, and is rather on the rise. Flouring mills begin to be erected, which will create a demand for this article, and if the price of flour abroad should advance, wheat in Illinois will rise in proportion. Considering the cheapness of land, the productiveness of the soil, and the ease with which a crop of wheat is cultivated, compared with the grain-growing States of the north, wheat is a profitable article for the Illinois farmer, at fifty cents per bushel. Harvest ordinary commences the last week in June, and is finished by the fourth of July. The richness of the soil brings the grain to its greatest perfection, while the dryness of the atmosphere protects it from those injuries which are produced by moisture. Few of our farmers have barns or threshing-floors; the grain is put up in stacks, exposed to the weather, and trod out with horses, on the ground, with considerable loss and injury; and yet, with all these disadvantages—which time and industry will overcome—the flour of Illinois and Missouri is superior to that of other western States, when properly manufactured.

Maize or Corn. I have already hinted that this species of grain is the staple of the country. An industrious man and one horse will cultivate twenty acres in a season. The product may be estimated, on an average, at one thousand bushels. The cultivation and harvesting of this crop, after deducting bad weather, and other hinderances, will occupy about four months. Corn often sells in the field, after gathering, in the fall, at twelve and a half cents per bushel, in the ears—three half bushels of ears heaped, equals one bushel of shelled corn. The value of the crop, then, before it is cribbed, is one hundred and twenty-five dollars. One shilling per bushel, New England currency, is a common price after being stored in the crib. In St. Louis it rarely sells for less than twenty-five cents. At this time, (June 1st, 1831,) not a bushel can be purchased for less than twenty-five cents; and in many places it sells at thirty-seven and a half, and even fifty cents. The unusually severe winter, and backward spring, with the influx of emigrants, has caused this scarcity.

A poor man, with a "cabin and cornfield," (and thousands of this class live on government land, without rent or molestation,) may easily support a large family in wholesome provisions. Two or three cows, and some hogs, which cost but little, and live and grow fat on the luxuriant range, are a necessary appendage.

Corn is the staple food for horses and cattle through the winter, for fattening swine, and is the sole article for bread in thousands of families. Many of the Kentuckians, Tennesseeans, and other western people, prefer it to the finest of wheat. There are many ways of preparing it which a Yankee farmer's wife knows nothing about.

The *pone*, is a large mass of meal, wet up with water, (sometimes milk,) and baked in the iron oven, by the fire.

Dodgers, are masses like small loaves of bread, prepared in a similar manner, and baked in the spider or skillet.

The *hoe-cake* of Virginia, is made of meal wet to a proper consistency, spread thin on the lid of an oven or thin board, and baked before the fire. The Yankees may tell us of their pies, and dough-nuts, and crulls, and ginger-cake, and bread—whether of rye or wheat, and all their other "notions," but give me the genuine hoe-cake for substantial diet. It bids defiance to the dyspepsy.

Waffles are baked in the hot irons of that name.

Pancakes, baked on the griddle, are a fine substitute for the buck-wheat cakes of New-Jersey.

The method of raising a crop of corn, after the prairie sward is broken up, and cultivated a season or two, is extremely simple and cheap. It is a bad practice, but a common one, to grow corn on the same ground for years in succession. The writer rented a farm in Missouri, in 1820, furnished team, tools, and board, and gave a man *one third* of the crop for planting and cultivating it. On one field, the old settlers informed me that it was the nineteenth crop of corn in succession, and it produced about forty bushels to the acre; and this on land of a second quality. There are spots in the American bottom, in the common fields of the French, that tradition says have produced corn more than one hundred years in succession.

In producing a crop of corn, the dry stalks are chopped down in the spring with a hoe, collected in heaps with a horse rake, and burned. A much better practice is to let them rot in the soil, and unless very large, they do not impede the plough. The ground is then ploughed up smooth, usually with two horses; but if light, one horse will often do this ploughing. Good managers then harrow the ground; but thousands do not. The next process is to "list" it; that is, to strike straight furrows through the field, in the proportion of four to a rod, and cross these at right angles. This is usually done with a single horse and a light plough. The corn is then dropped with the hand, in the intersection of the furrows, five or six grains in each hill, and covered with the hoe—sometimes with the plough, by passing a light furrow over it. Soon as the corn is of a suitable height, the horse and plough must be in the field at an early hour in the morning. An industrious farmer sees the sun rise in his cornfield. This is now the most busy season of the whole year for the farmer. Then comes the "tug of war" between industry and the weeds. The astonishing rapidity with which every species of vegetation puts forward at this season and in this climate, makes it indispensable for the farmer to be active. Even the class of frontier men, who spend one half of the year in indolence, or in hunting excursions, will not neglect the cornfield. I have repeatedly observed that the cornfields of our plodding yankees, before they become sufficiently acquainted with the country and its habits, look worse for weeds than those of the otherwise careless backwoodsman.

After the corn is planted, the hoe is thrown aside, unless casually used to chop down a few large weeds in the hills, and the whole process of cultivation is conducted by the plough. The unphilosophical notion of a New England farmer in *hilling* corn, is unknown here; and it is a very useless expedient anywhere. Nature has so organized the cornstalk, that it will throw out a set of roots, two or three inches above the ground, which strike the earth at a proper distance from the stalk, and serve as supporters. Raising a hill round the plant does a positive injury by preventing these shoots.

Corn ordinary requires three ploughings, the last of which is usually performed after wheat harvest, from the 4th to the 12th of July. In luxurious fields, it is necessary at this time, for the process of suckering to be performed. The sprouts that start out near the roots of the plant are pulled off, and the smaller stalks from the hill thinned out, so as to leave only four healthy stalks. To use the phrase of the country, the corn is then "laid by," and the leisure and lazy season of the farmer commences.

From the middle of July to the first of September is usually the hottest and most unpleasant part of the year for labor. It happens to be the time when the Illinois farmer has the least to do. The industrious farmer may clear the bushes from the corners of his fences, cut a few stacks of prairie hay for the winter, prepare his ground for winter wheat, or ride about and see his friends.

About the middle of September, the cornfields are again entered to gather the "blades;"—the leaves—which are stripped from the stalks below the ears, properly dried, bound in bundles, and saved for fodder. This is the common, rough food, in addition to corn, given to horses, calves, &c. The stalks are sometimes topped and saved. They make excellent food for milch cows during the winter.

If the season is dry, and frosts are early, corn is ready for gathering by the 10th of October. From this period till December, is another busy season in the cornfield to gather the crop. The corn is commonly plucked off by the hand, hauled to the vicinity of the crib, and the people in the settlement invited to the *corn-shucking*. Ordinarily, these gatherings end in sobriety and good feelings, but occasionally, (if whiskey is plenty,) they prove scenes of unbridled merriment. In slaveholding States, these annual corn-shuckings are the seasons of "fun and frolic" to the negroes. A fat ox or cow and two or three shoats are killed; pones of corn bread, smoking hot, are brought forward, the bottle of whiskey circulates, and the very woods and hills shake with the negro song of "'possum up a gum-tree." Whoever has passed down the Ohio in a November moon-light night, has heard the shores resound with the songs and shouts of merriment from the Kentucky side. It is the real harvest home of the slaves.

Corn is frequently planted late in June, and even the first week in July, and cut up before frost, for winter food for cattle; and it furnishes a cheap and nutricious diet for stock. The husks are appropriated to a similar purpose.

In breaking up prairie, after the grass starts in the spring, which is the best time to subdue the tough sward, corn is sometimes dropped in every fourth furrow, or planted in the newly turned up soil, by sticking an axe in the sod, and dropping the grain, where it is left to grow spontaneously. Sometimes large quantities of fodder are thus obtained.

The stalks of corn in the south and west, grow to a large size. The long grained Virginia corn is chiefly produced; the ears are usually five or six feet, and often more from the ground; on the rich bottom lands, the stalks attain to the height of twelve and fifteen feet. I saw a stalk measured, that grew on a rich bottom of the Missouri river, in 1818, that was twenty-two feet, six inches in length.

Oats have not been much raised till lately. They are very productive, often yielding from forty to fifty bushels on the acre, and usually sell from seventeen to twenty-five cents the bushel.

Hemp is an indigenous plant in the southern part of this state, as it is in Missouri. It has not been extensively cultivated, but wherever tried, is found very productive, and of an excellent quality. It might be made a staple of the country.

Tobacco, though a filthy and noxious weed, which no human being ought ever to use, can be produced in any quantity, and of the first quality, in Illinois. "From the county of Wayne, a good many hogsheads have been annually exported for some years past; and the result of the experiment has been altogether satisfactory. It has been raised to some extent throughout the southern counties. A few hogsheads, which were sent from Randolph county to New Orleans, some years since, was pronounced by the inspector to be the best ever brought to that market. We could not adduce a stronger proof than this, in favor of our soil and climate. The tobacco-plant, although coarse in its appearance, is one of the most delicate in the vegetable kingdom. It thrives only in a rich, light, and warm soil. It requires to be planted early in the spring, and is gathered late in autumn. In every stage of its growth it needs culture and attention, and is, at all times, sensitive to cold, and easily destroyed by frost. When we say, therefore, as we are authorised by repeated experiments, that ours is one of the best tobacco countries in the world, we produce the strongest evidence of the fertility of our soil, and the mildness of our climate."*

Cotton, for many years, has been successfully cultivated in this state for domestic use, and some for exportation. Two or three spinning factories are in operation, and produce cotton yarn from the growth of the country with promising success. This branch of business admits of enlargement, and invites the attention of eastern manufacturers with small capital. [See art. *manufactories*.] Much of the cloth made in families who have emigrated from states south of the Ohio, is from the cotton of the country.

Flax is produced, and of a tolerable quality, but not equal to that of the northern states. It is said to be productive and good in the northern counties. There is no oil-mill to manufacture oil from the seed, yet established.

Barley is raised in St. Clair county for the St. Louis breweries. It yields well, is a sure crop, and sells in St. Louis from thirty-seven and a half to fifty cents per bushel.

The *Palma christi*, or castor oil bean, is produced in considerable quantities in Madison,

---

* Illinois Magazine, p. 127.

Randolph, and other counties, and large quantities of oil are expressed and sent abroad. About twelve thousand gallons will be made in Edwardsville the present season. The bean is a more profitable crop to the farmer than corn, finds a ready market, and sells from seventy-five cents to one dollar per bushel.

Sweet potatoes are a delicious root, and yield abundantly, especially on the American bottom, and rich sandy prairies.

But little has been done to introduce cultivated grasses. The prairie grass looks coarse and unsavory, and yet our horses and cattle will leave the best timothy hay for it. It is already known to the reader that this grass disappears when the settlements extend round a prairie, and the cattle eat off the young growth in the spring. Consequently in a few years, the natural grass no longer exists. This, however, can be preserved by fencing in a tract of fresh prairie, and mowing it regularly every season, or burning it over in the fall. In this way, excellent meadows can be kept forever. It is thought by some that the seed might be gathered in the fall, sown on land that had been kept free from weeds, and by these means, meadows of the natural grass of the country might be formed.

It is to be regretted that so few have thought of providing themselves with natural meadows of 50 or more acres to each plantation, by a process so cheap as that of fencing in the prairie, before the cattle had subdued the natural grass, and preserving it with a very little care, in a perfectly natural state.

Timothy grass begins to be cultivated with success. For the first three or four years of my residence in this country, it was doubtful whether clover, timothy, or any other cultivated grasses could be made profitable for meadows in this rich soil and dry climate. I observed that in attempts to make meadows, the weeds soon overrun the grass. But this notion was entirely incorrect. To produce timothy with success, the ground must be well cultivated in the summer, either by an early crop, or by fallowing, and the seed sown about the 20th of September, at the rate of *ten or twelve quarts of clean seed to the acre*, and lightly brushed in.

If the season is in any way favorable, it will get a rapid start before winter. By the last week in June, it will produce from a ton and a half to two tons per acre, of the finest of hay. It then requires an annual dressing of stable or yard manure, and occasionally the turf may be scratched with a harrow, to prevent the roots from binding too hard. By this process, timothy meadows may be made and preserved. There are meadows in St. Clair county, which have yielded heavy crops of hay in succession, for seven years, and bid fair to continue for an indefinite period. Cattle, and especially horses, should never be permitted to run in meadows in Illinois.

The fall grass may be cropped down by calves and colts. There is but a little more labor required to produce a crop of timothy, than a crop of oats, and as there is not a stone or a pebble to interrupt, the soil may be turned up every third or fourth year for corn, and afterwards laid down to grass again.

A species of blue grass is cultivated by some farmers for pastures. If well set, and not eaten down in summer, blue grass pastures may be kept green and fresh till late in autumn, or even in the winter. The English spire grass has been cultivated with success in the Wabash country.

Of the trefoil, or clover, there is but little cultivated. A prejudice exists against it, as it is imagined to injure horses by affecting the glands of the mouth, and causing them to slaver. It grows luxuriantly, and may be cut for hay early in June. The white clover comes in naturally, where the ground has been cultivated, and thrown by, or along the sides of old roads and paths.

ANIMALS.

Of *wild animals* there are several species. The buffalo is not found on this side the Mississippi, nor within several hundred miles of St. Louis. This animal once roamed at large over the prairies of Illinois, and was found in plenty thirty years since. *Wolves, panthers,* and *wild* cats are still numerous on the frontiers, and through the unsettled portions of the country. Wolves harbor in almost every county, and annoy the farmer by destroying his sheep and pigs. There are three species found in Illinois:

1. The large grey wolf, or *canis lupus* of Linneus, is not very plenty, and not commonly found in the older settlements.

2. The black wolf, or *canis lycaon* of Linneus, is scarce. Occasionally they are killed by our hunters.

3. The *canis latrans* of Say, or common prairie wolf, is the most common, and found in considerable numbers. This mischievous animal is but little larger than the common fox, burrows in the prairies, and comes forth in the night to attack sheep, pigs, poultry, &c. Many of the settlers keep hounds to guard against the depredations of this animal.

Panthers and wild cats are less common, but occasionally do mischief.

Deer are also very numerous, and are valuable, particularly to that class of our population which have been raised to frontier habits; the flesh affording them food, and the skins, clothing. Fresh venison hams usually sell for twenty-five cents each, and when properly cured, are a delicious article. Many of the frontier people dress their skins, and make them into pantaloons and hunting shirts. These articles are indispensable to all who have occasion to travel in viewing land, or for any other purpose beyond the settlements, as cloth garments, in the shrubs and vines, would soon be in strings.

It is a novel and pleasant sight to a stranger, to see the deer in flocks of eight, ten, or fifteen in number, feeding on the grass of the prairies, or bounding away at the sight of the traveller.

The *brown bear* is also an inhabitant of this state, although he is continually retreating before the advance of civilization.

Foxes, rackoons, opossums, gophars, and squirrels, are also numerous, as are musk-rats, otters, and occasionally beaver, about our rivers and lakes. Rackoons are very common, and frequently do mischief in the fall to our corn. Opossums sometimes trouble the poultry. I have a few facts reported to me from sources entitled to great credit, that the production of the young of this singular and extraordinary animal, is different from the ordinary process of generation in viviparous animals. The fœtus is found adhering to the teat, within the false belly, at the very first stage of existence.

The *gophar* is a nondescript, and a singular little animal, about the size of a squirrel. It burrows in the ground, is seldom seen, but its *works* make it known. It labours during the night, in digging subterranean passages in the rich soil of the prairies, and throws up hillocks of fresh earth, within a few feet distance from each other, and from twelve to eighteen inches in height. I have seen a dozen of these hillocks, the production of one night's labor, and apparently from a single gophar. The passages are formed in such a labyrinth, that it is a difficult matter to find the animal by digging.

The grey and fox squirrels often do mischief in the corn fields, and the hunting of them makes fine sport for the boys. It is a rule amongst the Kentucky riflemen to shoot a squirrel only through his eyes, and that from the tops of the highest trees of the forest. It is evidence of a bad marksman, for a hunter to hit one in any other part.

Common rabbits exist in every thicket. These animals annoy nurseries and young orchards exceedingly. The fence around a nursery must always be so close as to shut out rabbits; and young apple trees must be secured at the approach of winter, by tying straw or corn-stalks around their bodies, for two or three feet in height, or the bark will be stripped off by these mischievous animals.

Wild horses are found ranging the prairies and forests in some parts of the state. They are small in size, of the Indian, or Canadian breed, and very hardy. They are caught in pens, or with ropes having nooses attached to them, and broken to the saddle and harness. The poor French, who monopolize the business of catching and breaking these horses, make them an article of traffic; their common price is from fifteen to thirty dollars. They are found chiefly in the lower end of the American Bottom, near the junction of the Kaskaskia and Mississippi rivers, called *the Point*. They are the offspring of the horses brought there by the first settlers, and which were suffered to run at large. The Indians of the west have many such horses, which are commonly called Indian ponies.

Domestic Animals. These are the same as are found in other portions of the United States. But little has been done to improve the breed of horses amongst us. Our common riding or working horses average about fifteen hands in height. Horses are much more used here than in the New England states, and many a farmer keeps half a dozen or more. Much of the travelling throughout the western country, both by men and women, is performed on horseback; and a large proportion of the land carriage is by means of large waggons, with from four to six stout horses for a team. A great proportion of the ploughing is performed by horse labor. Horses are more subject to diseases in this country than in the old states, which is thought to be occasioned by bad management, rather than by the climate. A good farm horse can be purchased for fifty dollars. Riding, or carriage horses, of a superior quality, cost about seventy-five or eighty dollars. Breeding mares are profitable stock for every farmer to keep, as their annual expense in keeping is but trifling, their labor is always needed, and their colts, when grown, find a ready market. Some farmers keep a stallion, and eight or ten brood mares.

Mules are brought into Missouri and find their way to Illinois, from the Mexican dominions. They are a hardy animal, grow to a good size, and are used by some both for labor and riding.

Our *neat cattle* are usually inferior in size to those of the old States. This is owing entirely to bad management. It is known already to the reader, that our cows are not penned up in pasture fields, but suffered to run at large over the commons. Hence *all* the calves are preserved, without respect to quality, to entice the cows homeward at evening. They are kept up through the day, and oftentimes without much pasture, and turned to the cows for a few minutes at night, and then permitted to graze through the night over the short and withered grass around the plantation.

In autumn their food is very scanty, and during the winter they are permitted to pick up a precarious subsistence amongst fifty or a hundred head of cattle. With such management, is it surprising, that our cows and steers are much inferior to those of the old States?

And yet, with due deference to the opinions of Mr. Flint, whom I have once before controverted, our beef is the finest in the world. It bears the best inspection of any in the New Orleans market. By the first of June, and often by the middle of May, our young cattle on the prairies are fit for market. They do not yield large quantities of tallow, but the fat is well proportioned throughout the carcase, and the meat tender and delicious. By inferiority, then, I mean the *size* of our cattle in general, and the quantity and quality of the milk of cows.

The writer killed a pair of aged oxen, on the 17th of last December. For the three preceding years they had been worked very hard, and at the close of the preceding winter were very poor. They were made to labor in the spring, till corn-planting was over, and then turned out to grass. In autumn they were shut up in a lot, fed with corn in the ear, and corn blades, with water. Occasionally they received a mess of oats. Their weight was as follows:

1. Hide, (green,)   62 lbs. value, 5 cts. $3,10
   Tallow, (rough,) 136 "   " 5 "   6,80
   Beef, (quarters,) 620 "   " $2\frac{1}{2}$ " 15,50

                                   Value, $25,40

2. Hide, ... 59 lbs. value, 5 cts. $2,95
   Tallow, . . . 80 "   " 5 "   4,00
   Beef, ... 668 "   " $2\frac{1}{2}$ " 16,70

                                   Value, 23,65

Making the value of both at $49,05, at the common selling price at that time. These oxen, in

1827, were valued at thirty-five dollars. The cost of fattening them cannot be easily estimated. They had what corn they would eat, which could be then purchased for twelve and a half cents per bushel, for about ten weeks. The beef was tender and excellent, some of which is now used in my family.

Common cows, if suffered to lose their milk in August, become sufficiently fat for table use by October. Farrow heifers and steers, are good beef, and fit for the knife at any period after the middle of May. Nothing is more common than for an Illinois farmer to go among his stock, select, shoot down, and dress a fine beef, whenever fresh meat is needed. This is often divided out amongst the neighbors, who in turn, kill and share likewise. It is common at camp and other large meetings, to kill a beef and three or four hogs for the subsistence of friends from a distance.

The following is the product of two other small beeves, the first killed Oct. 26th, and the second, Nov. 10th, 1830.

1. A three year old heifer. Hide, 42 lbs. tallow, (rough,) 25 lbs. beef in qrs. 356 lbs. valued at two cents per lb. Total, 423 lbs.—$8,46. The heifer would have cost about $5,50—the balance would be the butcher's profits.

2. A two year old steer. Hide, 40 lbs. tallow, 16 lbs. beef, quarters, 317 lbs. Total, 373—value, $7,46.

Guide for Emigrants.

At Coles' slaughter house, opposite St. Louis, in this county, (St. Clair) the prices for beef, for the two seasons past, delivered alive, and counting the weight of the quarters merely, has been as follows: For fat beef, weighing eight hundred or more, $3,00 per hundred; weighing less than eight, and more than six hundred, $2,50; weighing less than six hundred, $2,00.

Steers of three years old or more, have been purchased in great numbers in Illinois, by drovers from Ohio. They usually have sold from nine to twelve dollars per head. They are driven early in the spring to the Miami and Scioto country, in Ohio, fed in pastures through the summer, and in autumn drove to Pennsylvania, and turned over to the graziers there, to stall-feed for the Philadelphia and Baltimore markets. Cattle are sometimes sent in flat boats down the Mississippi and Ohio, for the New Orleans market.

We can hardly place limits upon the amount of beef cattle that Illinois is capable of producing. A farmer calls himself poor, with a hundred head of horned cattle around him. A cow in the spring is worth from seven to ten dollars. Some of the best quality will sell higher. And let it be distinctly understood, once for all, that a poor man can always purchase horses, cattle, hogs, and provisions for labor, either by the day, month, or job.

Cows, in general, do not produce the same amount of milk, nor of as rich a quality as in New England. Something is to be attributed to the nature of our pastures, and the warmth of our climate, but more to causes already assigned. If ever a land was characterized justly, as "flowing with milk and honey," it is Illinois and the adjacent States. From the springing of the grass till September, butter is made in great profusion. It sells at that season in St. Louis market for about ten cents; at Rock-Spring and the adjacent settlements, at eight cents; and in the interior of the state for six and a quarter cents per pound. With proper care it can be preserved in tolerable sweetness for winter's use. Late in autumn and early in winter, sometimes butter is not plenty. The feed becomes dry, the cows range further off, and do not come up readily for milking, and dry up. A very little trouble would enable a farmer to keep three or four good cows in fresh milk at the season most needed.

Cheese is made by many families, especially in the counties bordering on the Illinois river. A given quantity of milk will not make as much curd in the warm season as in New England; but if any family choose to perform the labor and care requisite, a dairy may be made very profitable. Good cheese sells for eight and sometimes ten cents, and finds a ready market in St. Louis. The most important arrangement for the dairy business in Illinois, and especially for cheese-making, is to persuade a few thousand families, from the dairy regions of New England, to emigrate, and continue their industrious habits after settling here.

Swine. This species of stock may be called a staple in the provision of Illinois. Thousands of hogs are raised without any expense, except a few breeders to start with, and a little attention in hunting them on the range, and keeping them tame.

In Maquapin county, and about twenty-five miles from Edwardsville, one of our Illinois frontier men, Mr. F. settled himself on Congress land three or four years since, with four or five sows for breeders, worth as many dollars. In 1829, he drove forty-two fat hogs to market, which he sold for one hundred and thirty-five dollars. The amount of corn given to the whole, before he drove them, did not exceed *one bushel.* They lived on the range, and grew fat on *mast*—the fruit of the oak, hickory, &c. Of the proceeds, one hundred dollars was applied to pay for eighty acres of land on which he had settled. The remainder served to pay some small debts, and purchase his salt, iron, and groceries for the ensuing year. This is not mentioned as an extraordinary occurrence, but as a circumstance that excited no special notice in Illinois. This kind of pork is by no means equal to that raised and fatted on corn, and in a domestic way. It is soft, oily, and will not bear inspection at New Orleans. It usually sells for $1,75 and $2,00 per hundred. Pork that is made in a domestic way and fatted on corn, will sell from two to three dollars, according to size, quality, and the time when it is delivered. With a pasture of clover, or blue grass, a well-filled corn crib, a dairy and slop barrel, and the usual industry and care that a New Englander bestows on his pigs, pork may be raised from the sow, fatted, and killed, and weigh from two hundred to two hundred and fifty, within twelve months; and this method of raising pork would be profitable.

In 1820, when the writer lived in Missouri, he bought a sow and three sucking pigs in April, and kept them in a blue grass pasture. Having to buy corn at a dear rate, none was given them till new corn was fit to cut up. They were fed regularly with the slop of the kitchen. During winter they run with the cattle, and eat the corn that would otherwise have been wasted. Two of the shoats were killed on the 2d day of March, 1821, and weighed, the one 216, and the other 219 pounds. The meat was remarkably solid, white, and fine flavored.

Few families in the west and south put up their pork in salt pickle. Their method is to salt it sufficiently to prepare it for smoking, and then make bacon of hams, shoulders, and midlings or broadsides. The price of bacon the last season and the present, taking the hog round, is six and seven cents. Good hams command eight cents in the St. Louis market. Stock hogs, weighing from 60 to 100 pounds, alive, usually sell from one dollar to one dollar and fifty cents per head. Families consume much more meat in Illinois, in proportion to numbers, than in the old States.

Sheep do very well in this country, especially in the older settlements, where the grass has become short, and they are less molested by wolves. But few are kept. The people from the south are more accustomed to cotton for clothing than wool. This article, when manufactured into rolls, sells for fifty cents per pound. Common wool is worth thirty-seven and a half cents in the fleece. Little is said or done to improve the breed of sheep, or introduce the marino, or saxony breed.

Poultry is raised in great profusion—and large numbers of fowls taken to the St. Louis market, and sell from ten to twelve and a half cents a head. It is no uncommon thing for some farmer's wives to raise three or four hundred fowls, besides geese, ducks, and turkies, in a season. Young fowls, butter, and eggs, are the three articles usually mustered from every farm in the counties adjacent to St. Louis, for that market. By these means, many families provide their coffee, sugar, tea, and various articles of apparel.

Eggs, when plenty, as at the close of winter and spring, sell for six and eight cents per dozen. I have often seen eggs brought to market in barrels, and sold in that manner by estimation.

In noticing poultry, I ought not to pass over some of our wild fowl.

Ducks, geese, swans, and many other aquatic birds, visit our waters in the spring. The small lakes and sloughs are often literally covered with them. Ducks, and some of the rest, frequently stay through the summer and breed.

The prairie fowl is seen in great numbers on the prairies in the summer, and about the cornfields in the winter. This is the grouse of the New York market. They are easily taken in the winter.

Partridges, (the quail of New England) are taken with nets, in the winter, by hundreds in a day, and furnish no trifling item in the luxuries of the city market.

Bees. This laborious and useful insect is to be found in the trees of every forest. Many of the frontier people make it a prominent business after the frost has killed the vegetation, to hunt them, for the honey and wax, both of which find a ready market. Honey is sold by the barrel, at the rate of fifty cents per gallon. The price of wax varies from eighteen to twenty-five cents per pound. Bees are profitable stock for the farmer, and are kept to a considerable extent. The cost is usually from one to two dollars the hive, in the spring.

Silkworms are raised by a few persons. They are capable of being produced to any extent, and fed on the common black mulberry of the country.

LOCATION, METHOD OF FARMING, BUILDING, &c.

Upon emigrating to this country, the *first* thing for an eastern farmer is, to throw off and forget many of his former habits and practices, and be prepared to accommodate himself to the nature of our soil, and the circumstances of the country, else he will throw away much labor uselessly, and expend money unprofitably.

The first object is to find a suitable situation; or, in the language of the country, to *locate* himself. An entire stranger to the country will judge incorrectly in relation to soil, and advantages and disadvantages of location. If he arrives in the dry season of autumn, he will be likely to select a level spot of prairie, with a deep black soil, determined to have rich land at any rate, and perhaps in the spring find himself ploughing in mud and water. If he looks at the appearance of the timber he will probably be deceived, and overlook some of the best tracts. Advice from those who have long been residents in the country would save many inconveniences in location. Unless a man has money for which he has no use, I would not advise an emigrant to purchase a large tract of land at first, even at the low price it sells by the government. If he locates on the border of a large prairie, he will secure timber and as much prairie as he will need, and at any future period he may enter the prairie land that joins him.

No emigrant need deceive himself with the notion that he can find a spot which will combine *all* the advantages, and none of the disadvantages of the country. On every spot he examines, some indispensable thing will appear to be lacking. Nor is it of any use for a man to travel the country to any great extent, to find as many natural advantages as may satisfy moderate desires. I have often observed that those who move about from place to place, to find a better location, never become satisfied. The best policy for an emigrant, after arriving in this country and fixing upon the district or county in which he intends to reside, is to locate himself on the first spot he finds that he thinks may answer his purpose, and resolve to abide there contentedly. Some years since, wealthy emigrants who came to the State, made serious mistakes about expending money in buildings, stock, and other personal property, under the notion of placing themselves at once in comfortable circumstances. They have never been able to count up the profits of their capital thus expended. Let an emigrant purchase no more cattle, horses, hogs, &c. than those for which he has immediate use, unless it is for breeders,—and calves, in the fall, at eight or nine months old. These usually sell for two dollars per head, and are profitable stock to purchase.

If an emigrant locates on the frontiers, or in the newly settled portions of the country, his first object will be to provide cabins for his family, and the less labor and expense in preparing these, the better. The most expensive buildings of the west, are log houses pretended to be finished. This I have demonstrated both theoretically and practically. Let a man and family come into any of our frontier settlements, get a shelter, or even encamp out, call upon the people to aid him, and in three days from the start he will have a comfortable cabin, and become identified as a settler. No matter how poor he may be, or how much an entire stranger, if he has the right *look*, makes no apologies, does not show a niggardly spirit, by contending about trifles, and especially if he does not begin to dole out complaints about the country, and the manners and habits of the people, and tell them the difference and superiority of these things from whence he came, he will be received with blunt frankness and unaffected hospitality.

But if a man begins, by affecting superior intelligence and virtue, and catechising the people for their habits of plainness and simplicity, and their apparent want of those things which he imagines indispensable to comfort, he may expect to be marked, shunned, and called in the way of sarcastic reproach, *a Yankee.*

Missionaries, in some instances, in these particulars, have failed most egregiously, for want of a little common sense, or common prudence, and in a little time have lost that influence, which, by a proper and conciliating course, they might have had. I earnestly recommend therefore to those who think of emigrating to this country, especially from the north, to come here with the fixed purpose of submitting cheerfully to many inconveniences, avoiding all complaint, and amalgamating and identifying themselves with the present population.

By this remark, I am not to be understood that they should connive at, or indulge in the vicious or idle habits of frontier people. This is not expected, and eastern emigrants will sink as fast in the estimation of "back-woods" people by such a course, as in any other.

The characteristic property of our western population, is blunt, unaffected hospitality. They will make every stranger welcome, provided he will accept of it in their own way. But he must make no complaints, throw out no insinuations, and manifest an equal readiness to be frank and hospitable in turn. Enter whatever house or cabin you may, if it is the time of meals, you are invited to share a portion; but you must eat what is set before you, asking no questions, and making no invidious comparisons. Nor must you offer remarks on the accommodations you have had, or the unpleasant things you may have encountered at other places where you have tarried, as such remarks are considered as reflections upon the people, and those by whom you are now hospitably entertained will infer that you will thus slander them when you have departed.

When an emigrant has fixed his location, he next selects his building spot. Much will depend upon a judicious selection, in regard to HEALTH.

As I shall devote an article specially to this subject in its proper place, I will merely observe here, that an elevated spot of ground, remote from lakes and marshes, and where the air circulates freely from all points of the compass, is desirable. If a river bottom is chosen, the house should be as near the stream, on the highest ground, as is possible, without risk from the washing in of the banks. Settlements directly on the margins of the Mississippi and Missouri, are healthy compared with a few hundred yards distance, in the interior of the bottom. Where all other circumstances are equal, the south or southwest side of the timber is the most desirable, as throughout the heat of summer our winds are usually from the southwest and west, and the timber affords protection from the cold north winds of winter. But an exposure to the north or northwest is far less disagreeable than would be imagined. In a very few years, by means of orchards and shade trees, sufficient protection can be had. All confined places should be avoided, such as ravines, and even coves, or points of prairie, surrounded by dense timber, unless an opening can be made immediately. The currents in the atmosphere appear to act on the same principles as currents in the water. Where eddies and counter currents are formed, there impure vapor will concentrate. This is not only true in theory, but holds good in practical observation. When sickness prevails in a family, or a little settlement, the intelligent and observing physician immediately looks about for the cause, and if he detects nothing in the immediate vicinity to generate miasmata, he will probably discover circumstances that cause an eddy, or a current of impure air, around the dwelling. I have frequently known, and the same remark has been made to me by observing physicians, that severe sickness has prevailed in a family located at the head of a small ravine, while other families at a few rods distance have entirely escaped. Physicians and philosophers have not yet determined what the thing is, called *miasma*, which invariably produces yellow, bilious, intermittent, and other summer and autumnal fevers; but if it is a species of *carbonic gas*, as some think, it is heavier than the surrounding atmosphere, is more dense on low grounds and bottoms, and in ravines, and naturally concentrates in confined places. But whatever may be its nature, as a remote cause of disease, it is enough for practical purposes to know that any spot where the air is confined, as a cove in the timber or bluff, or where it is forced through a passage, as the head of a ravine, is always less healthy than a spot freely ventilated, or on elevated ground.

Having fixed on the spot, the next step is to provide cabins or temporary buildings. These, and all other dwellings should be so arranged as to promote ventilation in the summer. The doors and other apertures should be opposite each other, the chimney at the end, and if a double cabin, or one of two rooms is designed, a space of ten or twelve feet between them should be left, and roofed over. Forks may be set in the ground, and porches or sheds may be made on the sides, eight feet in width. The cost is trifling, and they add greatly to the coolness of the dwelling in summer, and its warmth in winter, besides protecting the body of the house from rains. Hundreds of cabins are made without a nail or particle of iron about them, or a single piece of sawed plank. I have already described the structure of a cabin. If an emigrant can furnish a few pounds of nails, and a dozen panes of glass, he may add to his comforts, and if a saw-mill is near, and plank or boards cheap, he may save himself the labor of splitting puncheons or slabs for floors and doors. In addition to the cabin, he will need a meat house, a corn crib, and stables, all built of logs in the same rough manner. If an emigrant has plenty of money, and sawed lumber can be gotten conveniently, he may put up a frame barn as soon as he pleases. If he has not the advantage of a good spring, he should dig a well immediately, which will cost four or five days' labor, and will stand some time without walling. In making all these improvements, all cash expenses should be avoided as much as possible, unless a man has money to waste.

The next step is to prepare a farm. If a man locates himself in barrens, or in timbered land, he has to *grub* out the small growth, preparatory to ploughing—that is, dig them up by the roots with an instrument called a mattock. It is true that land covered with bushes can be ploughed, and the stumps left in the ground, as well or better than in the north. But it will require more labor in the end to subdue the sprouts that will strive for the mastery, than to clear the land at once. It usually requires from three to six days' labor to grub an acre. The small growth in timbered lands is taken out in the same manner. If a settler has located himself in a timbered tract, which, in this prairie country is wretched policy, he grubs up the small growth, girdles the trees, and puts in the plough.

Prairie land requires a strong team and a large plough, kept very sharp, to break it up thoroughly. This must be done well, and every particle of the sward turned over, or it had better be let alone.

The following calculations exhibit not the hypothetical, but the practical expenses of preparing farms or enclosures, of different sizes, for cultivation, according to the ordinary prices of labor, and supposing the employer to furnish timber.

1. Expense of a farm of 160 acres, in four fields, surrounded with a fence eight rails high, and staked, allowing two stakes to each pannel of fence, with two division fences crossing each other at right angles.

To enclose and divide the tract into four fields will require 15,360 rails, and 3,840 stakes—the rails ten feet, and the stakes eight feet, in length.

Making 15,360 rails, at 50 cts. per hund. $76,80
   Do. 3,840 stakes, $37\frac{1}{2}$ cts. do.   14,25
   Hauling same, say one mile,   45,00
   Laying up do.   20,00
   Extras, say,   3,95

    Cost of fencing, $1 per acre, $160,00

If no division fences are made, but the whole tract left in one field, the cost is just *one third* less for fencing.

   Breaking up 160 acres of prairie, at
    two dollars per acre, is $320,00

Expense of the plantation, $480,00
To this add the cost of cabins, stables, corncribs, &c. say, $200,00
Price of the land at $1,25 per acre, 200,00
Eighty acres of timber, and eighty acres of prairie, to join it, 200,00

Making cost of farm and improvements, $1080,00

J.... S...., from near Zanesville, Ohio, came to Illinois, in the fall of 1829. He brought a large waggon and six horses, with other teams, and eleven ploughs, none of which would do to break prairie. During the following winter and spring, he broke up one hundred acres of prairie, with one team of horses. With the aid of his sons, who were stout young men, he built his cabins, fenced his field, and raised a crop of corn, most of which, though on new prairie, produced forty bushels to the acre.

Lest every man should imagine he can do likewise, and in the end be disappointed, I will relate one or two other instances.

P— Q—, came from Tennessee, in the same autumn, spent part of his time in hunting, another portion at the grocery, and the rest in getting a little meal, wood, &c. He took possession of an old cabin, that was very open, and exposed his family to the weather; but as he contemplated moving again, not liking that part of the country, he could not afford to "chink and daub" it. By exposure his family got sick. He had a large family of children, but he would not send them to school, for divers reasons: 1. It was too far; 2. He did not like the teacher, though he knew nothing about school-teaching, not being able to read himself; 3. He could not afford to pay; 4. He thought they would learn best when they were older. In the spring he rented a piece of land and made a sorry crop, which he sold in the field, and moved to another county, to pursue the same course another year.

It must be understood then, that where one man breaks up and fences one hundred acres in a season, about fifty take the track of P. Q.

Expense of a farm of 80 acres, 160 rods long, and eighty rods wide, called in the land surveys *a half quarter section*, with division fences crossing at right angles, so as to make four fields of twenty acres each.

Fencing.

Making 11,520 rails, at 50 cts. per hund. $57,60
Do. 2,880 stakes, at $37\frac{1}{2}$ cts. do. 10,75
Hauling one mile, 40,00
Laying up fence, 20,00
Extras, 3,65

$132,00

The cost of enclosing eighty acres, without a division fence, at the same ratio, would be $88,70.

It will be perceived there is considerable disproportion in the expense of fencing one hundred and sixty and eighty acres. This arises from two circumstances: 1. The one hundred and sixty acre tract was a square, and the eighty acre tract, a parallelogram, the length of which was twice equal to the width. 2. The larger the field is, the fewer rails in proportioon are required to enclose it. Consequently, were twelve families to unite, and enclose one thousand acres, the proportionate expense of fencing would be vastly lessened.

Breaking up 80 acres of prairie,	$160,00
Cost of the land,	100,00
Cost of another 80 acre tract, of half timber, and half prairie, to furnish timber, pasture, meadow, &c.	100,00
Cabins and other improvements,	150,00
	$510,00
Add cost of fencing,	132,00
Whole cost,	$642,00

Expense of enclosing and breaking forty acres, in a square form, divided into two fields.

Making 6,400 rails,	$32,00
Do. 1,600 stakes,	6,00
Hauling do. one mile,	21,75
Making fence and extras,	13,75
	$73,50

(If but one field is made of the tract, the cost of enclosing will be $58,80.)

Breaking up prairie,	80,00
Cost,	$153,50
Add cost of eighty acres of land,	100,00
	$253,50

A farm of twenty acres in a square field.

3,650 rails, to enclose it,	$18,25
912 stakes,	3,40
Hauling, one mile,	10,00
Laying up fence,	5,00
Cost,	$35,65
Breaking up do.	40,00
	$75,65

Ten acres, or a field of forty rods square.

2,560 rails, to enclose,	$12,30
740 stakes,	2,75
Hauling,	7,50
Laying fence,	3,50
Breaking up ground,	20,00
Cost,	$45,05

In these calculations, the timber is supposed to be furnished, for which no account is made. In St. Clair county, rails cost one dollar per hundred, when purchased, which would increase the cost of fencing proportionably. When rails have lain in fence four or five years, they are estimated at half price, say fifty cents per hundred. These statements are sufficiently accurate for practical purposes, to enable emigrants to judge of the value of improvements. Of course proper estimates must be made for local advantages, the quality and extent of improvements made—for orchards, wells, barns, &c. and for the relative value of property in different counties.

COST OF BUILDINGS.

Brick usually sells at the kiln for $3,50, and $4,00 per thousand. Where a man finds yard, wood, team, tenders, and board, the price for moulding and burning is seventy-five cents per thousand. Pine plank or boards in St. Louis, from the lumber yards, and seasoned, costs from twenty-five to thirty dollars per thousand feet. It is purchased from the rafts on the river for fifteen dollars, and even $12,50 in an unseasoned state. Various kinds of oak for flooring sells at the mills from one dollar to one dollar and twenty-five cents per hundred feet.

The following table shows the prices of lumber in St. Clair county, at the mills.

Flooring, 1¼ inch thick,	$1,25
Weatherboarding,	80 to 1,00
Walnut, for ceiling, &c.	1,00 to 1,50
Lynn, (Basswood,)	1,25
Roofing,	,75

Scantling is usually estimated the same as plank or boards, one inch thick; that is, a piece of timber four inches wide and three inches thick, is estimated at twelve inches in width.

Nails by the keg sell for ten cents per pound;

in some instances cheaper. Glass, at five and six dollars per hundred square feet.

Carpenters and joiners' work is estimated either by the day, the job, or by the *square;* that is, one hundred square feet.

Common workmen usually receive one dollar per day and board. Framing, one dollar per square, when the timber is hewn previously. Putting on the siding, or enclosing buildings, one dollar per square. Roofing, one dollar and fifty cents, the materials being prepared for the workmen. Laying floors, four dollars per square, including the dressing of the plank. Making doors, fifty cents per pannel. Making window sash, six cents a light. Laying brick, where materials and tenders are furnished, two dollars per thousand. Putting on three coats of plaister, where materials are all found, including hands to carry mortar, and board, twelve and a half cents per square yard. Oil costs by the barrel, seventy-five cents per gallon. White lead, ground in oil, in kegs of twenty-eight pounds weight, from three dollars and fifty cents, to four dollars per keg. The usual wages for various mechanics per day, and board, is one dollar. Masterworkmen, millwrights, and some others, charge higher. Scientific millwrights, and machinists will command from two to three dollars per day, including their tools. Common laborers have ten dollars per month, or fifty cents per day. Men who can handle the broad-axe, saw, or plane, though they are not carpenters, get seventy-five cents per day.

These prices are the rates of the country, not of St. Louis, or any prominent town. Wages there are higher. Some variations will be found in different parts of the State, according to the scarcity of mechanics or laborers, and other circumstances. On the whole, wages and prices are rather on the rise, and the demand increases.

There are but few good buildings in the State. Even those of brick, in most cases, are slightly built. The people are obliged to use economy, and oftentimes, for want of a few dollars, or allowing a little more time, lose much more than they save.

A very large majority of the people, especially in the newer parts of the State, live in cabins. A good framed barn is seldom seen. This is a great drawback on both the convenience and interest of the farmer. A man who can hew timber may build a barn, thirty feet by forty, for about seventy-five dollars, besides his own labor and that of his sons. In some counties it is difficult to obtain sawed lumber in sufficient quantities, but this is an evil that will soon be removed, and better buildings be erected.

MANUFACTURES.

In the infancy of a country, little can be expected in machinery and manufactures. And in a region so much deficient in water power as is most parts of the State, still less may be looked for. Yet Illinois is not entirely destitute of manufacturing enterprise. This will be briefly noticed under appropriate general heads; but for particulars, the reader is referred to the statistics of each county.

1. *Salt.* The salines of this State have been mentioned in the account of minerals. The principal works are the United States or Gallatin salines, the Big Muddy, and the Vermillion salines. Of the extent of the works of the latter, I have no particular information, only that they are considered valuable, and manufacture large quantities of salt.

The following outline of Gallatin saline, and works has been politely furnished by Gen. Leonard White, clerk of the county.

There are nine furnaces, containing on an average, sixty kettles each, holding m thirty-six to sixty gallons, and which make upwards of three thousand bushels per week, averaging about 130,000 bushels per annum, after deducting lost time. The works are carried on by Messrs. B. White, J. Davis, John Crenshaw, W. Weed, and C. Guard. Salt sells at the works from thirty-seven and a half to fifty cents per bushel. A bushel of salt is fifty pounds. About one half of the salt manufactured here is exchanged for corn, corn meal, flour, beef, pork, potatoes, onions, and every article that can be raised in the country. The usual rates of exchange are two bushels of corn for one of salt; one and a half bushels of corn meal for one of salt. Four bushels of salt are given for one hundred pounds of beef; six bushels for one hundred pounds of pork; four bushels for one hundred pounds of flour; and the same in proportion for other articles of produce. Thus the farmers are supplied with salt at a cheap rate, and find a market for all their products at home.

The following account of the Big Muddy saline is taken from a communication from Conrad Will, Esq. one of the principal manufacturers.

"As to the salt works at this place, (Brownsville) there is one furnace with fifty-five kettles, that boil thirty-five gallons each, and which make one hundred bushels of salt per week. In the present situation of the works, it takes three hundred gallons of water, to make one bushel of salt. This is owing to the well being tubed, and the fresh water not being excluded, which will be effected during the present year. The well is two hundred and three feet deep, and the fountain is so strong that it gushes six feet above the surface of the ground, and in quantity sufficient to run five furnaces. Salt water can be had in many places in this county, and it is my opinion that much better water can be had by boring deeper, than in any other part of the State.

"Mr. William H. Nielson has commenced boring for salt water, one mile below Brownsville, on the banks of the Big Muddy river, and has gotten down one hundred and thirty-seven feet, at which distance he has plenty of water, fully as strong as mine. He intends boring three hundred feet deep, unless he gets water sufficiently strong at a less distance. He will erect this summer two furnaces of the following description. Two pans of twenty feet in length, and five feet in width, which will hold about twelve hundred gallons of water, and thirty kettles in each furnace of sixty gallons, all of which, together with copper tubes for the well, and sundry other articles necessary for the furnaces, have arrived at the place. The salt made here is superior to that made at the Ohio saline, near Shawneetown, and I have no doubt there will be large quantities made in a few years.

"Mr. Nielson has opened a very extensive coal bank about four miles above Brownsville. The mine is inexhaustible, as far as the experiment has been tried, and the coal equal to that at Pittsburgh in quality. He is preparing to send off ten boats loaded with coal this season; and contemplates sending sixty boats next season, Mr. Nielson's coal bank is immediately in the banks of the Big Muddy river, and is so convenient that the coal can be thrown from the bank into the boats. There are a number of beds of coal in this county, and equally good.

C. W."

Jackson county, where the above works are situated, lies on the Mississippi, about thirty-five miles below Kaskaskia. Brownsville is not marked on the map. It is on Muddy river, twelve miles from the Mississippi.

Salt has been made in the neighborhood of Carlyle, in the eastern part of Madison county, on the waters of Sangamon river, and perhaps in other parts of the State.

2. *Steam Mills.* There are ten steam mills, for either sawing or grinding, in the State, and many more contemplated; one of which, a steam sawmill, in Gallatin county, has been recently burnt. They are located as follows. One steam sawmill in Clark county; two saw and one flouring steam mill, in Randolph county; one saw and one flouring mill, in St. Clair county; one steam sawmill, in Madison county, near Alton; and two saw and grist mills in Morgan county. Of those in St. Clair county, I can speak with the most accuracy. The sawmill is at Lebanon, four miles east of Rock-Spring, was built by a company, and put in operation in the summer of 1830. The engine is twelve horse power, runs one saw, and will cut three thousand feet of plank in a day and night. The flouring mill is at Belleville, built in the autumn of 1830, and owned by a Mr. Harrison. It is of twelve horse power, and will manufacture thirty barrels of flour per day. The engine is on the high pressure principle, cylinder eight inches in diam-

eter, three feet stroke, one of which causes the stones to perform fifty revolutions. The water is pumped from a well thirty-feet deep, and five feet in diameter, which furnishes an abundant supply. The furnace burns two cords of wood, and seven bushels of coal. The coal is brought five miles, and costs five and a half cents per bushel; but enough can be dug within half a mile. The mill-house is thirty-eight feet by thirty-five, two stories, and the engine room eighteen feet by thirty-eight. It has two run of stones, one of which is four feet six inches, and the other four feet in diameter, with elevators, screens, coolers, and all the apparatus complete for manufacturing flour. The cost of the whole, including building, engine, &c. was $3,500.

Knapp & Pogne's steam flouring mill is at Beardstown, on the Illinois river, in the upper part of Morgan county. From the 12th of March to the 27th of April, they sent to Hill & McGunnegle, a mercantile commission house in St. Louis, eight hundred barrels, and three hundred half barrels of superfine flour, and will probably send seven hundred and fifty barrels more before harvest. This being the first year of its operation, or of any flouring mill in that quarter of the State, the farmers were not able to supply it with wheat.

Collins' steam mill is adjoining Naples, in the same county, and about four miles above the mouth of the Mauvresterre, and eighteen miles from Jacksonville. The sawmill is fifty feet by twenty, and calculated for three saws. It runs only one saw yet, and cuts fifteen hundred feet of plank in the day time, which readily sells at the mill for one dollar and fifty cents and two dollars per hundred. The flouring mill is thirty feet by fifty, four stories high, with two run of stones, and will manufacture forty barrels of flour in twenty-four hours.

As a general principle, steam power can be applied economically and profitably for propelling all kinds of machinery in Illinois. A steam sawmill, in complete order, can be built for fifteen hundred dollars. It can be placed in any convenient and healthy spot in the midst of timber; and when the timber is exhausted for a mile or two around, it can be pulled down and removed for far less cost than logs can be hauled from a distance, for the supply of six months.

Ox tread mills, on the inclined plane, and horse mills by draught, are very common through the country. Water mills are built in many parts; but it must be acknowledged there are but few *good* mill sites in the State, south of a line drawn across from Alton. There are many places where mills exist, and do considerable business for considerable portions of the year, and a few that are excellent sites. But in most cases some difficulty presents itself. At one time the water is too high, and the mill submerged; at another period, the stream is nearly dry, and the pond exhausted, leaving a deposite of mud to throw off noxious exhalations and generate disease. Very rarely in this part of the State, can a site be found where rock and bluffs line both sides of the stream. A projecting rock or a substantial bluff may be found on one side, and perhaps the bottom of the stream firm, but on the opposite side is a low bottom, of rich, porous soil, which will be swept away as soon as the current at its highest stage is stopped by a dam. In the counties bordering on the Illinois, and in the vast tract of country north of that river, there are many good sites for water mills and machinery. At the rapids of Illinois, the advantages of water power are not exceeded in the western country. I have not the least apprehension that the State will suffer any inconvenience for the supposed lack of water privileges.

3. *Castor Oil.* Considerable quantities of this article are manufactured in Illinois. There is one castor oil press in Edwards county, three in Randolph county, and two at Edwardsville, in Madison county. The manufacture of this article at Edwardsville, was commenced by Mr. John Adams, in 1825, in which season he made five hundred gallons, which sold at the rate of two dollars and fifty cents per gallon; in 1826, he made eight hundred gallons, at the price of one dollar and fifty cents; in 1827, one thousand gallons, at one dollar and twenty-five cents; in

1828, eighteen hundred gallons, which sold for one dollar; in 1829, he made five hundred and twenty-eight gallons, at the price of one dollar and twelve and a half cents; in 1830, two presses were started, and made ten thousand gallons, from seventy-five to eighty-seven and a half cents per gallon. The present season he will make about twelve thousand five hundred gallons, and the wholesale price is about seventy-five cents.

One bushel of the castor bean, or palma christi, will yield about seven quarts and a half pint of oil. The beans are cleaned and well dried or heated in a furnace, put in a cylinder, and the screw, which is an immense one of wood, forces down a follower with great power. The screw is turned by a horse and a large lever, precisely similar to that of a cider mill, in New England, called a nut mill. Beans are purchased from the farmers for seventy-five cents per bushel.

This species of manufactory is a happy commentary upon the system of protection to home industry against foreign competition. Some years since, when the duty upon imported castor oil was extremely light, it sold in the Philadelphia market at four dollars per gallon. The duty now is forty-five cents, amounting to a prohibition; the domestic competition is great, and it sells for seventy-five cents.

The farmers of Madison county produce large quantities of beans where they otherwise would raise corn; which they sell for cash and store goods, thus giving greater scope for market to the corn-growers, and giving an impulse to all kinds of business.

4. *Cotton Spinners.* I know of only two machines for the manufacture of cotton yarn in the State; but it is a business that ought to attract the attention of those acquainted with the business, as it may be conducted to great advantage on a small scale. The people would produce cotton, carry it to the machine in the seed, and receive yarn in pay. Coarse cotton yarn, in bales of five pounds each, usually sells from one dollar and twenty-five cents to one dollar and thirty-seven and a half cents a bale.

There is a spinning machine in Bond county, of one hundred and sixty spindles, and one at Jacksonville of one hundred and twenty-six spindles. They are carried by ox power, on an inclined plane.

In Jo Davies county are ten lead furnaces, which have been noticed already.

Many other branches of manufactures are carried on in a small way which will be seen in the tabular view of the counties, taken from the census table of last autumn. At Mount Carmel in Wabash county is an iron foundry. Alton will probably become a place for building steam boats, as it has around it one of the best bodies of oak timber in the State.

CLIMATE, DISEASES, &c.

I am aware of the difficulty, if not impossibility, of giving clear and definite ideas on this subject to those who have never seen this country. On the subject of health, all generalities are vague and indefinite. As the public mind abroad is extremely sensitive on this subject, and as certain sickness is the evil, which, most of all others, haunts the imagination of those who desire to emigrate to the west, I shall devote a number of pages to this subject. Besides presenting the opinions of several distinguished physicians, I shall exhibit such facts as have come under my own observation and experience.

The following is extracted from the introductory part of the FAMILY PHYSICIAN, published in Cincinnati, in 1826, by a physician of eminent standing in his profession, and long experience.

"OF THE CLIMATE OF THE WESTERN COUNTRY, ESPECIALLY WITH REFERENCE TO ITS INFLUENCE ON HEALTH.

"This extensive region may be considered as a great valley, lying between the Alleghany mountains on the east, and the mountains of New Mexico and Missouri on the west: its rivers, uniting from the east, the west, and the north, form one common channel, by which they are poured southwardly.

"From the gigantic scale on which this valley has been cast, we naturally look for varieties of climate; but owing to the remarkable junction of its waters, and their determined course, as well as in consequence of those ranges of mountains which we have mentioned, there are certain features of uniformity attached to its atmosphere, which pervade almost the whole western country, and only fade away, and become gradually more indistinct, as we recede northwardly from the Mexican Gulf, and enter into higher and colder latitudes.

"The Alleghany mountains, as well as distance from the Atlantic, prevent us from experiencing the cold, drizzling weather, which, in spring, and early part of summer, is so disagreeable along the eastern coast, and extends a considerable distance inland, propelled by north east winds: and a vast extent of continent, with lofty mountains, prevents the possibility of similar weather from the west. From the north, the winds also blow principally over land. The south and southwest winds,* in this country, are most apt to be loaded with vapors. That

---

* Perhaps the most common wind of long continuance, especially in the winter, which is charged with vapors, or with heavy clouds affording rain, is from one point to the southward of southwest.

part of these vapors is accumulated by the south wind, after it leaves the Gulf of Mexico, in passing over the Mississippi and its numerous attendant lakes and swamps, is not doubted; but the southwest winds, which oftener prevail, are equally, and as uniformly charged with vapor.*

"In the month of January, 1824, a warm southwest wind was observed by a gentleman near Cape Girardeau, in Missouri, on the Mississippi river, to blow for more than three weeks, frequently so hard as to threaten the buildings, and carrying an immense mass of clouds in a direction towards the upper lakes, and the head waters of the Mississippi. This is not mentioned as a solitary instance, but as an example of those currents of air: and there seems reason to suppose that long continued winds, of this description, have their origin over the vast Pacific ocean, and pass across the southern extremity of North America, the province of Texas, and the Arkansas country: a sufficient cause cannot be assigned for their long continuance, and peculiar humidity, short of this.

---

* Neither the celebrated Volney, nor professors Mitchell or Drake, in their views on this subject, seem to have considered that a southwest wind, felt in the heart of the western country, cannot come from any part of the Mexican Gulf in a direct line. There will be no difficulty in ascertaining this fact by reference to a correct map of the United States,

"Thus, besides the rain that falls from clouds proper to this country, there is a great accession of moisture from the Gulf of Mexico, and, according to our supposition, from the Pacific. It has been noticed that much rain seldom falls until the force of long continued and severe southwest winds is abated, when the vapor, compressed, probably, by counter currents of air, descend. This, in the winter, is one cause of floods in the rivers, which are further increased by the breaking up and dissolving of the ice.

"However some may be disposed to question the extent of space over which these southwest winds, (it appears reasonable to believe,) travel, yet the facts, which must be admitted, and their consequences, are of importance in assisting us to become acquainted with the climate.

"After such weather as we have described, has continued a length of time in winter, it is common for the wind to come out from between the northwest and northeast, intensely cold; this also was the case in Missouri, in 1824, and many neighborhoods were soon visited with peculiarly fatal fevers, of typhus kind, considerably resembling the disease which a few years since prevailed in Kentucky and elsewhere, called the cold plague. Nor was sickness confined to that section of the country; it extended largely through the Arkansas, Illinois, and elsewhere; especially in low situations, in very young settlements, and where the wilderness had been but partially cleared and cultivated. It was particularly noticed that those who lived in warm, close houses, and wore suitable clothing, were the most exempted from its attacks.

"The northwest wind, coming over the Rocky Mountains, and a bleak expanse of continent, is often in the winter extremely cold, especially in those states which lie most exposed. The weather is generally much more variable in the winter than it is in the same latitude on this continent, east of the mountains; but is, on an average, milder. In the summer the weather is less variable than it is east of the mountains, and the heat, though not greater, is more permanent.

"In level tracts of country, particularly prairies and barrens, the air is less elastic, and neither man nor beast can perform the same labor, with safety, that they have been accustomed to execute in the Atlantic states. This comparative want of elasticity in the atmosphere is partly owing to the absence of morning and evening breezes.

"Another peculiarity of the western country, and connected with its climate, well deserves to be noticed. The rivers, with very few if any exceptions, are dependent on periodical or casual rains or thaws, for what is considered their full volume of water: and at certain seasons, especially in summer, they become insignificant streams: a drought, in many places, succeeding to a superfluity of water on the face of the earth, vast quantities of decaying vegetable substances and stagnant waters in parts of the beds of creeks, in ponds and swamps, are thus left exposed to the rays of the sun. As we travel northward, these unpleasant appearances are less frequently noticed—but the lake country is not without them, being much of it swampy.

"Exhalations from the face of a country thus situated, have a tendency to impart at least the causes of languor to the atmosphere; and if we have not the raw and chilling northeasterly winds of the middle and eastern states, we lack, also, the invigorating influence which is derived from a constant agitation of the atmosphere, and a continual change and succession of its particles. A very material consequence in relation to health follows: there are fewer consumptions with us than in those states of which we have been speaking, but more bilious diseases. This last remark is applicable particularly to the upper part of Missouri, Indiana, Illinois, Kentucky, Ohio, and the Michigan territory, for farther south, on the waters of the Mississippi, the Santee, the Savannah, and Altamaha, the causes of diseases are more nearly the same. Notwithstanding, however, the general influence of those causes which tend to render this climate insalubrious, there are many situations in the western country, as healthy as any on the continent of North America; neither is there any other section of the Union which has not its disadvantages with regard to health.

"Having thus noticed some general and extensive coincidences of the climate, and some causes by which it is influenced, we will endeavour to examine a few distinguished characteristics which mark different parts of the country, and which have an influence on the human constitution.

"In the vicinity of rivers—as for instance in Kentucky, below the Tennessee; in Illinois, below fort Massae, and up the east side of the Mississippi; in Missouri, on the west side of the Mississippi, from Cape Girardeau to New Madrid, on parts of the Arkansas, and in many other places above the 34th degree of latitude, is found a great deal of low ground, which at times is partly covered with water, by floods coming down the rivers, and at other times by long continued and heavy rains, which are not uncommon; the growth of natural vegetation on this soil is exceedingly luxuriant.

"These low grounds are intersected by gullies, containing water the whole year, and by channels of permanent streams, which, in a dry season, are but rivulets: but in a time of heavy rains, some of them become a quarter of a mile wide. There are also frequently many small elevated spots of land well calculated for cultivation. During a flood, the water is often forced up through some opening, so as to cover large tracts of land, forming temporary lakes. The mosquetos in warm weather, in such situations, are innumerable. When a dry time commences, in the summer, and the waters begin to be exhaled from the surface of the earth, the air feels close and oppressive ; many of those who have been a considerable time resident, are attacked, as the heat and drought increases, with agues, that are evidently in a great measure dependent on, or at least connected with, diseased action of the liver ; and also of other glands contained in the cavity of the abdomen ; these agues frequently continue for months, and sometimes alternate with dysentery. Strangers, or new comers, are mostly attacked with greater violence by diseases more confirmedly bilious; and when they are released from the first and most alarming symptoms, find entailed upon them agues which last three, six or nine months, and seldom leave the constitution more than the wreck of what it was in health.

"From the thirty-fourth degree of latitude, southwards, many of those last mentioned causes which affect the atmosphere, and through it the human system,—are increased in all places during the summer season ; and in times of low water, the air communicates perceptibly a sense of lassitude ; in addition, winds are frequent from the southwest, which, passing over the marshy and unhealthy western shore of the Mexican gulf, still more unfit the air for the purposes of health. Those who navigate the Mississippi, at such times, smell distinctly the pestiferous effluvium that arises around, and is carried on the wings of the wind.

"At Natchez, which is more sickly than New Orleans, in consequence of being exposed to accumulated causes of disease, and at the same time destitute of breezes from the sea, these influences are but too sensibly perceived; and experience has shown that buildings erected under the bluff, nearly on a level with the water, are safer residences than those built on the top of the bluff; for it seems to be a fact, that when the whole mass of air is loaded with pestilential effluvia, a retreat from its direct and unqualified influence, by seeking unexposed situations, and even using fires and fumigations, is advisable.

"In the vicinity of New Orleans, the westerly winds, in addition to domestic miasmata, bring the same atmospheric poison which has been already noticed, from the border of the gulf; and the most grateful and refreshing breezes experienced in hot weather, are from the southeast; these come over an open expanse of salt water.

"It may be noticed generally, that as we proceed south, from its head waters, in the course of the Mississippi, the debilitating influence of extreme heat in summer, with the increased condensation of miasmata, cause the diseases to become more severe; ague and fever gradually give way to bilious fevers of the highest grade, and in Natchez and New Orleans, and the country between and around them, very frequently in a few hours after the attack of the disease, the hand of death presses heavy on the patient.

"The terms barren and prairie are not very definite, if we may judge from common usage. A barren is generally supposed to be land somewhat elevated, and tolerably level, frequently of good quality, the timber of which has been destroyed, probably for ages; and a prairie, a low, level tract, occasionally wet, and somewhat resembling meadow land; both barrens and prairies, in a natural state, are covered with long coarse grass.* The Big Prairie in Missouri, between Cape Girardeau and New Madrid, is, according to the above definition, perhaps more properly barren land. The same might be said of other prairies. The word prairie in the French language, signifies meadow.

"Many of the barrens, since they have been enclosed and preserved from fires, begin to be, when they are not cultivated, covered with young timber.

"Large tracts of barrens are found in perhaps all of the western States, and are tolerably healthy situations. Agues and fevers are not uncommon, however, among those who reside

---

* This distinction of prairie and barren is incorrect.

on them. The want of spring or elasticity in the atmosphere is sensibly perceived in summer and autumn, on the barrens and prairies. Ponds of stagnant water are common, and the running streams are few. From their exposed situation, the sudden changes in winter, acting upon systems relaxed by the influences of summer, are severely felt.

"It is in the high wooded country, at a distance from stagnant waters and swamps, that we find in most of the western States an atmosphere conducive to health, and to a full developement of all the physical powers of man.

"That some who have been born, or who have become climatized, in places, which to a stranger prove unhealthy—are generally free from disease, and live to be aged, proves little; for it is a well known truth, that the constitution of man is calculated for adaptation to every clime, and almost every mode of living. The same argument might be adduced by the Asiatics, as favoring the habitual use of opium, or even of corrosive sublimate, and these practices are not uncommon among them.

"There are certain situations which universal consent has allowed to be more healthy than others; thus, the hills of East Jersey, on the Atlantic coast, with their pure, bracing atmosphere, are acknowledged to afford a more salubrious residence than can be found in the vicinity of the wooded swamps and the morasses, with which the southern part of that State terminates. And yet on the southern extremity of New Jersey live some of our hardiest and most robust fellow-citizens.

"There is, however, little doubt but that many situations in this country, now unhealthy, or deemed so, will become, in the gradual course of improvement, safe places of residence. A barbarous mode of half cultivating the soil, neglecting a proper attention to precautionary means for the preservation of health, suffering stagnant ponds to remain near dwellings, and the like causes, which will be spoken of in the next chapter, have placed many residents in an unnecessary state of liability to disease.

"Limestone water is the most common throughout the western country, and is generally good; but sometimes it passes through impure or imperfectly formed beds of this earth—it then has a disagreeable taste, and is unwholesome.

"Among the large towns, Pittsburgh, Lexington, Cincinnati, and Nashville, may be esteemed the most healthy.

"If any, deceived by erroneous statements, think that we have been too severe in estimating the climate of this country, our reply is, that truth, not always told, and but seldom at first popular, will stand the test of examination, and must eventually prove beneficial to all who come within the sphere of its influence."

To the above opinions, I take the liberty of appending a few remarks.

1. I doubt the correctness of the assertion, that southwestern winds in Illinois and Missouri are charged with vapor. Much less rain falls in this country in a year than in the Atlantic States. In most parts of Illinois, and in the vicinity of St. Louis, it is always wet when the periodical rise of the Missouri takes place. And then the clouds always come from the west, and a few degrees north of west, following precisely the course of that river. In the latter part of summer and autumn, our atmosphere is dry, and were it not for the smoke at that season, arising from the burning of the prairies, it would be remarkably clear.

It is true that throughout the year our winds are from the southwest, more than from all other points of compass.

2. I cannot agree to the assertion that in prairies and barrens the air is less elastic than in timber, or in the Atlantic States. I have uniformly thought there is more elasticity. Asthmatic persons never fail to find relief in this climate. I have corrected in a note the mistake about the characters of barrens and prairies, as I have heretofore done in the description of the country.

3. It is not correct that a "high wooded country" furnishes better health than our high prairies. This is contrary both to nature and fact.

From the same source of the last article, I make the following extract, entitled,

"ADVICE TO EMIGRANTS, RECENT SETTLERS, AND TO THOSE VISITING THE SOUTHERN COUNTRY.

"The outlines which have already been given will afford some information to emigrants from other sections of the Union, or from Europe. We will now offer a few cautionary remarks, particularly intended for such as are about to settle, or have recently settled in this section of the United States.

"Of new comers, there are two tolerably distinct classes; the one comprising farmers, mechanics, and indeed all those who calculate on obtaining a subsistence by manual industry; the other is composed of professional men, tradesmen, and adventurers of every description. Towards the first class our attention is now directed, premising that throughout a great portion of the western country, except in large towns, almost every mechanic is almost necessarily a farmer; the population being in but few places sufficiently dense to support that designation of mechanical employments which is common in the eastern and middle States.

"For the industrious and temperate of this class, our country holds forth inducements which are not generally known or understood.

"The language of indiscriminate panegyric, which has been bestowed on its climate and soil, has conveyed little information, and is the source of many fears and suspicions in the minds of people at a distance. Other accounts have described the western country as uniformly sickly; but the habit of exaggeration in its favor has been most prevalent; neither need we wonder, when much of the information communicated, has been afforded by interested landholders, or speculators, and by travellers, whose views have been superficial, and whose journeys have been performed generally either on the rivers or by post roads.

"The first inquiry of a substantial farmer, from one of the old settled States, is mostly for good land in the vicinity of a market; and afterwards, whether the situation be healthy. It is true that there are many places in the western country, affording the qualities expressed in this description, but they are perhaps all occupied; and it would be, in several respects, more advisable for a farmer, possessing even a considerable sum of money in hand, to inquire first for a healthy situation, and then good land.

"The spirit of improvement throughout the United States, especially evidenced in canalling, will, it is hoped, in a few years, open modes of communication, which as yet are wanting, with the markets.

"The same remarks will apply to the poorer class of emigrants. If they value their own health, and that of their families, the main object of their attention will be to secure, if possible, a situation remote from the fogs that hover over the channels of large rivers, which become partly dry in summer, and from the neighborhoods of swamps, marshes, ponds, and small lakes.

"Every person on coming from beyond the mountains, and especially from the eastern States, or Europe, will have to undergo some degree of change in his constitution, before it becomes naturalized to the climate; and all who move from a cold to a considerably warmer part of the western country will experience the same alteration; it will, therefore, be wisdom for the individual brought up in a more rigorous climate, that he seek a situation where the circulation of the air is unimpeded and free, and that he avoid those flat and marshy districts, which have been already described.

"Those who settle in new countries are almost universally exposed to inconveniences which have an unfavorable influence on health. They are seldom able for a length of time to erect comfortable places of residence, and indeed, many postpone this important object of attention even after their circumstances will permit them to build comfortable dwelling houses.

"Wool is mostly a scarce article in new settlements, so that cotton and linen garments are too frequently worn in winter. There is another circumstance, which no doubt has an unfavorable influence on health, especially among the poorer class; it is the want, during the summer season particularly, of substantial food. This is sometimes owing to indolence or improvidence; but perhaps oftener, to the circumstances in which a few families are placed, at a distance from any established or opulent settlement.

"Erroneous views are too generally entertained in relation to hardening the human system, and the analogies drawn from savage life, are altogether inconclusive. The manners of the North American Indians are essentially different from those of the whites. It is true, there is a portion of the latter, especially in Illinois and Missouri, who from infancy are educated almost in the habits of the aborigines.

"We have frequently heard the example of savages referred to, as an argument in favor of attempting to strengthen the constitution by exposure.* There is plausibility in this; but

---

* Uniform exposure to the weather is favorable to health. I can affirm this from long experience and observation. Our hunters, and surveyors, who uniformly spend their time for weeks in the woods and prairies, who wade in the water, swim creeks, are drenched in the rains and dews, and sleep in the open air or a camp at night, very rarely are attacked with

might not the example of the negroes in the lower parts of South Carolina and Georgia, be also quoted as evidencing the propriety of living on corn meal and sweet potatoes, and working every day in the water of a rice field during the sickly season. They are generally more healthy than the whites who own them, and who reside on the plantations in the summer. The civilized man may turn to savage life perhaps with safety, as regards health; but then he must plunge with the Indian into the depths of the forest, and observe consistency in all his habits. These pages are not written, however, for such

---

fevers. I have known repeated instances of young men brought up delicately in the eastern cities, accustomed, as clerks, to a sedentary life, with feeble constitutions—I have known such repeatedly to enter upon the business of surveying the public lands, or in the hunting and trapping business, be absent for months, and return with robust health. It is a common thing for a frontier man, whose health is on the decline, and especially when indications of pulmonary affection appear, to engage in a hunting expedition to renovate his health. I state these facts, and leave it to the medical faculty to explain the *why and wherefore*. One circumstance may deserve attention. All these men, as do the Indians, *sleep with their feet towards the fire at night*. And it is a common notion with this class, that if the feet are kept hot through the night, however cold the atmosphere, or however

as are disposed to consider themselves beyond the pale of civilized society; but for the reflecting part of the community, who can estimate the advantages to be derived from a prudent care of health.

"Much disease, especially in the more recently settled parts of this country, is consequent to neglecting simple and comfortable precautionary means; sometimes this neglect is owing to misdirected industry, and at others to laziness or evil habits.

"To have a dry house, if it be a log one, with the openings between the logs well filled up, so that it may be kept warm in winter; to fill up all holes in its vicinity which may contain stag-

---

much exposed the rest of the body, no evil consequences will ensue. I have passed many a night in this position, after fatiguing rides of thirty or forty miles in the day on our extreme frontiers, and through rains, and never experienced any inconvenience to health, if I could get a pallet on the cabin floor, and my feet to the fire.

Those who are exposed to these hardships but occasionally, when compelled by necessity, and endeavor to protect themselves at all other times, usually suffer after such exposure.

I have observed that children, when left to run in the open air and weather, who go barefoot, and oftentimes with a single light garment around them, who sleep on the floor at night, are more healthy than those who are protected.

nant water; to have a good clean spring or well, sufficient clothing, and a reasonable supply of provisions, should be the first object of a settler's attention: but frequently a little, wet, smoky cabin or hovel is erected, with the floor scarcely separated from the ground, and admitting the damp and unwholesome air. All hands that can work, are impelled, by the father's example, to labor beyond their strength, and more land is cleared and planted with corn than is well tended; for over exertion, change in the manner of living, and the influence of other debilitating causes, which have been mentioned, bring sickness on at least a part of the family, before the summer is half over.

"It is unnecessary for even the poorest emigrant to encounter these causes of distress, unless seduced by the misrepresentations of some interested land holder, or by the fantasies of his own brain to an unhealthy and desolate situation, where he can neither help himself, nor be assisted by others.

"Many persons on moving into the *back woods*, who have been accustomed to the decencies of life, think it is little matter how they live, because *no one sees them*. Thus we have known a family of some opulence to reside for years in a cabin unfit for the abode of any human being, because they could not find time to build a house; and whenever it rained hard, the females were necessarily engaged in rolling the beds from one corner of the room to another, in order to save them from the water that poured in through the roof. This cabin was intended at first as only a very temporary residence, and was erected on the edge of a swamp, for the convenience of being near to a spring. How unreasonable must such people be if they expect health!

"Clothing for winter should be prepared in summer. It is a common, but very incorrect practice, among many farmers, both west and east of the Alleghany mountains, to postpone wearing winter clothing until the weather has become extremely cold: this is a fruitful source of pulmonary diseases, of rheumatisms, and of fevers.

"With regard to providing a sufficiency of nourishing food, no specific directions can be given, further than to recommend what is much neglected—particular attention to a good garden spot; and to remark that those who devote undivided attention to cultivating the soil, receive more uniform supplies of suitable nourishment than the more indolent, who spend a considerable portion of their time in hunting.

"New settlers are not unfrequently troubled with diseases of the skin, which are often supposed to be the itch: for these eruptions they generally use repellant external applications; this plan of treatment is prejudicial.

"The most proper time for the removal of families to this country from the Atlantic states, is early in the spring, while the rivers are full; or if the journey be made by land, as soon as the roads are sufficiently settled, and the waters abated. But if the fall be a more convenient season, one or two hard frosts should be waited for, and these rarely occur until the latter end of October.

"Persons coming from a distance, who have not resolved in their minds on the place of their future residence, unless they mean to establish themselves high up in the country, in which case Pittsburgh or Wheeling would be recommended, are advised to make Cincinnati *a post of observation.**

"It possesses, for this purpose, many advantages over any other town in the western country. The terms of living are moderate, the situation is central and healthy, it is a city of industry, and from its situation on the bank of the Ohio, affords superior facilities of information. If it be supposed by any, that partiality has instigated this eulogium, we can appeal fearlessly for the correctness of our observations,

---

* It will be recollected by the reader, that the work from which the extract is made, was written and published in Cincinnati. The same remarks may be made in relation to St. Louis, as the thoroughfare for Missouri and Illinois.

to all well informed persons who are practically acquainted with this country.

"Persons unaccustomed to the climate of the lower Mississippi country, are necessarily exposed, whilst there in the summer season, to many causes of disease. It will be advisable for such to have a prudent care of their health, and yet a care distinct from that finical timidity which renders them liable to early attacks of sickness.

"There is one important consideration, which perhaps has been somewhat overlooked by medical men, who have written on this subject. Natives of colder and healthier regions, when exposed in southern and sickly climates, experience, if they remain any length of time without evident and violent disease, an alteration in the condition of the liver, and of the secreted bile itself; when it passes through the bowels, its color being much darker than usual. Sometimes, indeed, it appears to be "locked up in the liver," the stools having an ashy appearance. This state of the biliary secretion is frequently accompanied, although the patient is otherwise apparently in tolerable health, by a pain over the eye-balls, particularly when the eyes are rolled upward.

"The proper mode of treatment for such symptoms, is to take without delay, not less than twenty grains of calomel, and in eight hours a wine glass full of castor oil. The tone of the stomach should not be suffered to sink too much after the operation of the medicine, which, if necessary, may be repeated in twenty-four hours. Wine, brandy, or porter, in quantities sufficient to renovate the feelings, ought to be used, when the cathartics have performed their office.* Nutritive food, which is easy of digestion, should also be taken in moderate portions at a time.

"Where diseases are rapid in their progress, and dangerous, no time is to be lost. The practice of taking salts and other aperients, when in exposed situations, and for the purpose of preventing disease, is injurious. It is sufficient that the bowels be kept in a natural and healthy state; for all cathartics, even the mildest, have a tendency to nauseate the stomach, create debility, and weaken the digestive faculty.

---

* I dissent altogether from the opinion of the distinguished physician, as to the use of spiritous liquors, or even wine, as restoratives to the system: and in this, I have the decided opinions of several medical gentlemen of my acquaintance. Either as a preventive, or a restorative, ardent spirits are wholly unnecessary, and often decidedly injurious. The sulphate of quinine is much more than a substitute. It is to be hoped that the prevalence of temperance principles will correct these notions, and that the professor of chemistry and the medical profession will unite their influence to convince the world, what every man of science knows already, that ardent spirits are not *tonics.*

A reduction of tone in the system, which is always advantageous, will be more safely effected by using somewhat less than usual of animal food, and of spirituous, strong vinous, or fermented liquors. The robust will derive benefit from losing a little blood.

"It ought to be well understood, that as we approximate tropical climates, the doses of medicine, when taken, should be increased in quantity, and repeated with less delay than is admissible in colder countries. Exposure to the night air is certainly prejudicial; so also is the intense heat of the sun, in the middle of the day. Violent exercise should be also avoided. Bathing daily in water of a comfortable temperature, is a very commendable practice; and cotton worn next the skin is preferable to linen.

"It is impossible to prevent the influence of an atmosphere pregnant with the causes of disease; but the operation of those causes may generally be counteracted by attention to the rules laid down; and it is no small consolation, to be aware that on recovery from the first attack, the system is better adapted to meet and sustain a second of a similar nature. The reader will understand that we do not allude to relapses, occurring while the system is enfeebled by the consequences of disease."

To the foregoing remarks, I add the following from an address of Judge Hall to the "Antiquarian and Historical Society of Illinois," December 10, 1827.

"The climate, particularly in reference to its influence on the human system, presents another subject of investigation. The western country has been considered unhealthy; and there have been writers whose disturbed imaginations have misled them into a belief that the whole land was continually exposed to the most awful visitations of Providence, among which have been numbered the hurricane, the pestilence, and the earthquake. If we have been content to smile at such exaggerations, while few had leisure to attempt a serious refutation, and while the facts upon any deliberate opinion must have been based, had not been sufficiently tested by experience, the time has now-arrived when it is no longer excusable to submit in silence to the reproaches of ignorance or malice. It is proper, however, to remark, as well in extenuation of those who have assailed our country, as in the support of the confidential denial, which I feel authorised to make to their assertions, that a vast improvement in the article of health has taken place within a few years. Diseases are now mild which were once malignant, and their occurrence is annually becoming less frequent. This happy change affords strong authority for the belief, that although the maladies which have heretofore afflicted us, were partly imputable to the climate, other, and more powerful causes of disease must have existed, which have vanished. We who came to the frontier, while the axe was still busy in the forest, and when thousands of the acres which now yield abundance to the farmer, were unreclaimed and tenantless, have seen the existence of our fellow citizens assailed by other than the ordinary ministers of death. Toil, privation and exposure, have hurried many to the grave; imprudence and carelessness of life, have sent crowds of victims prematurely to the tomb. It is not to be denied that the margins of our great streams in general, and many spots in the vicinity of extensive marshes, are subject to bilious diseases; but it may be as confidently asserted, that the interior country is healthy. Yet the first settlers invariably selected the rich alluvion lands upon the navigable rivers, in preference to the scarcely less fertile soil of the priaries, lying in situations less accessible, and more remote from market. They came to a wilderness in which houses were not prepared for their reception, nor food, other than that supplied by nature, provided for their sustenance. They often encamped on the margin of the river exposed to its chilly atmosphere, without a tent to shelter, with scarcely a blanket to protect them. Their first habitations were rude cabins, affording scarcely a shelter from the rain, and too frail to afford protection from the burning heat of the noonday sun, or the chiling effects of the midnight blast. As their families increased, another and another cabin was added, as crazy and as cheerless as the first, until admonished of the increase of their own substance, the influx of wealthier neighbors, and the general improvement of the country around them, they were allured by pride to do that to which they never would have been impelled by suffering. The gratuitous exposure to the climate, which the backwoodsmen seem rather to court than to avoid, is a subject of common remark. No extremity of weather confines him to the shelter of his own roof. Whether the object be business or pleasure, it is pursued with the same composure amid the shadows of the night, or the howling of the tempest, as in the most genial season. Nor is this trait of character confined to woodsmen or to farmers; examples of hardihood are contagious, and in this country all ranks of people neglect, or despise the ordinary precautions with respect to health. Judges and lawyers, merchants, physicians and ministers of the gospel, set the seasons at defiance in the pursuit of their respective callings. They prosecute their journies regardless of weather, and learn at last to feel little inconvenience from the exposure, which is silently undermining their constitutions. Is it extraordinary that people thus exposed should be attacked by violent maladies? Would it not be more wonderful that such a careless prodigality of life could pass with impunity? These remarks might be extended; the food of the first settler, consisting chiefly of fresh meat without vegetables and often without salt; the common use of ardent spirits, the want of medical aid, by which diseases, at first simple being neglected, become dangerous; and other evils peculiar to a new country, might be noticed as fruitful sources of disease; but I have already dwelt sufficiently on this subject. That this country is decidedly healthy, I feel no hesitation in declaring; but neither argument nor naked assertions will convince the world. Let us collect such facts as amount to evidence, and establish the truth by undeniable demonstration."

From my own observations, I subjoin the following remarks. The impression has gone abroad and exists to some extent, that Illinois is a sickly region. This impression probably had its origin from the circumstance that the first settlements were made in and adjacent to the most sickly portion of the American bottom, and especially from a mortal sickness that swept through a little settlement near the bluffs, in what is now Monroe county, about forty years since. A large majority of the population was taken off within a few weeks, by the dysentery, or some analagous disease. As in all countries, there are spots, which from local causes are more liable to sickness than others, but in general *Illinois is as healthy as any other western State.*

This opinion can be abundantly supported by facts. Let a candid observer compare the health of the early settlers of New England, with that of the early settlers of the west, and he will find the scale to preponderate in favor of the latter. Unless there is some strange fatality attending Illinois, its population must be more healthy than the early settlers of a timbered region. But in no period of its history have sickness and death triumphed, in any respect equal to what they did two or three years since, in the lake country of New York.

1811, is recorded in the memories of the early settlers, as a season of unusual sickness near the banks of the Mississippi and Missouri. The latter river rose to an unusual height in June, the waters of the small creeks were backed up, and a large surface of luxuriant vegetation was covered and deadened. This was succeeded by hot and dry weather. Bilious and intermittent fevers prevailed extensively. The seasons of 1819, 20, and 21 were usually sickly in Illinois and Missouri. Emigrants, in shoals, had spread over a wide range of country within a year or two preceding. Multitudes were placed under circumstances the most unfavorable to the preservation of health, in new and open cabins of green timber, often using the stagnant water of creeks and ponds, with a luxuriant vegetation around them undergoing decomposition, and all the other evils attendant on the settlement of a new and unbroken country. Under such circumstances, can it be surprising that many were sick, and that many died? The summer of 1820 was the hottest and driest ever known in this country. For weeks in succession the thermometer in the shade at St. Louis, was up to 96° for hours in the day. Not a cloud came over the sun, to afford a partial relief from its burning influence. The fevers of that season were unusually rapid, malignant, and unmanageable. Almost every mark of the yellow fever, as laid down in the books, was exhibited in many cases, both in town and country. The bilious fever put on its most malignant type. Black fœted matter was discharged from the stomach, and by stools. The writer and all his family suffered severely that season. He lived seventeen miles from St. Louis, on the road to St. Charles in Missouri, on a farm. The settlement had been called healthy. The Missouri bottom was one mile distant. Three miles west south-west, was the Creve Cœur lake, a body of water several miles in length and half a mile in width, connected by an outlet with the Missouri river. The water of this lake was entirely stagnant, covered with a thick scum, and sent forth a noisome smell. Fish in it died. My oldest son, a robust youth of ten years of age, and my brother-in-law, a hale and stout young man, sickened and died the first week in October. I was attacked the 5th day of July, came as near dying as a person could and recover. All my children were sick. While convalescent in September I took a long journey to Cape Girardeau country, 120 miles south, and back through the lead mine country to the Missouri river, 60 miles west of St. Louis, and in all the route found that sickness had prevailed to the same extent.

At Vincennes and other parts of Indiana, disease triumphed. The country around Vincennes, on the east side of the Wabash, is a sandy plain. A gentleman who escaped the ravages of fever in that place, and who was much engaged in nursing the sick and consoling the dying, stated to me that nothing was so disheartening as the cloudless sky and burning-sun that continued unchanged for weeks in succession. Mortality prevailed to a great extent along the banks of the Wabash. Hindostan, a town on the east fork of White river, 38 miles from Vincennes on the road to Louisville, was begun the preceding year. Seventy or eighty families had crowded in at the commencement of the year 1820. The heavy timber of poplar, (whitewood) oak and beech, had been cut down, the brush burned, and the logs left on the ground. By June the bark was loosened, an intolerable stench proceeded from the timber—sickness followed, and about two thirds of the population died! And yet to look about the place, there is no local cause that would indicate sickness. In the summer of 1821, sickness prevailed very extensively, but in a much milder form. Its type was intermittent, and usually yielded to ordinary remedies. During that year the number of deaths in St. Louis was 136—the population 5000. At least one third of that number were strangers and transient persons, who either arrived sick, or were taken sick within two or three days after arrival. St. Louis had then no *police* regulations—the streets were filthy in the extreme—and the population were crowded into every hole and corner. This was the most sickly and dying season St. Louis ever knew.

The same years (1820—21) were noted for unusual sickness throughout the United States, and indeed the whole world. The bilious fever prevailed in the hilly and mountainous districts of Virginia and Pennsylvania, and even among the Green Mountains of Vermont.

And yet, I have never seen the time in Illinois and Missouri, during the most sickly period, when death made such ravages, and the arm of the physician was so completely paralyzed, as in the epidemic that prevailed throughout the northern states in 1812 and 13! A very large majority of the cases of autumnal fever in this country can be managed with great ease. Nor have I ever felt half the anxiety under the utmost pressure of disease and debility, to get from this climate as I did in September, 1826, when laboring under considerable pulmonary affection, after considerable exposure in the bleak moist atmosphere and eastern winds of New England, to get back into the soft and genial atmosphere of autumn in Illinois. Nor was it till I reached the shores of Lake Erie, that I began to breathe freely, and enjoy the blessing of renovated health.

This climate is subject to sudden changes from heat to cold; from wet to dry; especially from December to May, and yet cases of pulmonary affection are rare. I have not yet seen half a dozen cases of the genuine New England consumption in all my travels, and but few of asthma. Many persons afflicted with the latter disease in the old states have found relief in the west. Affections of the liver are more common. Pleurisies and other inflammatory diseases sometimes prevail in the winter and spring. Ophthalmia is more frequent than in the north. Dysentery has prevailed in a limited extent in some settlements, but not as a general disease. Those persons who have been unaccustomed to lime stone water, until they become acclimated, frequently have eruptions on the skin, and in some cases are grievously tormented with boils. These are rather indications of the future enjoyment of health than otherwise. A slight diarrhœa is a common occurrence, and always a favorable symptom. It is an effort of nature to relieve itself from the elements of disease. In Illinois and Missouri, but few infants and children die in proportion to the number of births. Occular demonstrations can be furnished in almost every cabin, in favor of this region for raising well-formed and healthy children. They are subject to the exposure of all kinds of weather, to play and romp in the air and dirt, with scarcely any covering but a shirt, and frequently sleep at night in a blanket spread upon the floor, and in the hot season with the doors of the cabin open. A practice prevails generally, even amongst the mose indolent class as well as others, favorable to the preservation of health: Children and adults are habituated to bath the feet and legs in cold water, before retiring to rest.

The more common diseases of the country are intermittents, frequently accompanied with bilious symptoms. Those which prove fatal are generally bilious remittents. I have no doubt that more than one half of the cases of sickness and death arise from imprudence and bad management, or the want of proper nursing. A notion prevails abroad, and this has been confirmed by some writers of this country, that emigrants from the north must necessarily pass through a time of sickness by way of seasoning. To this subject, I have paid some particular attention while travelling, by making inquiries of emigrants from various parts, and those who have been some years in the country. In 1825, I found the result of my inquiries for the eight years preceding to be as follows.

About one half the emigrants had been attacked, in various degrees, with the summer and autumnal fevers. In a majority of cases the attacks were light and easily yielded to medicine; a single dose in many cases being sufficient. At least one half the emigrant population had not been sick. Many acknowledged relief from chronic complaints, under which they had suffered before they came to this country; and what rather surprised me, I could find no material difference in regard to sickness between those who came from the south and those who came from the north. This was not a hasty conclusion. It was the deliberate result of inquiries patiently pursued in almost every county in Missouri and Illinois, as these States were then located, and about 10 counties in Indiana; and made in hundreds of families.

It is readily admitted that our climate is more enervating, and that the system is more readily debilitated, than in the bracing atmosphere of the granite regions of the north. It is not convenient to perform as much severe labor in this climate as in that. But I am confident more labor can be comfortably performed out of doors in this climate than in New England. In twelve months there are more pleasant days when the air is not oppressively hot. It has been intimated already that in the most oppressive season, the month of August, our farmers have the least to do. But frequently throughout the whole autumn and winter, it is very frequently a pleasant season to labor. It is usually dry, and though the frost is sometimes severe, the air is not colder than a laboring man of the north would prefer for convenience.

In case of sickness, physicians are to be found in almost every county, and every season adds to their number. In St. Clair county, with a population of 7000, there are four physicians, neither of which can find a lucrative employment in the practice of medicine. Charges are somewhat higher than in the northern States. Many families keep a few simple articles of medicine, and administer for themselves. Calomel is a specific, and is taken by multitudes without hesitation, or fear of danger. From fifteen to twenty grains are an ordinary dose for a cathartic. Whenever nausea of the stomach, pains in the limbs, and yawning, or a chill, indicate the approach of disease, a dose of calomel is taken at night, in a little apple honey, or other suitable substance, and followed up in the morning with a dose of castor oil, or salts, to produce a brisk purge. Sometimes an emetic is preferred. Either a cathartic or an emetic will leave the system under some debility. The mistake frequently made is, in not following up the evacuating medicine with tonics. This should be done invariably, unless the paroxysm of a fever has commenced. A few doses of sulphate of quinine or Peruvian bark in its crude state, will restore the system to its natural tone. To prevent an attack of fever, medicine should be taken on the very first symptoms of a diseased stomach; it should not be tampered with, but taken in sufficient doses to relieve the system from morbid effects, and then followed up by tonics to restore its vigor and prevent relapse.

New comers will find it advantageous to protect themselves from the damp atmosphere at night to provide close dwellings, yet when the air is clear to leave open doors, and windows at night for free circulation, but not to sleep directly in the current of air, and invariably wear their clothing in the heat of the day, and put on thicker garments at night, and in wet and cloudy weather.

I have observed those families are seldom sick who live in comfortable houses with tight floors, well ventilated rooms, and who upon a change of weather, and especially in time of rains, make a little fire in the chimney, although the thermometer might not indicate the necessity.

In fine, I am prepared to give my opinion decidedly in favor of the general health of this country and climate. I would not certainly be answerable for all the bad locations, the imprudences, and whims of all classes of emigrants, which may operate unfavorably to health. I only speak for myself and family. I decidedly prefer this climate with all its miasma, to New-England with its north-east winds, and damp "raw" and pulmonary atmosphere. We very seldom have fogs in Illinois and Missouri. My memorandums, kept with considerable accuracy for twelve years, give not more than half a dozen foggy mornings in a year.

The following comparisons between St. Louis and several eastern cities, will afford some evidence of the opinions expressed above. I have remarked already, that 1821, was more sickly in St. Louis, than any preceding year, and deaths were more numerous in proportion to the population. Some cases of fever were more malignant in 1820, in that place, but deaths were more frequent the following season. I solemnized the marriage of a young lady of my acquaintance, who was under the age of fourteen years. In eight days she was a widow. At the funeral of a gentleman the same season, who left a widow under twenty years, there were present thirteen widows, all under twenty-four years of age, and all had lost their companions that season. Young men were victims more than any other age or condition. And yet I am prepared to show, that St. Louis that summer was not more sickly than several eastern cities were in 1820, and 1823.

The population of St. Louis in 1821, varied but little from 5000, the number of deaths during that year was one hundred and thirty-six. This account was taken by the Rev. Salmon Giddings, who was particular in collecting the facts. The proportion of the deaths to the population was one to thirty-five.

In 1820, Boston contained a population of 43,893—number of deaths 1,103; proportion one to thirty-nine and three fourths.

New York the same year contained a population of 123,000—deaths 3,515; being a proportion of one to a fraction less than thirty-five.

In Philadelphia, the population then was 108,000—deaths 3374: being a proportion of one to thirty-two.

Baltimore had a population of 62,000—deaths 1,625; being a proportion of one to thirty-eight.

The aggregate population of these four cities in 1820, was 336,893; the aggregate number of deaths, 9,617; the proportion of one to thirty-five, the same as that of St. Louis.

In 1823.

Boston. Population estimated at 45,000; number of deaths by official returns, 1,154; the proportion of one to thirty-nine.

New-York. Population about 130,000—deaths 3,444; proportion of one to thirty-seven and two thirds.

Philadelphia. Population about 120,000—deaths 4,600; proportion of one to twenty-six. [This was an uncommonly sickly season in Philadelphia.]

Baltimore. Population estimated at, 65,000;

deaths were 2,108; proportion of one to thirty and two thirds.

I have thus selected the mortality of St. Louis, during the most sickly season, since my residence in this country, and compared it with the bills of mortality of four eastern cities for two years, those of 1820 and 1823, and the result is favorable to the health of St. Louis, and by consequence to the adjoining States. For eight years past there has been no general sickness in St. Louis, during the summer and autumnal months.

Last season there was more sickness in the country and particularly near the rivers and creeks, than in any former season since 1822. But the emigrants from the north, unless located in some very unfavorable spot, were in general highly delighted with the health of the country.

About twenty families entered the town of Lower Alton, on the Mississippi, and under high bluffs in the spring of 1830. But three or four families were residents the preceding years. The emigrants were unprovided with comfortable habitations, much exposed, and the surface of the earth was cleared of trees and shrubs, and exposed to the sun. Every circumstance made it unfavorable to health. Some sickness was felt by almost every family. A gentleman from Boston visited this place in August, and from the appearance of sickness became much alarmed, and left the country with unfavorable impressions. Yet one person died in Lower Alton, and this death was caused by imprudence. Most of those who were attacked, experienced only a slight intermittent.

In the months of August and September, I took a journey through the counties of Madison, Green, and Morgan, attended a number of large meetings, and visited different and populous settlements, and in all the route I saw but two persons ill, and those cases of the ague.

Some parts of Indiana and Ohio are unquestionably more subject to bilious attacks than Illinois. The reason is obvious. Much of that region is heavily timbered, and upon cutting it away in spots, and letting in the rays of the sun upon vegetable matter undergoing decomposition, miasmata is generated. These regions will become comparatively healthy when put under general cultivation.

The story is told that the late emperor of France, lay encamped with one of his armies near a place reputed unhealthy, when one of his officers requested a furlough. The reason being asked and given that the place was unhealthy and the applicant feared to die an inglorious death from fever: Napolean replied in his accustomed laconic style, "Go to your post, men die every where."

If a family emigrate to a new and distant country, and any of the number sicken and die, we are apt to indulge in unavailing regret at the removal, whereas had the same afflictive event happened before removal, it would have been regarded in quite a different light. Let, then none come to Illinois who do not expect to be sick and to die, whenever Divine providence shall see fit so to order events.

The *milk-sickness* is a disease of a singular character, which prevails in certain places. It first affects animals, especially cows, and from them is communicated to the human system by eating the milk, or flesh. The symptoms of the disease indicate poison, and the patient is affected nearly in the same way, as when poisonous ingredients have been received into the system. Cattle, when attacked by it, usually die. In many instances it proves mortal in the human system, in others, it yields to the skill of the physician. Much speculation has been had upon its cause, which is still unknown. The prevailing idea is, that it is caused by some poisonous substance eaten by the cattle, but whether vegetable or mineral, remains undetermined. Physicians and others have attempted to ascertain the cause of this disease, but hitherto without success.

It infests only particular spots, or small districts, and these are soon found out. There are places in Ohio, Indiana, and the southern states, where it exists. Its effects are more frequent in autumn than any other season, and to guard against it, the people either keep their cows in a pasture, or refuse to use their milk. Some have supposed this disease to be produced by the cattle feeding on the *cicuta-virosa*, or water hemlock, as a similar disease once infested the cattle in the north of Europe, the cause of which was traced out by the great Naturalist Linnæus; but it is not known that this species of plant exists amongst the botanical productions of Missouri and Illinois.

EDUCATION.

Education in Illinois is still in its infancy, and many of the settlers have no proper view of its necessity and importance. Many adults, especially females, are unable to read or write, and many more, who are able to read a little, cannot readily understand what they attempt to read, and therefore take no pleasure in books and study. Common schools are usually taught some part of the year in most of the settlements, but more frequently by teachers wholly incompetent to the task than otherwise. This has been the case particularly in former years. Some are decidedly immoral, especially intemperate, and many parents have not felt the absolute necessity of having teachers of unblemished morals, and correct principles.

In 1818 and '19, the author travelled through most of the settlements then formed in Missouri, and made it an especial object to visit and inquire into the character of the schools then taught, which was done by a visit to every school, or an inquiry of proper persons from every settlement where a school had been taught in the Territory. According to my judgment, the result was, that one third of the schools were public nuisances, and decidedly injurious to the children from the immorality and incompetency of the teachers. One third did about as much harm as good, and the remainder were of some public utility.

It is presumed the same investigation would have brought forth similar results in Illinois. It must not be presumed by the reader that this is now the state of things, and the character of the schools in either state. The character, habits, feelings, and manners of the population are undergoing rapid changes every year; and the influx of emigrants, better qualified to appreciate good schools, is producing a rapid change in common education. In a short time the facilities for common schools in the more populous portions of the state, and even for an academical or collegiate course, will be equal to most of the states in the union,

The legislature has done very little yet to aid the cause of common schools. Popular feeling has to be set right first in this, as well as other subjects of legislation. A law was passed in 1825, which was brought forward by General

Duncan, our present representative in congress, then a member of the state senate, authorizing the people to form school districts. Each district was to become a corporate power to a limited extent, and the voters were authorized to appoint trustees to manage the concern, and by the votes (I think) of three fourths of the people within the district, to levy a tax to support the school. The law was unpopular. Designing and selfish politicians seized hold of it to raise popular ferment, and at the next session of the legislature it was repealed.

A complete common school system must sooner or later be organized, and will be sanctioned by the people. The lands and education funds, now held in reserve, will make this indispensable.

Many good common schools now exist, and where three or four leading families in a settlement are disposed to unite and exert their influence in favor of the measure, it is not difficult to get up and sustain a good English school. Qualified teachers are becoming more numerous. Some young men, natives of the State, have received an education that will enable them to teach with facility the rudiments of an English education. Others are now pursuing studies with the same design. Both male and female instructers are emigrating to the State, with the view of teaching. The Sunday school system is awakening attention to that of common schools, and eventually, in aid of other means, will change the current of feeling on this subject.

Several seminaries, and institutions of a higher grade than mere common schools, are in successful operation, and promise much to the country. Taking them according to priority of existence, the following brief sketch of each will suffice.

Belleville Academy. This institution is a select boarding school for boys, under the management and instruction of John H. Dennis, Esq. a liberally educated gentleman from Virginia, and well qualified for the station. The pupils are limited to twenty-five, one third of which are from the village and vicinity; the rest boarders from a distance, chiefly from St. Louis. The cost of boarding and tuition is seventy-five dollars per annum. There are two vacations of one month each, when the scholars return to their friends. It is altogether a private institution. The various branches of an English education, with Latin, Greek, and the mathematics, are taught here. Belleville, as placed on the map, is in St. Clair county, fourteen miles from St. Louis. This academy commenced in 1826.

Rock-Spring Seminary is located in the same county at the residence of the author, eighteen miles from St. Louis, on the principal stage road to Vincennes, entirely in the country, and intended in its original plan to be remote from the habits and influence of a village population.

The buildings, which are framed, are as follows. A *Seminary* which consists of a main building twenty by thirty feet, two stories, with wings on each side, fourteen feet by twelve, and forming a front of forty-four feet. The lower story of the main building is a public hall for recitations and school exercises, the left wing for the library and teachers' room, and the upper rooms for dormitories. A *boarding-house*, including a dining hall, fifteen feet by thirty, two kitchens, a pantry, and two chambers for the use of the family. The students lodge in the upper rooms of the seminary, and in cabins on the premises. A *small building*, originally designed for a carpenter's shop, but now fitted up and occupied as a printing office, and tract depository. The land on which the buildings are erected, consisting of twenty-five acres, including never failing springs of water, is held by a deed of trust for the sole use and benefit of the Institution forever. Considerable vacant land adjoins the premises which can be purchased for the Institution at congress price. Two tracts of land of one hundred and sixty acres each, lying on the military tract, are owned by the Institution. The upper rooms of the seminary and boarding house have never been finished, nor has the land been enclosed and cultivated for want of funds. The library consists of about twelve hundred volumes, a number of valuable maps, a pair of globes, &c.

The original plan of the institution embraced two departments.

1. A high school, conducted upon the plan of a New-England academy, with the modern improvements in education, and admitting students without distinction of age or previous study.

2. A theological department designed for preachers of the gospel, of any age and acquirements. The fact that multitudes of professors of religion, in the western country, become preachers of the gospel without any previous literary or theological knowledge, and who will continue to preach in their way whether sufficiently qualified or not, and these men, with all their errors and false notions, will gain influence over the uninformed; all these things point out the necessity of an Institution and a mode of study that will accommodate their circumstances, expand their minds, and thus convince them of the necessity of a learned ministry.

This seminary was gotten up partly by donations obtained in the eastern states by the author in 1826, and partly by subscriptions of shares from individuals in Illinois and vicinity.

The trustees are chosen annually by the share holders, who manage the Institution. It opened November 15, 1827. The number of students generally have averaged from forty to fifty, several of whom have supported themselves by their own industry and the aid of an individual.

There are three sessions in a year, one of fourteen weeks, and the other two of fifteen weeks each, with a vacation of one week at Christmas, and another of seven weeks in August and September. Owing to the failure of the health of the late Principal, it is suspended for the present season; but its friends are about to adopt measures to revive and raise it to a higher rank as a literary Institution.

Illinois College is located near Jacksonville, on a delightful eminence that overlooks the town and surrounding country. The following sketch has been politely furnished the author by the Rev. J. M. Sturtevant, professor of mathematics in the Institution.

"This Institution, under God, owes its existence and present state of forwardness to the efforts of two distinct associations of individuals, formed at the distance of fifteen hundred miles from each other. One of these was composed of individuals residing in various sections of the state of Illinois who were deeply impressed with the importance of education, to all the great interests of society and government; and who had been, for years, thinking, acting, and praying, with reference to the establishment of a seminary to accomplish the ends now contemplated by the friends and trustees of Illinois college.

"Of the difficulties attending such an undertaking, they only could form an adequate conception, who have themselves attempted it under similar circumstances. Population was every where sparse, and the inhabitants were almost without exception, contending with the embarrassments of a recent settlement in a new and uncultivated country.

"In this state of things, a site was to be selected, which should meet the views of the friends of the cause living hundreds of miles distant from each other; public opinion was to be enlisted in favor of the object; and the funds for erecting and endowing such an institution were to be obtained.

"But enlightened and decided benevolence, when once convinced of the necessity and importance of its ends, is never deterred from prosecuting them by the want of means. After much time spent by the active friends of the cause in visiting different sections of the state, and comparing the advantages of different locations, a site was selected one mile west of the village of Jacksonville, on a commanding eminence, overlooking the village and surrounding country, and now occupied by the college buildings. A subscription was opened, and 2,000 dollars were pledged to the object by various benevolent and patriotic individuals in different sections of the state, and notice of their plans and operations was inserted in an eastern periodical.

"This was much indeed to have accomplished in a section of the country, which eight years previously was in all the wildness of uncultivated nature; but it was little towards the accomplishment of an object of such magnitude and importance as the establishment of a well endowed literary institution. So the friends of the enterprise regarded it, and have ever looked for aid in the accomplishment of their noble undertaking to the benevolent and patriotic in the older, and for that reason more wealthy portions of our country.

"Such aid they were to receive from a source quite unexpected and quite providential.

"While these operations were going forward in Illinois, seven young gentlemen, then members of the Theological Department of Yale college, had associated themselves together, with the view of devoting their lives to the cause of education and religion in some of the new settlements of our rapidly extending country. Their plan of operations was to locate themselves in the vicinity of each other, and to unite their efforts for the establishment of a literary Institution on the most enlarged and liberal principles, and, by the blessing of God, and the aid of their Christian brethren, and fellow-citizens, to raise it to the rank of the most favored and useful Institutions of education in our land.

"No sooner had the design been formed, than the notice above alluded to, of the contemplated seminary at Jacksonville, met the eye of its projector. The idea of a union of the two efforts was at once suggested, and a correspondence was opened with the trustees of the seminary at Jacksonville, which resulted in the consummation of such a union, on the conditions that the gentlemen above referred to should raise the sume of 10,000 dollars for the benefit of the Institution, and become members of its Board of Trustees. These conditions have been on both sides complied with, and under these auspices, the Institution was opened for the reception of students on the first Monday in January, 1830: it having previously received by a vote of its patrons, assembled within the walls of its first, and then unfinished edifice, the name of *Illinois College.*

"Since that time the trustees have been employed in unremitting efforts to extend their buildings, their system of instruction, and all their arrangements, in order fully to meet the wants of this rising community. Something has been accomplished.

"The buildings of the Institution at the present time are the following: one brick edifice, designed partly for recitation rooms, and partly for lodging of students; sixty-five feet in length, by thirty-six in breadth, and two stories high, and affording at present, a chapel sufficiently large to accommodate from one hundred and fifty to two hundred persons, and recitation rooms, with lodgings for about thirty students. A framed house sufficiently large to accommodate a family, now employed for a boarding house, but designed for a farm house, as soon as present arrangements can be completed. Connected with the Institution and owned by it, is a farm of two hundred and twenty-eight acres, extending from one fourth to one half a mile in every direction around the college edifice, and as well suited for cultivation as any which this most fertile country affords. A part of this farm is already under cultivation, and one half of the remainder is to be brought under cultivation the present season.

"A shop is also to be fitted up, and furnished with the requisite tools for performing most of those mechanical operations which are concerned in the working of wood; and both farm and shop are to be provided with a competent superintendent. The object of the Trustees is, to furnish the students with the means of pursuing a regular system of exercise for the preservation of health, and at the same time to render that exercise as far as possible available for the reduction of their expenses.

"One half of all the profits arising from the farm and shop is to be divided among the laboring students in proportion to the amount of labor done by each.

"In respect to the system of instruction, it will be made to meet the wants and circumstances of the community. The Institution has a library of from 600 to 800 volumes, and a small collection of philosophical apparatus. The number of students at present is about forty, being more than three times the number which entered at the opening of the Institution. But though something has been done, much remains to be done. Every step taken in this enterprise has served to impress more deeply upon the trustees a conviction of the great importance and entire practicability of what they have undertaken, and to fix more deeply in their minds the deliberate resolution to persevere in their work till all obstacles are removed;—till 'Illinois College' shall be furnished with every requisite advantage for training the youthful mind to habits of vigorous action, and till it shall pour forth in copious abundance, pure streams to bless this rising community."

Since the date of the above communication, which was in March, 1831, considerable progress has been made. The funds of the Institution, already secured (including the expense of buildings, land, and improvements,) amount to about $13,000. The Rev. Mr. Baldwin, one of the trustees, is now at the east, obtaining additional aid, and additional buildings are under contemplation.

The Faculty, already chosen, are the Rev. Edward Beecher, late pastor of the Park-Street Church, Boston, President, who has accepted of the office; the Rev. J. M. Sturtevant, Professor of Mathematics, with a temporary instructer in the Latin and Greek languages.

Vandalia High School. This is an institution gotten up by the enterprise and public spirit of the citizens of Vandalia. It is taught in the public meeting-house, and at present is under the charge of Rev. William K. Stewart, a Presbyterian clergyman, of some celebrity, as a teacher from Kentucky. The number of students are supposed to be about fifty.

Individuals of the Methodist denomination have raised funds, and erected buildings at Apple Creek, in Green county, and at Lebanon, in St. Clair county, but they have never been finished so as to organize schools.

Several young ladies have recently opened boarding schools for females. One is taught in Hillsborough, in Montgomery county; another in Carrollton, Green county. At Edwardsville is a female academy, designed as the commencement of a public institution, and managed by trustees. It is now under the superintendence of Miss Chapin, aided by Miss Hitchcock.

The Rev. Mr. Loomis and his daughter, are employed by gentlemen in Kaskaskia, to teach a select school, where the ordinary, and some of the higher branches, are taught successfully.

At a meeting of the Illinois Presbytery, Oct. 13, 1830, the *Illinois Branch of the American Education Society* was organized. The object is, "to educate pious, indigent young men for the gospel ministry." Its officers are Elihu Wolcott, Esq. President, Rev. Hubbel Loomis,

Vice President, David B. Ayres, Secretary, and James G. Edwards, Treasurer. Its first annual meeting was appointed to be held at Jacksonville, at the time of the college commencement, in August, 1831.

The public provision for purposes of education are lands, and the proceeds of land sales derived from the general government. One thirty-sixth part of all the lands in the state, on the section numbered 16, in every township, is set apart for common schools, and belongs to the people of that township. If such section was sold, or otherwise disposed of previously, other lands, equivalent thereto, and as contiguous as may be, are given.

Two entire townships, granted for the use of a seminary of learning, and vested in the legislature of the state, were also given. In addition to this, three per cent of the nett proceeds of lands lying within the state and which should be sold by Congress from and after the 1st of January, 1819, of which one sixth part is to be exclusively bestowed on a state college or university. This three per cent fund has already accumulated to more than $40,000. Estimating the lands at Congress price, the aggregate value of this provision for education cannot be much less than $2,000,000. It is true that much of this will not be realized by the present generation; but it is an important fund, which, if managed prudently, will pour its blessings upon succeeding generations.

PUBLIC LANDS.

The public lands in all the states and territories, when owned by the general government, are all surveyed and sold on one general plan. A district of country is first divided into townships, of thirty-six square miles, or as sections, as they are called in the surveys. Each section is subdivided into quarters, and each quarter may be divided again by a line running north and south if the purchaser desire, leaving eighty acres the smallest tract, a section being six hundred and forty acres.

For the convenience of sale, the State is divided into land districts, which are designated by Congress. There are six land districts in the State, in which offices are opened and doing business, and two others not yet in operation. Those where sales are now made, are Shawneetown, Kaskaskia, Edwardsville, Springfield, Palestine, and Vandalia. Of the two districts not yet in readiness, the office of one is located at Danville, Vermillion county, and the other to be located north of the Military Tract, probably at the mouth of Rock river.

The officers in a land district are a Register and Receiver, appointed and paid by government.

The lands, by proclamation of the President, are set up first at public sale, by half quarter sections. If no one calls for the tract at one dollar twenty-five cents per acre, or bids for it, it remains subject to private entry at any time after, upon payment at the time of entry. No credit is allowed. Whoever pays the money first obtains the land. And yet so seldom is it that one man enters the land, upon which another man has settled, that thousands settle on public lands, make improvements, and live for years unmolested.

RELIGION AND RELIGIOUS SOCIETIES.

On this subject I shall be brief. The Methodists are the most numerous in the State. There are three districts, the Illinois, the Kaskaskia, and the Wabash districts, over each of which is a presiding Elder. The society includes about 9000 members.

The Reformers, or Methodist Protestant church, have several societies and preachers in the State, chiefly in the upper counties. The local Methodist preachers are numerous, probably double the number of those on the circuits, and the whole may be estimated at 100.

The Baptists rank next in numbers. Unpleasant divisions exist in this denomination, and portions of them, from their erroneous doctrines and mistaken views, probably would not be owned by the denomination in the old States.

There are in the State, thirteen Associations, and upon an estimate, one hundred and twenty churches, 80 preachers, and three thousand five hundred members.* Except the Roman Catholics, the Baptists were the first religious people in the territory. The first preacher of any denomination who visited the early settlement was a Baptist from Kentucky, by the name of *Smith*, who was taken prisoner by the Indians, near New Dosign, in Monroe county, carried towards Detroit, and afterwards ransomed by the people, who paid one hundred and seventy dollars, for his release.

The Presbyterians may be classed next in numbers. Presbyteries three, churches thirty, ministers twenty-five, communicants seven hundred. The churches are located in the following counties: Madison, Bond, Randolph, Morgan, Sangamon, Fulton, Schuyler, Adams, Tazewell, Montgomery, White, Green, Fayette, Gallatin, Pope, Shetley, Clark, Edgar, Wabash, Franklin, Wayne, and Jo Davies. The above information was obtained in part from the Rev. John M. Ellis, of Jacksonville, who was stated clerk when the three Presbyteries were in one.

The *Cumberland Presbyterians* deserve notice in the next place. These are a large and respectable body of Christians in the western states.

---

*Of these, two associations, nineteen churches, twenty-five ministers, and six hundred members, call themselves " Friends of Humanity," because they refuse to correspond with slaveholding churches.

They are united under a General Assembly, and have four Synods, and twenty Presbyteries, scattered through Kentucky, Tennessee, Alabama, Indiana, Illinois, Missouri, and Arkansas. I have no means of ascertaining their numbers, nor does the General Assembly know, owing to defects in returns from Presbyteries. They may probably be estimated at fifteen or twenty thousand communicants. In doctrinal sentiments, and views about qualifications to the ministry, they are on a line between the old Presbyterians and Methodists. In church government they are strictly Presbyterians.

I have no certain information of their numbers in Illinois, but shall estimate them as follows: churches 15, preachers 12, communicants 375.

The *Christ-ians*, as they are termed, have some societies in Illinois, particularly in the Wabash country, but the exact number cannot be given.

The *Dunkards* have three or four societies, and some preachers in the state. They are known by their long beards, by trine immersion, inoffensive manners, and refusal to bear arms.

There is a society of *Seceders* in Randolph county, and another of *Covenanters*, both supplied with pastors of their own orders.

Amongst the different religious societies there is much interchange of good feelings, and the members frequently hear each other preach.

There are but few instances where a minister officiates with a congregation every Sabbath. It is a common, though unfortunate custom, throughout the western country for a congregation to have regular meetings only once a month. The qualifications of the preachers are various. There are a number of men of talents, learning, and unblemished piety. Others have had but few advantages in acquiring either literary or theological information, and yet are good speakers and useful men. Not a few are very illiterate, and make utter confusion of the word of God. Such are usually proud, conceited, and influenced by a spirit far removed from the meek, docile, benevolent, and charitable spirit of the gospel. Of the various sects in Illinois, the number of preachers may be estimated at about two hundred and forty, and the members of society at about 15,000 souls. Of the preachers, considered in the aggregate, one third may be rated as doing positive injury to religion, one third as of minor service, and the rest as possessing various qualifications, of a higher grade for usefulness in the ministry. This supposition is made without respect to acquirements purely of a literary character.

HISTORY.

The following historical sketch of Illinois, and the adjacent regions, is copied from Beck's Gazetteer of Illinois and Missouri.

"About the middle of the seventeenth century, the French began to turn their attention to the discovery of the Mississippi. They had heard from some Indians who visited Canada, that there was towards the west a large river, but they could obtain no information in regard to its course or extent. The attention of the enterprising had for a long time been directed to the discovery of a north-west passage; and the hints which they received of the existence of a river west of the lakes, were calculated to give additional confidence, and render them more sanguine. They supposed that this river emptied itself into the Pacific ocean, and that it also formed a communication with the Lakes, and thus vainly imagined that they had at once discovered the great object of their wishes. Anxious to signalize himself and his nation, M. Talon, the intendant of New-France, a man of superior genius, determined to settle this important question previously to leaving America. He gave charge of the investigation to P. Marquetta, a Jesuit, who had already travelled over almost all the Canadas, and who was much respected by the savages; and associated with him a man of courage and experience, named Joliet. Having made the necessary preparations, they embarked from the mouth of Fox river, and ascended it to near its source; then crossed westward by land, until they intersected the Wisconsin, and descending this, they reached the Mississippi on the 17th of June, 1673. They found that river much larger and deeper than it had been represented to them by the savages. They were delighted with the beauty and fertility of its banks, and every day's journey furnished them with new subjects of admiration. Unfortunately, the regular journal which they kept, was lost when on their return to Canada. It appears, however, from the account of Joliet, that they found the natives friendly, and with the assistance of a few presents, they obtained such provisions as they were in need of. But a tradition existed among the savages, that there was on the banks of the Mississippi, below the Missouri, a Maniteau or Spirit, which it was impossible for any being to pass. This information was communicated to the adventurers, and being but few in number, they determined not to pursue their journey south, but to return to Canada by the way of the Illinois. It is uncertain how far they descended the Mississippi; it being asserted by some that they reached the mouth of the Arkansas, (or Arkanceas, as it was then called;) by others, that they did not proceed farther south than the mouth of the Missouri.

"Upon ascending the Illinois,* they found new objects of admiration. It formed such a contrast

---

* According to Hennepin, this name is derived from *Illini*, which in the language of the Illinois signifies *a perfect and accomplished man.*

with the stream which they had just left, its waters being clear, its current gentle, and its banks interspersed with plains and woodlands, that they were enraptured with its beauty. They were well received, and were treated very hospitably by the natives, particularly by the Illinois. They found this tribe destitute of that savage cruelty, so characteristic of the natives of that day: on the contrary, they prided themselves much on their hospitality and generosity. The pious Marquette, touched with their deplorable situation, and their desire of learning the arts of civilization, determined to remain among them, and spend the remainder of his life in the service of his God.* Thus we see, that even at that early period, there were those who were willing to endure every privation, that they might be servicable to their fellow creatures ; and it is but justice to observe that the Jesuits were at that day foremost on the list of philanthropists throughout the world.

"Joliet parted with Marquette, and in a short time reached Canada, where he gave an account of the discoveries he had made.

"After the return of Joliet, and the departure of M. Talon from Canada, the French appear to have lost sight of the Mississippi, and no measures were taken to prosecute a discovery com-

* Charlevoix gives an affecting account of the extraordinary death of this good old man.

menced under such favourable auspices; and although an extensive field of speculation was opened to the adventurous, several years elapsed before any one attempted to follow the track of Marquette and Joliet.

"M. de la Salle, a native of Rouen, in Normandy, who had resided for many years in Canada, and who was a man of enterprise and intelligence, was the first to revive the plan of M. Talon, in regard to the discovery of the Mississippi, and the country which it watered. When Joliet arrived in Montreal with the news of his discoveries, La Salle was engaged in the favourite project of a northwest passage to China and Japan.* He did not doubt what was asserted by this traveller, that the Mississippi discharges itself into the Gulf of Mexico; but he flattered himself that by ascending it he should discover the object of his researches. Should he fail in this, however, he had no doubt but the discovery of its junction with the ocean would have a tendency to establish his fortune and his reputation. Being zealous for the honour of his nation, he determined to signalize the French name by a plan of operations, than which none could be more important, none more splendid. Having already given frequent proofs of his uncommon talents, he had gained the esteem of

---

* Charlevoix's History of New France.

the governors of Canada, and had several times been employed in expeditions which contributed much to the honour and advantage of the colony; this facilitated, in a material degree, the prosecution of his plans. He accordingly left Canada for France, to obtain the sanction and assistance of his sovereign, and to make the necessary arrangements for the prosecution of the discovery. When he arrived at Court, he unfolded his plans, proved their vast importance to the French nation, and the facility with which they might be accomplished. The king was so well pleased with the views of La Salle, that he not only sanctioned his enterprise, but supplied him with men and means for the prosecution of his discovery. In the language of Fonti, 'his Majesty not content with merely approving his design, caused orders to be given him, granting him permission to go and put it into execution, and to assist him to carry so vast a project into effect.' Shortly after, the necessary succours were furnished him, with entire liberty to dispose of all the countries which he should discover.

"La Salle, after making the necessary arrangements, left France in July, 1678, and arrived in Quebec during the month of September of that year. He then proceeded to fort Frontenac, on Lake Ontario, of which he had been appointed governor. Here he made some repairs, and leaving a few men as a garrison, proceeded on his journey. On the 18th of November, of this year, he left the fort, with the Chevalier Fonti as his lieutenant, father Hennepin as his chaplain, and thirty or forty men. La Salle now engaged himself for about a year in examining the country bordering on the lakes, and in selecting proper sites for the erection of forts. His object in this was to secure to the Canadas the whole trade of the Indians residing in the country now known as the northern and western parts of the States of New-York, Pennsylvania, and Ohio. This was rendered the more necessary, on account of the exertions which were made by the English and Dutch to divert the trade to the south. After La Salle had effected this object, and had commenced a profitable trade at his different posts, he determined to continue his discovery. Previously to his departure, however, he commenced a considerable fort at Niagara, then a village of the Iroquois, which he intended as his place of *entrepot* between Canada and the countries he should discover. The Iroquois, who were then a powerful nation, viewed this with considerable jealousy; and La Salle, fearing that it might be the cause of hostility, abandoned the project, and contented himself with the erection of palisadoes merely for the protection of his magazine. His object was to influence the savages by mild and conciliatory measures, and he was therefore unwilling to persevere in any plan which had to them the appearance of coercion or force, unless it was absolutely necessary for the protection of himself or his party. After he had built a small vessel at Niagara, and left a few men for the defence of the fort and stores, he passed through lake Erie, and entered the Huron, where he had to encounter much difficulty, on account of the storms which now prevailed. He, however, passed through in safety, and entered lake Michigan; and after remaining a short time at the Bay of Puants, (Green Bay,) for the purpose of trading, he proceeded with his men in canoes to the southern extremity of the lake, and landed at the mouth of the river of the Miamis, on the first of November, 1679.* After building a small fort at this place, and leaving it in the charge of eight or ten men, he passed over to the head waters of the Illinois, and descended that stream for a considerabe distance, but was obliged to stop for the want of supplies. This was occasioned by the loss of a boat which had been sent from his establishment at the Bay of Puants. Necessity now compelled him to turn his attention to the construction of a fort for his defence; and after selecting a suitable site, he commenced building it, which, when completed, he called *Creve-cœur*, (broken heart;) for he had suffered much anxiety and distress of mind, on account of the disappointments he had met with, and the appearance of hostility among the Indians. This

---

* Fonti's account of the voyage of La Salle.

hostility, strange as it may appear, was occasioned by the perfidy of some of his own men. The French, as has been before mentioned, ever since their first visit to this country, had been well treated by the Illinois, and were considered by them as their true friends. The Illinois being engaged in a war with the Iroquois, a numerous, warlike, and cruel tribe, according to their savage, and perhaps correct notions of friendship, expected assistance from the French. La Salle, however, being convinced that his safety as well as his success depended upon the termination of this warfare, used all his efforts to accomplish this object. This was construed by some of the evil spirits of the Illinois into treachery; and their suspicions were strengthened by the wicked and malicious representations of some of the French, who told them that it was La Salle's intention to form an alliance with their enemies, the Iroquois. The Illinois now pronounced the sentence of death against La Salle, and would have put it in execution, had it not been for the firmness and courage which he afterwards evinced. As soon as he was apprized of what had taken place, he went forth alone to the camp of the Illinois, and addressing the chiefs, stated, that in coming among them, he had the most honorable, as well as the most peaceful intentions; that he always considered them as his friends, and that he was ready and willing to give them all the assistance in his power. He stated to them the impropriety of being thus engaged in war, as he wished to be friendly with all the tribes, which he could not under existing circumstances. He declared to them, that he had never offered any assistance to the Iroquois, but that his object in visiting them was to terminate the war. He then concluded, by demanding of them the author of this base and wilful misrepresentation; stating that if *he* would now appear and substantiate the charge, he was willing to suffer the sentence which they had so hastily passed upon him. The savages were lost in astonishment. The coolness and bravery which La Salle displayed, together with the eloquence of his harangue, had such an overpowering effect, that they instantly abandoned the purposes of revenge upon which they had determined. The calumet of peace was now smoked, presents were mutually exchanged, and the Illinois made the most solemn promises that they would be the friends of La Salle, and would never again give credence to the accusations which might be brought against him.[*]

"Peace being now established, La Salle again turned his attention to the prosecution of his discoveries; and in order the more expeditiously to explore the northern and southern country, his plan was, that Father Hennepin should as-

---

[*] Fonti, as before referred to.

cend the Mississippi, to its source; that Fonti should remain at Creve-cœur, while he would descend the river to its mouth. Accordingly, Hennipin embarked on the 28th of February, 1680; and having passed down the Illinois into the Missisippi, ascending the latter as high as the falls of St. Anthony. Shortly after, he was taken prisoner, robbed of his property, and carried to some Indian villages. But he soon made his escape, and returned to Canada by the way of the Wisconsin, and from thence he sailed immediately for France, where he published an account of his travels.*

"La Salle, after having visited Canada for the purpose of making further arrangements, returned to Creve-cœur; and shortly after descended the Illinois to the Mississippi, where he arrived in February, 1683. He then descended the latter stream, built one or two forts on its banks, and took a formal possession of the country in the name of the king of France, and in honour of him called it *Louisiana*. It is not necessary, to my present purpose, to give a detailed account of the subsequent operations of La Salle. Suffice it to say, that after descending the Mississippi to its mouth, he returned to

---

* In a subsequent edition of this work, Hennepin asserts that he descended the Mississippi to the sea; but in this he has been detected in attempting a most shameful imposture.

Canada by the way of the Illinois; that from Canada he went to France, where an expedition was immediately fitted for the purpose of forming a colony at the mouth of the Mississippi; that he sailed from France to the Gulf of Mexico, where he made several unsuccessful attempts to accomplish his purpose; that being unable to discover the mouth of the Mississippi, he determined on going by land to his fort on the Illinois; and that on this journey he was basely assassinated by two of his own men, in 1687.

"Fonti, who had been left in command on the Illinois, after building a new fort* a short distance above Creve-cœur, descended the Mississippi to meet La Salle according to an agreement between them. But this plan being frustrated by the unfortunate events already related, he again returned to the Illinois. On his return, his companions were pleased with many parts of the country through which they passed, and some of them requested permission to remain, which was readily granted. It is probable that this was the first commencement of the settlement of Kaskaskia, Prairie du Rocher, and Cahokia.

"After the death of La Salle, no attempts were made to discover the mouth of the Mississippi, until about the year 1699. In the mean time, however, the settlements on the Illinois

---

* Fort St. Louis, probably a few miles above Peoria.

were gradually increasing in population, by emigration from Canada.

"In 1712, the whole colony of Louisiana was granted to M. Crosat, by letters patent from the king of France. This grant secured to him all the commerce of the colony, and all the profits accruing from the mines and minerals he should discover, with the exception of one fifth of the gold and silver, which was reserved to the king. But Crosat was disappointed in his expectations in regard to the profits of the trade of Louisiana. There were many causes which operated to produce this effect. Without paying the least attention to the cultivation of the soil, which possessed in itself hidden treasure, the whole object of his search was the precious metals. These he supposed to exist in large quantities; and such was his folly and infatuation, that when he failed in this, he considered the country of little or no consequence. He therefore gave up his privilege to the king in 1717. The colony was soon after granted to the Mississippi company, projected by the celebrated Law. This company, which had engrossed almost the whole commerce of France, under the name of the "Company of the Indies," took possession of Louisiana, and appointed M. Bienville governor of the colony. At this time, the most extravagant accounts of this country were industriously circulated throughout all Europe, and 'the Mississippi became the centre of all men's wishes, hopes, and expectations.'

"Shortly after this, several forts were built within the present limits of the State of Illinois, the most considerable of which were fort Chartres, and one at Kaskaskia. By this means they were enabled not only to protect their trade, but to form a complete chain of communication and defence from the Canadas to the French forts at the mouth of the Mississippi.

"For some time previous to, and after the time that the Mississippi company relinquished their concerns to the government, the settlements of the Illinois country, as well as those of the whole colony, appear to have been in a languishing condition. An unhappy dispute now arose between the English and French, in regard to the true boundary between their colonies, which had never been defined. The French, anticipating a struggle for their American possessions, strengthened their posts along the Mississippi and the lakes, by which means they intended to engross the whole fur trade of the west. This was a new measure which excited the jealousy of the English, who, by virtue of their charters, conceived they had a right to navigate the Mississippi. With these views, a company of merchants and planters obtained a considerable tract of land near the Ohio, but within the province of Virginia: and were established by a charter under the name of the Ohio company, with the exclusive privilege of trading to that river.* This was cause of hostilities between the two powers, which continued till 1763, when the Illinois country was ceded to the English.

"In 1765, Capt. Sterling, of the royal Highlanders, in his majesty's name, took possession of that part of the Illinois country which had been ceded to Great Britain. He continued in command but a short time, and was succeeded by Major Farmer, who was relieved by Col. Reed, in 1766. With the administration of the latter the inhabitants were much displeased. The administration of justice which was wholly in the hands of the military commandant, was an engine of the most grievous oppression. Complaints were made by the inhabitants, but they produced little or no effect. Col. Reed, however, left the colony in 1768, and was succeeded by Lieut. Col. Wilkins, who arrived at Kaskaskia on the 5th of September in the same year.

"On the 21st of November, 1768, Col. Wilkins made a proclamation, in which he stated that he had received orders from general Gage, commander-in-chief in America, to establish a court of justice, for settling and determining all differences and affairs which the inhabitants might

* Bissett's continuation of Hume and Smollet's History of England.

have among themselves. In pursuance of these orders, he appointed seven judges, to settle all matters in relation to debt, and property both personal and real. They were ordered to meet for the first time at fort Chartres, on the 6th of December following, and afterwards once in every month. Although this was far preferable to the former judiciary system, the inhabitants remonstrated against it, and insisted on the right of trial by jury, which was denied them.

"Little change was produced in the situation of this colony, until the breaking out of the American revolution. In 1778, in consequence of the outrages committed by the savages at the instigation of the English, the Virginia militia made some successful incursions into the Illinois country, and took possession of the British posts on the Mississippi. These, by an act of the Virginia legislature, were erected into a county called the county of Illinois; and a regiment of infantry, with a troop of cavalry, were voted for its protection. The command of these troops was given to Col. George Rodgers Clark, a gentleman whose great courage, uncommon hardihood, and capacity for Indian warfare, had given him repeated successive enterprises against the savages. He remained a short time at Kaskaskia, and then conducted a successful expedition against Post St. Vincent, now Vincennes.*

---

* Marshall's Life of Washington.

"This territory, which by conquest became the property of Virginia, was afterwards ceded to the United States, and was included within the limits of Indiana territory, established in 1800; at which time, the country within the present boundaries of Illinois, contained about 3000 inhabitants. But on account of the fertility of the lands, and the inducements which were presented to enterprising men, the population rapidly increased. In 1809, it was erected into a territory, the population of which, in 1810, amounted to 12,282.

"During the last contest between the United States and Great Britain, the inhabitants of Illinois, in common with the other frontier districts, felt the evils of warfare. The most barbarous and cruel acts were continually committed by the savages, many of which were caused by the intrigue and perfidy of the British Indian agents and traders. Fearful that the Americans would share with them in their profitable trade, their agents had, for a long time, used every exertion to attach the tribes to the interests of the British government. Presents of arms, ammunition and clothing, were profusely made to the warriors, their women and children; and promises were made, that ample aid should be given to them to regain all their former possessions, and to drive the Americans beyond the mountains.

"The effects of this disgraceful system were perceived some time previous to, but were not fully developed until after the declaration of war. In consequence of the surrender of General Hull, the garrison at Chiago had been ordered to evacuate the fort. On the 15th of August, 1812, Captain Heald, with the troops, amounting to sixty or seventy men, the women and children, marched from the fort, and had proceeded but a short distance, when they were attacked by a large body of savages. A determined resistance was made, but it proved ineffectual against the superior force of the enemy. At length Captain Heald finding his number of soldiers much diminished, consented to surrender upon the promise of protection. But no sooner did the Americans lay down their arms, than the savages commenced an indiscriminate massacre.* This affair, added to the other acts of cruelty which had been committed by the Indians, induced Governor Edwards to prepare an expedition against them. Accordingly in October, 1812, after having despatched two boats up the Illinois, with ammunition and provisions, the governor, with Col. Russell and four or five hundred men, marched for Peoria, which was the head-quarters of the enemy. About the same time General Hopkins, with three or four

---

* M'Affee's History of the War in the Western Country.

thousand Kentucky volunteers, left Vincennes, in order to form a junction with Governor Edwards. Unfortunately, however, the general was deceived by his guides, who led him in various directions through the grand prairie, where his army suffered much from the excessive coldness of the weather. The Indians observing their approach from an eminence, fired the prairie, and obliged the general to retreat in disorder and confusion. Governor Edwards remained for some time near Peoria, waiting for the expected reinforcements; but being disappointed in this, and thinking his force not sufficiently large to cope with that of the Indians, he was obliged to abandon his favourite project, and retire to winter-quarters; not, however, without having destroyed all the Indian villages which lay in his route. Captain Craig, who commanded the boats, also returned, after having reduced to ashes the village of Peoria. It is much to be regretted, that through want of concert between the commanding officers of the different detachments, the principal design of this campaign was completely frustrated. After this, the seat of military operations was transferred to Michigan and Missouri; and during the remainder of the war, no events of consequence transpired in Illinois."

In 1818, this Territory was formed into a State, and admitted into the Union upon an equal footing with the original States. The constitution was adopted by a convention held at Kaskaskia, in August. It provides for the distribution of the powers of government into three distinct departments—the legislative, executive, and judiciary. The legislative authority is vested in a general assembly consisting of a senate and house of representatives. The members of the senate are elected every four years, and the representatives every two years, by the people. The executive is vested in the governor, who, with the lieutenant governor, is chosen every fourth year by the electors for representatives, and the same person is not eligible two terms in succession. The lieutenant governor is president of the senate. The judicial power is vested in a supreme court, and such inferior courts as the general assembly shall from time to time establish. The supreme court consists of a chief justice, and three associate judges, who, by law, hold circuit courts in their respective circuits. The supreme court sits once a year, and at the seat of government; the circuit courts are attended twice a year, in each county. An additional judge, besides the members of the supreme court, officiates in a circuit in the northern part of the State. The governor and judges of the supreme court, constitute a council of revision, to which all bills that have passed the assembly, must be presented. If the council returns a bill as rejected, two thirds of the members may pass it into a law.

The judges are chosen by joint ballot of the legislature, and continue in office during good behaviour. The governor nominates, and with the approbation of the senate appoints to all offices not otherwise provided for by the constitution. Slavery is prohibited in this State. All free white male inhabitants, who have resided in the State six months preceding elections, enjoy the right of suffrage.

SECTION III.

STATISTICS OF COUNTIES, TOWNS, &c.

THE census of Illinois is taken under the authority of the State, every five years, upon which the apportionment of the representation in the legislature is fixed by law for the same period. In September, 1830, the following census was taken, and the population of each county, then organized, was ascertained. Since then, the legislature has made the following new counties: viz. *Cook*, *La Salle*, *Mc Lean*, *Putnam*, *Coles* and *Rock Island*. As the census was taken before the fall emigrants arrived, we may safely estimate the present population, (1831,) at

175,000, and the ratio of increase for some years to come, at 20,000 annually.

CENSUS.

Sangamon,	13,793	Hamilton,	2,685
Morgan,	13,281	Jefferson,	2,628
Greene,	7,874	Wayne,	2,596
St. Clair,	7,082	Pike,	2,542
Gallatin,	6,970	Adams,	2,406
Madison,	6,540	Clinton,	2,375
Vermilion,	6,389	Fulton, Knox,	
White,	6,033	and Henry,	2,284
Tazewell,	5,300	Marion,	2,200
Randolph,	4,448	Jackson,	2,008
Edgar,	4,362	Monroe,	1,994
Franklin,	4,023	Macoupin,	1,919
Clark,	3,968	Jo Davies,	1,829
Lawrence,	3,000	Peoria,	1,782
Pope,	3,340	Johnson,	1,699
Schuyler and		Edwards,	1,688
M'Donough,	3,235	Washington,	1,673
Union,	3,218	Alexander,	1,404
Bond,	3,184	Perry,	1,228
Crawford,	3,165	Macon,	1,161
Fayette,	3,046	Calhoun,	1,130
Montgomery,	3,037	Clay,	751
Shelby,	3,019		
Wabash,	2,766	Total,	161,055

In my statistical view of the counties, which follows, I shall begin at the mouth of the Ohio, proceed in a line up the Mississippi to the mouth of the Illinois, thence up and on the right hand side of that river; thence across to the Wabash, and down that side of the State, and along the boundary of the Ohio river, to the place of beginning. From thence, I shall describe the line of counties interior, and which border on or approximate to the Kaskaskia river, and finish the interior portion of the State, south of the Illinois river, then proceed to describe the counties north and west of said river, on the military tract, and the lead mine district.

The impossibility of defining the boundaries of all these counties on the map, makes it necessary that the reader should have the foregoing arrangement in his mind, if he desires to have a well-defined idea in what part of the State any given county is located.

ALEXANDER COUNTY comprises the peninsula between the Ohio and Missisippi. It has a fertile soil, covered with a heavy growth of valuable timber, amongst which is white oak of the first quality, and poplar.

The following extract from the letter of an intelligent and observing correspondent will show the advantages of the location of this county in a commercial point of view. After alluding to that concentration of business to the mouth of the Ohio, by the only outlets from several States and Territories, he observes, in reference to the location of America, the first town site above the mouth of the Ohio, and on its bank, "About six miles above is what is called the Grand Chain, a reef of rocks across the bed of the Ohio river, which, at low water, is impassable by steamboats of any considerable magnitude. This reef of rocks is supposed to extend (below the surface of the earth) across our county to the Mississippi river, and causes the obstruction to the passage of boats in the vicinity of the Grand Tower. But in this vicinity, boats of the largest size may come at all times; for, notwithstanding the severity of last winter, there was not a day that boats could not pass in safety, although the Mississippi river was shut with ice within a mile or two of the mouth of the Ohio."

America is the seat of justice of Alexander county, situated on the first bluff, ten miles above the mouth of the Ohio, and near the mouth of Cash river. From this, to the mouth of the Ohio river, and for some distance above that on the Mississippi, there is no good site for a town, owing to the bottoms being inundated lands, and oftentimes eight or ten feet under water. If the landing at this place could be improved and made convenient for steamboats, it might be made a place of great commercial importance. This we understand is about to be done. It has about one hundred inhabitants.

Trinity is a landing place and post office a little distance below.

Alexander county has five horse or ox mills, one steam mill erecting, six stores, one physician, six schools, two post offices, and a few mechanics. Population, 1,404.

UNION COUNTY lies on the Mississippi, and north of Alexander. The county seat is Jonesboro', fifteen miles from the Mississippi, and near the centre of the county. It is a flourishing little village, with several stores, sundry mechanics' shops, and about one hundred and fifty inhabitants. The land in Union county is timbered, rolling, and much of it is of a good quality. It has an extensive bottom on the Mississippi, resembling the American bottom. The interior is watered by the sources of Cash river, which passes through Alexander county, and Clear creek, which discharges itself into the Mississippi. It has seven water grist, and two water saw mills, fourteen grist mills carried by horse or ox power, four cotton gins, ten distilleries, one threshing machine, one reed and two slæ shops, 3118 inhabitants, and twenty schools, or settlements, where schools should be taught. A portion of the population of this county are Germans, who still retain some of their native customs. These are subdivided into Lutherans and Dunkards, both of which have religious societies.

JACKSON COUNTY lies next as we journey north, still keeping the Mississippi on our left hand. This county contains much valuable timber and good land, considerable portions of which is still unoccupied. It is watered by Muddy river and its branches. Twelve miles up this stream is the village of Brownsville, and the salt works already noticed. The village now contains only fifteen or twenty families; but the preparations that are making to manufacture salt, and dig coal will be likely to cause an increase. Adjoining the Mississippi, and above the Grand Tower, is the Big Hill. This is a natural bluff one mile in width, and several miles in length, and from which, and on each side, flow some cold and excellent springs. This county has six mills, three distilleries, one carding machine, nine schools, several mechanics, and 2,008 inhabitants.

RANDOLPH COUNTY, of which Kaskaskia is the seat of justice, lies at the mouth of the river of the same name, and is about equally proportioned into timber and prairie. It is watered by the Kaskaskia river, Praire de Long, St. Mary's, and Beaucoup creeks. The soil is unequal. Some is of the richest quality of bottom land; other portions, rolling and of second rate; while some parts, in the interior, is poor and rocky. In this county are upwards of twenty mills—of which three are moved by steam; five by water, and the rest by animal power. Here are nine distilleries, three carding machines, five cotton gins, three spinning machines, three castor oil presses, seven schools, one select academical school, and 4,448 inhabitants.

Kaskaskia is the oldest settlement in the valley of the Mississippi, it being made shortly after the visit of La Salle, in 1683. While the French held possession of Illinois, Kaskaskia was the seat of government, and a populous town. In 1721, it contained a college of Jesuits. The country east of the Mississippi was ceded to the British in 1763, at which time Kaskaskia contained one hundred families. After the revolutionary war it declined, until within a few years past. The town contains about one hundred and fifty houses, scattered over a large plain, and is situated on the Kaskaskia river, six miles above its mouth.

Chester is a landing place, and a river port on the Mississippi, one mile below the mouth of the Kaskaskia. It may probably become a place of considerable business, having a rock bluff for a wharf, and an excellent landing for steamboats at all seasons. Mather, Lamb & Co. and S. Smith are proprietors, and will give considerable encouragement to mechanics and men of business.

MONROE is a small county, taken off from Randolph and St. Clair. Its area is about 300 square miles. The west side of the county contains a portion of the American bottom; the middle section is cut up with bluffs, ravines, and sink holes.

The settlements about Waterloo and New Design are the oldest American settlements in the State, and contain good land. Monroe has eight mills, six distilleries, one carding machine, six schools, and 1,994 population.

Waterloo is the seat of justice. It is a small

village on the hill road from St. Louis to Kaskaskia.

ST. CLAIR COUNTY was organized as a county about 1794, and is the oldest in the State. This tract of country originally was about equally divided into timber and prairie, and contains much excellent land. The prairies are High, Ridge, Ogle's, Bottom, and Looking-glass prairies. High prairie commences one mile south of Belleville, and extends to Monroe County. Ridge prairie begins west of Belleville, and extends northward into Madison county. Ogle's prairie is intersected by the road from Rock Spring to St. Louis, and unites with Ridge praire. The prairie on the Bottom is intersected by a slough and a strip of timber. Looking-glass prairie lies east of Silver creek, and extends from the mouth of that creek indefinitely north. Each of these prairies is undulating, rich, and contains much land unlocated. As I have intimated in another place, much of the prairie land has turned to barrens, and is fast growing up with timber.

The streams that water this county are Silver creek, Ogle's creek, Richland creek, Prairie du Pont, and a part of Canteen and Cahokia creeks.

Improved farms in this county can be purchased, from $2,50 to $8,00 per acre.

St. Clair county has the following mills and mechanics. Two steam mills, nine ox mills, on the inclined plane, five geared horse mills, seven water saw, and four water grist mills, eight distilleries, two machines for threshing wheat, fifteen blacksmith's shops, six coopers, eight tanyards, three machines for carding wool, three waggon maker's shops, one tobacconist, two hatter's shops, three shoemaker's shops, five cabinet maker's shops, one tinner's shop, two cotton gins, one machine for reeling silk cocoons, three turner's shops, one silversmith, two patent grist mills, and four tailor's shops.

The towns are Belleville, Lebanon, Cahokia, and Illinois.

Belleville is the seat of justice, and situated fourteen miles from St. Louis, on Richland creek, and seven miles from the bluffs which bound the American bottom. It contains a handsome court house, a jail, and a public hall for literary purposes, all of brick. Here is a public library of three or four hundred volumes, a select academy, and two common schools, three taverns, four merchant's stores, two groceries, and various mechanic's shops.

It has a steam flouring mill, which makes thirty barrels of flour per day. The engine is of twelve horse power. Water is pumped from a well thirty feet deep, and five feet in diameter, which furnishes an ample supply. The fire consumes two cords of wood and seven bushels of bituminous coal in twenty four hours. The wood costs one dollar per cord, and the coal five and one half cents per bushel, and is hauled five miles from the bluffs. The mill house is thirty feet by thirty eight, a frame building two stories high—the engine room eighteen feet by thirty eight. The engine is high pressure, cylinder eight inches in diameter, and the piston three feet stroke. There are two run of stones, one of four and one half, and the other of four feet diameter. The whole cost of buildings, machinery and mill work for a complete flouring mill, was $3,500.

Belleville at present is a place of considerable business, which will admit of indefinite increase. A saw mill and a small water mill are in the immediate vicinity. Town lots sell from twenty-five to fifty dollars. Many tradesmen are still wanted, and would find immediate employ at profitable rates. A Baptist and a Methodist society have been formed here, which keep up regular meetings, and the population in, and around the place, are as moral and intelligent as any portion of the state. This is the residence of the Ex-Governor Edwards and the present Governor Reynolds. Population about 500.

Turkey Hill is a settlement a little to the east of Belleville, and, next to New Design, is the oldest American settlement in the state.

Lebanon is a port town one mile east of Silver-creek, on the stage road from St. Louis to Vincennes. It has two taverns, five stores, a number of mechanic's shops, an ox flouring mill, and a steam saw mill, and is a thriving place. The

Methodist denomination have put up a large framed building, adjoining Lebanon, for a Seminary; but it is not yet finished.

Cahokia is an ancient French village, of about eighty houses, five miles southeast from the ferry opposite St. Louis, inhabited chiefly by French. It was settled about the same time of Kaskaskia.

Illinois-town is a small village, of not much consequence, opposite St. Louis. There is a distillery, two or three stores, and a slaughter-house. The business of killing and packing some thousands of barrels of beef and pork annually, is here carried on by N. Cole and his sons. He commenced the business in 1823, on a small scale, as supplies in large quantities could not be then obtained. The business has steadily increased, competition has been excited, until now there are two large establishments in St. Louis, one at Alton, and several up the Illinois river.

Mr. Cole writes me, "There is a great improvement in the quality of pork the last winter over preceding years. *The beef made from the prairies of Illinois and Missouri, is in all respects equal, if not superior to any grass beef in the world.* In this, I am fully sustained by the opinion of the inspector of New Orleans, as well as many other gentlemen."

Rock Spring offers no claim to the rank of a village or town. It is a location in the midst of a tract of barrens, with only a few families within two miles. It was selected by the writer, in 1820, after having explored the country to some extent, as a site for a family residence and a small literary institution. It possesses the advantages of being removed from the contaminating influence of a village, is unquestionably healthy, has an abundance of excellent water, and a back country as range for stock. The Seminary and appurtenances have been described already. St. Clair county has a population of 7,082, and requires about thirty schools in as many settlements.

MADISON COUNTY is situated north of St. Clair, and on account of soil and situation possesses considerable advantages. The soil is various, but generally good, and proportionately divided into timber and prairies. It is well watered, having Silver and Sugar creeks towards its eastern side, Cahokia running diagonally through it from northeast to southwest, Indian creek, Wood river, and its branches, and the Piasau, in two forks, on its northern and northwestern parts.

Goshen, Marine, Wood river, Gilham's, and Ridge prairie, are all fine and flourishing settlements of industrious farmers. Its towns are Alton, (Upper and Lower,) Edwardsville, and Collinsville.

Alton, from its locality and prospects, demands special attention. There are two villages of this name, about two miles distant from each other, and distinguished as Upper and Lower Alton, the former being on the high ground back from the river, and the latter at the landing.

Lower Alton is thought by many to present superior advantages for commerce and business than any other spot in the State. It is at the place where the curve of the Mississippi penetrates the farthest into the interior of Illinois. (See map.) It is within one mile of the mouth of the great Missouri, sixteen miles below the mouth of the Illinois, and at the junction where the business and commerce of the wide spread regions of the northeast, north, and northwest, must arrive. The great road from all the northern portions of Illinois, and from the counties that extend along the eastern side of the Illinois river, in the direction of St. Louis, and the mouth of the Ohio, passes through this place. The legislature of Illinois, at its last session, memorialized Congress to have the great National Road, now constructing through Ohio, Indiana, and Illinois, to the seat of government in Missouri, pass at or near this place; and many are sanguine in their expectations of this result. If it crosses the Mississippi *above* the mouth of the Missouri, Alton lies directly in its route. It has the best landing for steamboats on the east bank of the Mississippi, having a solid rock of level surface, of suitable height, and to which boats at any stage of water can come and discharge and receive cargoes. It has been selected as the site for the State penitentiary, which is now building; and it is thought by many it will yet become the seat of government for the State.

This town is laid out on fractional sections thirteen and fourteen, in township 5 north, in range 10, west of the third principal meridian, latitude 38° 52' north; twenty miles north of St. Louis, and sixty miles west from Vandalia. One of the finest bodies of timber in the State surrounds it for several miles in extent. Bituminous coal of a good quality and in common use by the blacksmiths, exists in abundance, and but a short distance from this place. Inexhaustible beds of limestone of a good quality for buildings, and easily quarried, and a species of sandstone, possessing a fine grain, which is quarried and dressed for monuments and architectural purposes. Here also is an abundance of that peculiar species of lime, used for water cement. The population of this place is rapidly increasing, and improvements are going on with great activity.

"Alton, although yet small, possesses natural advantages rarely equalled. Situated as it is, at the junction of three large and navigable rivers; possessing a fine commodious harbour, and landing for boats at all seasons of the year; surrounded by a fertile country rapidly settling, it bids fair to become a populous, wealthy, and commercial town."*

* Beck's Gazetteer.

Building lots sell from twenty to one hundred dollars, according to situation. The policy of the principal proprietors is to sell lots thus low, but on condition that good buildings shall be erected on them within one year, on penalty of a forfeiture. A large number of lots were sold a few months past, subject to these conditions. This is the finest place on the river for building and repairing steamboats. Land is reserved for a large boat yard, and a steamboat is contemplated to be built shortly to run between this place and St. Louis.

With all these advantages, Lower Alton is not without its disadvantages. As my object is to give an impartial statement relative to this place, I shall not pass over them. It is too much confined for a pleasant situation, being surrounded on the west and north with abrupt hills and bluffs. As the business part of the town will necessarily be about the river and landing, it will be a confined place. The south and southeast is open; but across the river, an extensive low bottom stretches up the Missouri, and along the Mississippi. From these circumstances it will be more exposed to fall fevers than an elevated and airy situation. St. Louis is within twenty miles—a place admirably located, and of great business. It now draws a considerable portion of the trade of Illinois, and will be a powerful rival to compete with. These difficulties leave the future prospects of the rise of a great commercial city shortly at this point, a little problematical at the present. Still it is a place that merits the attention of men of capital and business. Three or four mercantile houses are already established, are erecting warehouses, and calculate upon doing a large business in trade with the interior. Eight or ten merchants, in the wholesale and retail line, and a suitable number of mechanics and manufacturers would soon determine the question of a commercial town. Mechanics of almost every trade are wanted here. Coopers to supply not only the demand here, but the St. Louis market, in casks, barrels, and firkins. Another large tannery, with shoemaking. One slaughter house here, now in operation, will furnish five hundred hides yearly. A soap and tallow chandler. Cabinet makers to supply the St. Louis market with furniture. Much of the supply of that market is now brought from Cincinnati. Stone and brick masons, plaisterers, carpenters, and joiners are much needed. Hardly any mechanic, needed in a new and rapidly increasing country, but might do well at Alton. We advise, however, that none but sober, industrious, and enterprising men come to Alton, either Upper or Lower. The idle, profligate, and *intemperate*, will find the leading men, and a large majority of the people, combined against them.

Lower Alton, in March last, had thirty-two families, and one hundred and seventy souls, to which there has been considerable increase. There were at that time one steam saw mill, one ware house for packing beef and pork, one carpenter, one waggon maker, one tannery, one cooper with six journeymen and three apprentices, two brickmakers, one brick mason, one stone mason, one blacksmith, two shoemakers, one lawyer, one tavern, and boarding-house, and one retail store. There are now in addition, one penitentiary with warden's house and officers, mechanic shops, yard, and twenty four cells for convicts, three or four wholesale and retail stores, one physician, one week day and Sabbath school, several mechanic's shops, and a plan under consideration to establish a seminary of learning in the immediate vicinity. A steam flouring mile is about being built.

Upper Alton is from one half to two miles east from Lower Alton, in section 7 of township 5 north, range 9 west of the third principal meridian.

Its situation is high and healthy, and contained last spring thirty-five families and two hundred souls. Its numbers, within a few months, have augmented nearly one third. The soil of the surrounding country is fertile, and rolling; the prevailing timber, walnut, hickory, and oak.

In March it had two stores, one tavern, one blacksmith, one ox flouring mill, one waggon maker, one tannery, one saddler, one shoe maker, one brickmaker, two carpenters, two physicians, one pottery, for coarse earthen ware, one post office, and a brick school-house building.

Methodists, Baptists, and Presbyterians, have organized societies, and preaching alternately by one of these denominations every Sabbath. A flourishing Sabbath school is kept up. At Upper Alton, the first Sunday school in Illinois was opened in 1819.

Alton has been retarded in growth from several causes, but especially from several conflicting claims to the soil, which have happily terminated in a decision of court according to the mutual agreement of *all* the claimants. Titles are now perfectly secure.

North of Madison lie the counties of Greene, and Maquapin, or Macoupen, as it is frequently written, and usually pronounced with the French sound.

Greene has the Mississippi on its southwest, and the Illinois on its north west side.

MAQUAPIN has Greene on the west, Montgomery on the east, and Morgan north. It is watered by the Cahokia, and Maquapin creeks. The county seat is *Carlinville*, situated a few miles to the left of the main road from Edwardsville to Springfield. This county is about equally proportioned in timber and prairie, rather level than otherwise, and contains much good land unlocated, and is conveniently situated for Alton market. It has several horse mills, and three or four by water power, five schools, and 1,919 inhabitants.

Green County is watered by the Maquapin and Apple creeks, having the Mississippi and the Illinois rivers on two sides. This is a fine, flourishing, and rich county, with proportionate quantities of prairie and timber, and contains 7,871 inhabitants, with a rapid increase. The surface approaches nearer to a level than the counties further north. This county has twelve grist mills by animal power, and seven grist and eight saw mills carried by water, twenty-five schools, twelve stores, nine physicians, three attorneys, two coal banks opened, fifteen blacksmiths, two gunsmiths, one silversmith, one tinner's shop, thirteen carpenters, seven waggon makers, four coopers, two millwrights, five tanneries, four saddlers, four shoe makers, three tailors, one rope maker, three brick makers, six brick layers, and two hatters.

Carrollton is the county seat, and is a pleasant and flourishing town of about 400 inhabitants, situated in a central part of the county.

Bluffdale is a retired and romantic settlement under the bluffs that overhang the bottoms of the Illinois. Here the lime stone rocks and precipices overhang the settlement, from the foot of which some of the finest springs gush out, and meander through the adjacent prairie. The prevailing population of this settlement came from Vermont, amongst whom is Mr. John

Russell, who stands deservedly high in the ranks of literature and science. Apple creek settlement, lies north of the creek from whence it derives its name, and is a flourishing settlement of thrifty farmers. As a drawback to the prosperity of this county, it has eleven distilleries, seven of which are by steam.

MORGAN COUNTY is destined to become one of the richest agricultural counties in the State, lying north of Greene, with the Illinois river on the left. In 1821, the tract of country embraced within the limits of this county, contained only twenty families. Its population in 1830 was 13,281. It is well proportioned into timber and prairie, tolerably well watered, and contains the finest tract of farming land around Jacksonville I have ever seen. In this county are about thirty mills for sawing and grinding, carried by animal power, water and steam. There are two large steam grist and saw mills, one at Naples, and the other at Beardstown. In this county are forty-six schools, twenty-six stores, of which eleven are in Jacksonville, eighteen physicians, six attorneys, six coal banks opened, thirty-five blacksmiths, two coppersmiths, one tinner, thirty-one carpenters, fifteen cabinet makers, five waggon makers, one carriage maker, fifteen coopers, ten millwrights, ten tanneries, six saddlers, twenty shoe makers, twelve tailors, one cloth dresser, twenty brickmakers, twenty-nine bricklayers, six hatters, and one college.

Jacksonville, the seat of justice, is conveniently located in the centre of the county, in a beautiful prairie, and contains a population of about 750, and rapidly increasing. This will doubtless become one of the largest inland towns in the State. Here is a factory for making cotton yarn, which runs one hundred and twenty-six spindles.

Diamond Grove is a beautiful eminence, two miles south-west from Jacksonville. It is a tract of timber of about eight hundred acres, surrounded on all sides by prairie.

Naples is a landing and village on the Illinois river, three miles above the mouth of the Mauvresterre, and is a place of business.

Beardstown is another landing and village on the river towards the northeastern part of the county.

Exeter is a post office and small village on the Mauvresterre, twelve miles from Jacksonville.

Winchester is a new village begun near the southern border of the country.

Jersey Prairie is a beautiful settlement near Indian creek towards the northern side of the county.

The streams in this county are the *Mauvresterre*, and its four branches, Indiana creek, Sandy, Apple creek, and a branch of Maquapin.

Mauvresterre, which means *poor land*, is a most unfortunate name—for the county on its borders is one of the richest bodies of land in the Great Valley.

SANGAMON COUNTY lies north and east of Morgan, and is watered by the Sangamon and its branches. Here the prairies widen, and the settlements which are always in the boarders of the timber, are farther removed from each other. In this county, which is the most populous in the State, containing 13,793 souls, there are upwards of fifty mills. Here are fifteen water grist, and seventeen water saw mills, and the remainder by animal power. Here are sixty schools, fifteen stores, eight physicians, six attorneys, and about the same proportion of mechanics as in Morgan county.

Springfield is the seat of justice, and contains a population of between nine hundred and one thousand. It is beautifully situated on the borders of a prairie, seven miles from Sangamon river, and twenty miles from the Illinois.

Sangamon is a small village on the river of that name, seven miles from Springfield.

TAZEWELL COUNTY lies above Sangamon, with the Illinois river on the left. This county is new, but emigrants are fast filling it up. Here the priarie predominates, and timber becomes comparatively scarce. The land in general is of an excellent quality, and many desirable locations yet remain unsettled. Population, 4,055.

Pekin is a town site, and landing on the Illinois river, and its prospects to become a town are thought by some to be promising. In this county are eight or ten mills.

McLean county is next in succession; this and the two following ones were made last winter. Here the timber no longer exists in large bodies, but rather in groves and copses, while the prairies embrace a larger proportion of the county. This county contains about 450 souls, but will become equal to many others in the State.

La Salle, another new county, is next, and exhibits about the same characteristics as Mc Lean. Population about 300.

Cook County adjoins Lake Michigan, and has the port of *Chicago* for its county seat, which must eventually become a place of considerable commercial importance. The three last named counties lie in the course of the projected canal which is to unite the navigable part of the Illinois river with Lake Michigan.

The practicability and utility of this project is scarcely doubted. A survey was made under authority from the State in 1823, and the distance ascertained to be a little over 70 miles from Chicago, an arm of the Lake, to the proposed junction with the Illinois below the rapids of the latter, and near the mouth of the Fox river. The cost was estimated at about 750,000 dollars. Four or five routes were examined, which varied a little in distance, quality of ground, and cost of construction.

In March, 1827, Congress granted to the State of Illinois each alternate section of land bordering on the canal route, the proceeds of which were to be appropriated to its construction. Part of these lands have been sold and produced a revenue of 13,500 dollars. The commissioners also laid off the town of *Chicago* at the contemplated junction of the canal with that river, and the town of *Ottawa*, at its junction with the Illinois, and lots have been sold to the value of 4,545 dollars. The canal commissioners, in their report made to the legislature of Illinois, Dec. 27, 1830, describe the town site of Chicago, which is located on section 9, township 39 north, range 14 east from the third principal meridian, as follows.

"This town is situated on Chicago river, near its mouth, and possesses many advantages, natural and adventitious. It is the only eligible site for a town on the Lake shore, within the limits of Illinois, surrounded by a beautiful campaign country, surpassed by none in the richness of its products; and from the long experience of its inhabitants, is decidedly healthy. Its prominence in a commercial point of view has already prompted merchants from the northeastern part of this State, and from Indiana, to take their produce to Chicago, ship for Detroit, Buffaloe, and New York, and return by the same route, as the safest and cheapest. The circumstance of Chicago being located at the head of the contemplated canal, will make it the future depot of all the surplus products of the country on the Illinois river, and its tributaries. The town of *Ottawa*, at the mouth of Fox river of the Illinois, is advantageously situated in the heart of a most beautiful, fertile, and healthy region of country, and, as connected with the canal, deserves the legislative care of the State." This is the county seat of Mc Lean county.

The route of the canal has been partially surveyed by the United States engineers, under the direction of the general government. Until last winter it has been contemplated to use Lake Michigan as the feeder for the canal. The distance from the Chicago to the river Des Plaines, a principal branch of the Illinois, is eighteen and a half miles, and for about nine miles the elevation of the surface above the bottom of the canal, to use the lake as a feeder, is nearly sixteen feet. This was supposed to present no serious difficulty, until, by repeated borings, it was ascertained, that of this depth, ten feet must be excavated through a solid bed of limestone, making the whole cost of the first eighteen and a half miles, to exceed a million and a half of dollars. The Commissioners have been instructed by the legislature to ascertain if the waters of the Calimick river, which empty into Lake Michigan, south of Chicago, can be employed for a feeder, and also to estimate the comparative cost of a rail road across this portage. It is understood that the Commissioners are ready to report upon the entire feasibility of the Calumick as a feeder, and that the cost of this section will not exceed 161,000 dollars.

It may be safely calculated, therefore, that either a canal or a rail road will soon form a line of commercial intercourse from the navigable waters of the Illinois to Lake Michigan, and thus open a direct communication with the commerce of Ohio, New York, and the Canadas.

The country on the lake shore north of Chicago is low, level, and in many places wet. South of the Lake, and betwixt Cook and Vermillion counties, is much good land, intermixed with strips of swampy, wet land. Here is room for two or three new counties.

VERMILLION COUNTY adjoins the State of Indiana, and is equal to Sangamon in quality of soil. Here, too, there is more prairie than timber, but of an excellent quality. *Danville* is the seat of justice, situated in the forks of the Vermillion river, and is a place of considerable promise. Its mills, schools, professional men, and mechanics, are about equal to those counties which I have particularized. The salt works in this county are considered valuable. Vermillion has 6,389 population.

EDGAR COUNTY lies south of Vermillion, hav-

and surrounded with an industrious population. The population of the county is 3,702.

CLAY COUNTY lies west of Lawrence, and is watered by the Little Wabash and its tributaries. On the bottoms of these streams are fine bodies of valuable timber, but much of the upland is prairie.

Maysville, the seat of justice, is a pleasant little village, of about twenty families, on the borders of the twelve mile prairie. Here the roads to St. Louis and Vandalia separate. But a small portion of the land in Clay county is yet located, and many good settlements might be formed. Its population is 751.

WAYNE COUNTY lies south and southwest of Clay, having Edwards and Wabash counties betwixt it and the Wabash river. It is well proportioned into timber and prairie, and contains many tracts of good land. The Little Wabash and Skillet Fork are its principal streams. Wayne has a population of 2,596. *Fairfield*, a small village, is the seat of justice.

EDWARDS COUNTY is situated east of Wayne, having Wabash county lying between it and the Wabash river. Its land is about the same as the last named counties. In the centre of this county is the British settlement of which Richard Flowers, Esq. and Morris Birbeck, Esq. were the leaders. Mr. Birbeck is known for his letters on Illinois, which, in general, were accurate descriptions of the country in a state of nature.

He was afterwards drowned in crossing an inconsiderable stream. The English emigrants have never succeeded equally to their expectations.

Albion is the seat of justice, a small, and not very flourishing village. *Wanborough* is the name of the settlement made by Mr. Birbeck.

WABASH COUNTY adjoins the Wabash river, and lies east of Edwards. It has considerable good land, the prairies small and well located for settlements. Population, 2,766. *Barney's Prairie* lies four miles northwest from Palmyra, and is an extensive tract of excellent land, surrounded with industrious farmers. *Bald Hill Prairie* lies four miles west northwest from Mount Carmel, and is a high ridge of rich land.

Mount Carmel, the seat of justice, is situated on the Wabash, opposite the mouth of White river, and contains about five hundred inhabitants. It is a flourishing town; the population moral, industrious, and enterprising. Amongst other improvements is an iron foundry, for castings, the only one in the State. *Palmyra* is a small village on the Wabash, towards the northern part of the county, going to decay.

WHITE COUNTY is situated south of Wabash and Edwards, and is bisected by the Little Wabash. The banks of this stream and its tributaries, and of the Big Wabash, are heavily timbered. In the interior are considerable prairies. There is much good land in the county.

Carmi is the seat of justice, situated on the west bank of the Little Wabash, about twenty miles above its mouth. *Bon Pas* is a small village in the northeastern part of the county. *Big Prairie* is a rich tract of country lying between the Big and Little Wabash. The population of White county is 6,033. White county has about the same proportion of mills, stores, schools, mechanics, &c. as other counties already specified.

GALLATIN COUNTY is south of White, and in the southeastern part of the State ; it joins the Wabash on the east, and the Ohio on the south. The interior is watered by the Saline creek and its tributaries. Population 6,970. In this part of the State sand predominates in the soil. The basis rock in all the counties on the Wabash is sandstone, resting, it is thought, on clay slate. This county contains a large proportion of timbered land, and the soil is well adapted to grass, and has great facilities for raising stock, as but little food is required in the winter. The counties bordering on the Ohio river have milder winters than other parts of the State. This is thought to be owing in part to the more compact bodies of timber for thirty or forty miles north.

The salines or salt springs in this county must be a source of much wealth. The most valuable is known by the name of the *Ohio saline*, which is situated on Saline creek, fifteen miles northwest from Shawneetown. The Indians, who formerly possessed it, called it the "Great Salt Spring," from which they had long been in the habit of making salt. Large fragments of earthen pans and kettles are found near the works, buried in the earth. The same is true at the Big Muddy Saline in Jackson county. Several tribes of Indians in conjunction, ceded these works to the United States in 1803, for which the United States engaged to give them one hundred and fifty bushels of salt per annum. The works, with 97,000 acres of land, were ceded to the State of Illinois in 1818, and are now leased by the State for a term of years. Of the land, 30,000 acres have been offered for sale, the proceeds of which are to be appropriated in building a penitentiary, and in improving certain roads and navigable streams. There are now in operation four different establishments, including nine furnaces, averaging sixty kettles each, which hold from thirty-six to sixty gallons. These make on an average 3,000 bushels of salt per week, and 130,000 bushels per annum. Salt sells at the works from thirty-seven and a half to fifty cents per bushel, of fifty pounds.

Equality is the present seat of justice, situated on the Saline about fifteen miles from Shawneetown. It is a pleasant village, of 250 inhabitants, in the midst of the salt manufactories.

Shawneetown is on the Ohio river, in latitude 37° 40′ north, 110 miles southeast of Vandalia. It is probably the largest river town in Illinois, contains about six hundred inhabitants, and is a place of business and commerce. It is subject to be overflowed at the high floods of the Ohio.

POPE COUNTY lies down the Ohio from Gallatin. It is a rolling, timbered county; but contains considerable good land, of a sandy soil, and is watered by Big Bay creek, and other smaller streams that fall into the Ohio.

Golconda is the seat of justice, and situated on the Ohio river, twenty miles below the mouth of the Cumberland, and has about one hundred and fifty inhabitants.

JOHNSON COUNTY lies next, and joins Alexander. This is chiefly a timbered county, with some small prairies, tolerably level; excepting the Ohio bluffs, and of a good sandy soil. Population, 1,699. County seat, *Vienna*, a small village.

In this county are six common horse mills, three water mills, three distilleries, six schools, five stores, two physicians, one lawyer, nine blacksmiths, one gunsmith, seven cabinet makers, two plough makers, one carriage maker, three coopers, two millwrights, one saddler, two shoemakers, one brickmaker, and two bricklayers.

I give these particulars of Johnson county as a specimen of the proportion of mills, mechanics, &c. to the population in most of the southern counties in the State.

FRANKLIN COUNTY, (proceeding northward again, in the same order as before, and taking the interior counties,) lies north of Johnson county and part of Pope. It is watered by the Big Muddy and its branches, and lies east of Jackson county. It is well timbered, the prairies are small and generally fertile, and the banks of the streams are low and subject to annual inundations. It does not differ materially from the neighbouring counties. Population, 4,023. Seat of justice is *Frankfort*, a small village.

PERRY COUNTY lies northwest from Franklin. This was formed a few years since, from a part of Randolph and Jackson. The Little Muddy and Beaucoup are its principal streams. Timber and prairie about equally divided, soil good, tolerably level and healthy. *Pinckneyville* is its county seat. Population of the county is 1,228.

WASHINGTON COUNTY lies north of Perry. It joins the southeastern part of St. Clair county, and is watered by the Kaskaskia, Elkhorn, and some other small streams. The banks of the streams are well timbered; but in the interior are considerable prairies.

Nashville is the seat of justice. *Covington*, the former seat of justice, is a small town on the Kaskaskia, in the northern side of the county. Population of the county, 1,673.

CLINTON COUNTY lies north of Washington and east of St. Clair. It is a small county taken from Washington and Bond, about equally proportioned in timber and prairie, and good soil. It is watered by the Kaskaskia river, and Shoal and Sugar creeks. Arrangements have been made by the legislature to improve the navigation of the Kaskaskia, which will add much to the facilities of commercial intercourse with this county.

Carlyle is the seat of justice, and is situated on a prairie near the Kaskaskia river, at the junction of the roads from Vincennes and Shawneetown to St. Louis, and to the northern counties, which will make it eventually a considerable thoroughfare. This town contains about seventy-five industrious and enterprising families, and is increasing. Here is an excellent water grist and saw mill, and salt water has been discovered in the vicinity, about thirty feet from the surface, which is said to be valuable.

BOND COUNTY lies north of Clinton, and is small in extent, but well proportioned into timber and prairie, and contains a population of industrious farmers.

Greenville is the seat of justice, situated on the east fork of Shoal creek, and contains about fifty families, and a factory for making cotton yarn. The inhabitants of this county have been foremost to promote temperance, Sunday schools, and to supply every family with the Bible. It is watered by the two forks of shoal creek, and has a population of 3,181; eleven grist mills, five water saw mills, four distilleries, one carding machine, one cotton spinning factory, sixteen schools, four stores, two physicians, two blacksmiths, five carpenters, four cabinet makers, two waggon makers, two coopers, four millwrights, two tanneries, two saddlers, six shoemakers, four tailors, four brickmakers, four bricklayers, two hatters, and one spinning wheel factory.

MONTGOMERY COUNTY lies north of Bond, and is watered by the branches of Shoal creek. It is an elevated tract of country, equally proportioned into timber and prairie, of good soil, and contains many desirable tracts unlocated.

Hillsboro' is the seat of justice, and contains forty families, and two hundred inhabitants; four stores, three taverns, two blacksmiths, two carpenters, one cabinet maker, two physicians, two tanneries, one shoemaker, two tailors, one tinner, a post office, a land agency office by John Tillson, Esq., and a Presbyterian meeting-house of brick, 44 feet by 46, one story, and is a flourishing little inland town. Population of the county, 3,037.

MACON COUNTY lies northeast of Montgomery county, high up the Kaskaskia river, of which *Decatur* is the seat of justice. Macon contains 1,161 inhabitants, is a rich body of land, more than one half prairie, and is settling rapidly.

SHELBY COUNTY, farther down the Kaskaskia, lies south of Macon. The seat of justice is *Shelbyville*, a considerable village on the west bank of the river. Shelby county in character and quality of soil, is similar to the others in this region, having large bodies of excellent land suitably proportioned into timber and prairie. Population 3,019, and increasing fast.

FAYETTE COUNTY is next south, including *Vandalia* the seat of government. Fayette is very much like Shelby, is watered by the Kaskaskia, and its tributaries, and contains much good land yet unlocated.

Vandalia, the capital of the State, and also the seat of justice for this county, is situated on the west bank of the Kaskaskia river, in sections eight, nine, sixteen and seventeen, of township six north, and in range one, west of the third principal meridian. The site is high and undulating—the public square is elevated, and commands a considerable prospect. The "National Road" which enters the State in Edgar county, and passes through Coles and Fayette counties, to this place, is already located thus far, the ground cleared off, and contracts now made to grade the road, and bridge the streams fit for use.

The State house is of brick, two stories, fifty feet by forty, a plain, economical building, not designed for permanent use. Another public building erected for the State bank, but now used for the public offices, is of brick, two stories, forty-four feet by forty. The church, which is a neat, white frame, forty by thirty-six, with a cupola and bell, is built for all denominations.

Vandalia contains seven stores, three taverns, three blacksmiths, four carpenters, one tailor, two tanneries, one shoemaker, two bricklayers, two physicians, three lawyers, one water grist mill, one water saw mill, one ox mill, one horse mill, and two schools. The population is estimated at five hundred inhabitants. Here is a Presbyterian society of upwards of twenty members, a Methodist society, and a Sunday school of twelve teachers and seventy scholars. The population of Fayette county is 3,046.

MARION COUNTY lies south of Fayette and east of Clinton. It includes a considerable proportion of the grand prairie, and is watered by Crooked creek, and some of the branches of the Little Wabash, on the borders of which is good timber; but in the interior are extensive prairies.

Salem, a small village on the east side of the Grand Prairie, is the seat of justice Population of the county 2,200.

JEFFERSON COUNTY is situated south of Marion, and lies north of Franklin, and east of Washington and Perry counties, and does not materially differ in surface and soil from them.

Mount Vernon is the seat of justice, an inconsiderable village, on the principal road from Carlyle to Shawneetown. Jefferson county has five horse and two ox mills, one water power sawmill, one cotton gin, seven schools, three stores, two physicians, seven blacksmiths, one gunsmith, three carpenters, one ploughmaker, one waggon maker, two coopers, three millwrights, three tanneries, one shoe maker, two tailors, two brick makers and bricklayers, and one hatter. Population, 2,628.

HAMILTON COUNTY lies east of Jefferson, principally a timbered county, and has Wayne on the north, White on the east, and Gallatin south. Seat of justice is *Mc Leansboro'*, a small village.

We have now examined the counties south and east of the Illinois river, and shall proceed to the Military tract and the northern portion of the State.

The *Military Bounty Tract* lies in the forks of the Mississippi and Illinois rivers, and contains 3,500,000 acres, which was set apart by Congress and patented for soldiers who served in the last war. It extends from the mouth of the Illinois river on a meridian line north, one hundred and sixty-two miles, but its width varies, its shape being that of an irregular triangle, as may be seen on the map. Its soil and surface very much resemble the country on the opposite side of the Illinois river, excepting the northern part of the tract, which has a much greater proportion of prairie. Along the bottoms of the Mississippi and Illinois, as has been noticed in another place, there is much inundated land. This tract, until recently, has not populated equal to the other parts of the State south. But very little of the land is now in possession of the soldiers to whom it was patented, and much of it has been sold for taxes, and is passed redemption. All lands owned by individuals, whether residents or non-residents, have been assessed for taxes by the State, at the rate of one, two, and three cents per acre according to quality of soil. If the taxes for the year are not paid by the 31st of December, the lands, or such portion as is bid off, are sold for the taxes according to previous advertisement, subject to redemption within *two* years from the time of sale, upon the claimant paying double the amount of tax and costs of sale.

Large portions of this tract have thus passed out of the hands of the original proprietors. Purchasers for taxes, now offer and sell quarters thus held by tax-titles, and give general warrantee deeds for one dollar per acre. These and other circumstances have heretofore retarded the population of this section of the country, which is now rapidly filling up with industrious and enterprising emigrants.

In our sketch of the counties in this tract, we shall commence with that of

CALHOUN, which lies immediately in the forks of the Mississippi and Illinois rivers. This county contains all the variety of soil I have described. Considerable portions are inundated bottoms, ravines, bluffs, and sink-holes. Its width is quite disproportionate to its length, being in most places from three to ten miles from one river to the other. Still there is much good land unoccupied. An intelligent gentleman, who resides in the county, calculates that 1,000 families can be supplied with land for first rate farms. The bottoms furnish excellent range for stock. There are but few mechanics. Population, 1,130. *Gilead* is the seat of justice.

SCHUYLER, following up the Illinois river, is the next county. This is a valuable county, being well proportioned into timber and prairie, a fertile soil, and generally healthy. In it are six mills, six schools, a number of stores, mechanics, &c.

Rushville is the seat of justice, a thriving and pleasant village. This county lies directly opposite Morgan county. Population, 2,385.

FULTON COUNTY lies next, on Spoon river, and opposite Sangamon, equal to Schuyler in quality of soil, and contains a population of 1,962. *Lewistown* is the seat of justice. This county is improving rapidly.

PEORIA COUNTY lies above Fulton. In this county prairie predominates. It contains much good land, and has 1,782 inhabitants.

Peoria or *Fort Clark* is the seat of justice, a most delightful town site on the bank of the Illinois. Here is an expansion of the Illinois river into a kind of lake for twenty miles above

Peoria. Its water is clear, its bottom gravelly, and abounds with fish of various kinds, such as sturgeon, buffalo, bass of several species, pickerel, perch, white fish, &c. Steam boats run regularly now from St. Louis to Peoria, and occasionally to the rapids of Illinois.

PUTNAM COUNTY is situated above Peoria. It is a new county, located last session of the legislature, and much of the character of the other counties in this region.

The *Rapids of Illinois* are at the termination of the Illinois and Michigan canal, sixty miles by land, and ninety miles by water, above Peoria. It is thought, by competent judges, that here is water power equal, if not superior to any in the Western States, and doubtless at some future day will be used for some manufacturing purposes to a vast extent.

INDIANA.

THIS State is divided into sixty-three counties, and according to the census of June, 1830, contained 344,508 inhabitants. In 1808, (including Illinois,) the population amounted to 5,641; in 1810, the population of Indiana Territory was 24,520; in 1820, it was 147,178.

Guide for Emigrants.

The following table exhibits the counties, and the census of each for 1830.

Allen,	1,000	Madison,	2,242
Bartholomew,	5,480	Martin,	2,010
Boon,	622	Monroe,	6,578
Clark,	10,719	Montgomery,	7,389
Clay,	1,616	Morgan,	5,579
Crawford,	3,234	Orange,	7,906
Carroll,	2,614	Owen,	4,060
Cass,	1,150	Parke,	5,734
Clinton,	1,423	Perry,	3,378
Dearborn,	14,575	Pike,	2,464
Decatur,	5,851	Posey,	6,883
Daviess,	4,512	Putnam,	8,195
Dubois,	1,774	Randolph,	3,912
Delaware,	2,372	Ripley,	3,957
Elkhart,	935	Rush,	9,918
Fayette,	9,112	Scott,	3,097
Floyd,	6,363	Shelby,	6,294
Franklin,	10,199	Spencer,	3,187
Fountain,	7,644	Sullivan,	4,696
Gibson,	5,417	Switzerland,	7,111
Green,	4,253	St. Joseph's,	287
Hamilton,	1,750	Tippacanoe,	7,167
Harrison,	10,088	Union,	7,657
Henricks,	3,967	Vanderburgh,	2,510
Henry,	6,498	Vermillion,	5,706
Hancock,	1,569	Vigo,	5,737
Jackson,	4,894	Warrick,	2,973
Jefferson,	11,465	Washington,	13,072
Jennings,	3,950	Wayne,	18,589
Johnson,	4,436	Warren,	2,854
Knox,	6,554		
Lawrence,	9,239	Total,	344,508
Marion,	7,181		

The southern portion of the State, towards the Ohio river, contains much broken, hilly land, and very little prairie. The northern half contains considerable tracts of prairie, and in general is quite level. Much of the timbered land is heavily covered with beech, sugar maple, yellow poplar, lyme, and various species of oaks.

Along the Wabash, the soil inclines to sand, but is fertile. In the interior, it becomes clayey and adhesive. The country up the Wabash is more level and wet than Illinois. This river is navigable for steamboats at a rise of the water for more than two hundred miles. From the fifth of March to the 15th of April, the present year, there were 54 arrivals and departures of steamboats at the port of Vincennes. The number of flat boats that passed Vincennes on their way *down* the river was estimated at five hundred: As many were supposed to have descended the two forks of White river. One tenth of these flat boats, it is calculated, are loaded with pork, at the rate of three hundred barrels to a boat. Another tenth are said to be loaded with lard, cattle, horses, oats, cornmeal, &c.; and the remainder loaded with corn in the ear. The estimated value of produce and stock sent off in flat boats, all which leaves the mouth of the Wabash is $740,000.

In 1821, no white family was settled twenty miles north of Terre Hante. Since that time, the following counties have been formed on or in the vicinity of the river, viz. Cass, Carroll, Tippecanoe, Fountain, Warren, Vermillion, Parke, Putnam, Montgomery, and Clinton. These counties now contain a population of 70,000.

Terre Hante is a flourishing town on the banks

of the Wabash, sixty miles above Vincennes, and two and a half miles from the site of Old Fort Harrison. The National Road from Indianapolis to Vandalia passes through this place. It must eventually become a place of considerable commerce and business.

In Parke county the land is excellent, well watered, generally heavily timbered with beech, poplar, sugar maple, oaks, and lyme. There is but little prairie.

Fountain county lies north of Parke and west of Montgomery. The land generally is good.

Montgomery, east of Fountain, has much wet land, most of it heavily timbered; a part is of excellent quality. Crawfordsville is the seat of justice.

Tippacanoe lies northeast of Fountain, and has Lafayette for its county seat. Steamboats now ascend the Wabash to this place. This is a promising town, and must become a place of considerable importance. In this county there is considerable prairie and much good land.

Warren county lies above, has excellent land, and well proportioned into timber and prairie.

Vermillion county lies on the west side of the Wabash opposite Park, and joins the State of Illinois. It is a long narrow county, and contains considerable good land.

Putnam lies east of Parke, and south of Montgomery. The land in general is heavily timbered.

It is watered by Eel river, and Rackoon creek, and contains considerable tracts of excellent land; but some portions are too level and wet for convenience. This is a common fault of much of the land that joins the Wabash.

Around Indianopolis, for thirty miles in extent, the land is level and the soil rich. The northern portion of Indiana is about equally divided into timber and prairie, and is but little rolling. Towards Lake Michigan in the northwestern part of the State is some inundated land, and small lakes, and swamps. The general characteristics of the people of this State resemble those of Illinois.

There are twenty weekly newspapers published in this State, and it has been the policy of the legislature to encourage the establishment of academies in the principal counties.

RELIGIOUS DENOMINATIONS.

Presbyterians. There is one synod, five presbyteries; 35 ministers; seventy-one churches, and 2,816 communicants.

Baptists. Associations fourteen: churches about two hundred; ministers estimated at one hundred and twenty-five; communicants estimated at eight thousand. The above estimate is made by ascertaining the numbers in seven Associations, and giving the same ratio for the rest.

Methodists. In this State and Illinois the Methodists are united in one conference. The last minutes give for both States eighty-eight preachers, exclusive of local preachers, which may be estimated at about three local preachers to one who rides the circuit, and 24,440 members. Probably three fifths are in Indiana. Besides these, are Christ-ians, Quakers or Friends, and some smaller sects, the numbers of which are not known.

The State college is at Bloomington, and the Presbyterians have a Theological school at Hanover.

OHIO.

The settlement of this State commenced at Marietta in 1788; in 1789, the first grade of territorial government was organized, and called the "Western Territory," afterwards altered to the "Territory Northwest of the Ohio."

In 1802, it became an independent State. Its growth has been rapid, and is now the fourth State in the Union in point of population, which is 937,000. In 1820, its population was 581,434; showing an increase of sixty-one per cent. I have room only to give the census of the counties for 1830, from which the reader may draw general conclusions of its improved condition.

CENSUS OF OHIO.

Adams,	12,278	Madison,	6,191
Athens,	8,778	Marion,	6,558
Belmont,	28,543	Medina,	7,560
Brown,	17,866	Meigs,	6,159
Butler,	27,143	Mercer,	1,088
Champaign,	12,137	Miami,	12,807
Clark,	13,074	Monroe,	8,770
Clermont,	20,466	Montgomery,	24,374
Clinton,	11,406	Morgan,	11,800
Columbiana,	35,661	Muskingum,	29,335
Coshocton,	11,162	Perry,	14,063
Crawford,	4,788	Pickaway,	15,931
Cuyahoga,	10,362	Pike,	6,024
Dark,	6,204	Portage,	18,747
Delaware,	11,522	Preble,	16,296
Fairfield,	24,753	Richland,	24,007
Fayette,	8,183	Ross,	24,060
Franklin,	14,756	Sandusky,	2,851
Gallia,	9,733	Scioto,	8,730
Geauga,	15,606	Seneca,	5,157
Green,	15,122	Shelby,	3,671
Guernsey,	18,036	Stark,	26,941
Hamilton,	52,380	Trumbull,	26,200
Hancock,	813	Tuscarawas,	14,298
Harrison,	20,920	Union,	3,192
Highland,	16,347	Warren,	21,474
Hocking,	4,008	Washington,	11,731
Holmes,	9,123	Wayne,	23,327
Huron,	13,340	Williams,	1,039
Jackson,	5,941	Wood,	1,096
Jefferson,	22,489		
Knox,	17,125		922,900
Lawrence,	5,366	Ashtabula,	
Licking,	20,864	estimated,	14,100
Logan,	6,432		
Lorain,	5,696	Total,	937,000

APPENDIX.

ATLANTIC AND MICHIGAN RAILWAY.

Extract from the Sketch of the Geographical Route of a great Railway, by which it is proposed to connect the Canals and navigable waters of the States of New York, Pennsylvania, Ohio, Indiana, Illinois, Missouri; and the Michigan, Northwest, and Missouri Territories.

"THE route commences on the Hudson river, in the vicinity of New York, at a point accessible at all seasons to steam ferry-boats, and from thence proceeds through a favourable and productive country to the valley of the Delaware river, near the southwest corner of New Jersey. Here it forms a junction with the route of the Delaware, Lehigh, and Lackawaxen canals, which are in progress in Pennsylvania, and with the Delaware and Hudson canal in New York. From thence the route ascends the valley of the Delaware to a point that affords the nearest and most favourable crossing to the valley of the Susquehannah, at or near the great bend of that river. Pursuing a westerly course through the fertile valleys of the Susquehannah and Tioga rivers, the route crosses the head waters of the Gennessee; having in its course intersected the terminating points of the Ithica and Oswego railway; the Chenango and Chemung canals in New York; the great Susquehannah canal in Pennsylvania; and several other points that afford important facilities for internal communication.

From the Gennessee river, our route enters the valley of the Alleghany, and proceeds along that river, which affords a navigable communication with Pittsburgh, the Pennsylvania canals, and the Ohio river. From the Alleghany the route intersects the outlet of

Chetauque lake, opening thereby a communication with lake Erie, and proceeds to the head waters of French creek, in Pennsylvania, from whence it again communicates with the Alleghany and the Pennsylvania canals, on the one hand, and with the harbour of Erie on the other.

The benefits that would result from the construction of a railway on the route which we have followed, and its capacity to multiply the elements of individual and national prosperity, can be best appreciated by those who have carefully observed the effects of such improvements; but that portion of our route, which remains to be considered, offers to our view results of the highest and most invaluable character.

From French creek, the western branch of the Alleghany, we proceed into the rich northern counties of Ohio, intersecting various streams, and the great canal of that State in a direction parallel to the shore of lake Erie, till we arrive at the rivers which empty into the western extremity of that lake.

Having crossed the Sandusky, Maumee, and St. Joseph rivers, tributaries to lake Erie, the route enters Indiana, passes the head waters of the Wabash and the St. Joseph of lake Michigan; crosses the canal which is to unite the Wabash river with the lakes; enters the State of Illinois, and passing along the course of the Kankakee, continues to the head of steamboat navigation on the Illinois river; from whence provision has been made for opening a communication with lake Michigan. This portion of the Railway would open to immediate occupation, immense tracts of the public lands, of the most exuberant fertility; and offers to the enterprising industry of our hardy settlers, such facilities in the pursuit of wealth and prosperity, as even the giant growth of our young and flourishing country has never afforded.

The Illinois affords good depth of water for steamboats, and its current is so slight, as to be in many places hardly perceptible. It affords, perhaps, the best navigation in America for two hundred and fifty miles, through a country of unbounded fertility, to the Mississippi river near the mouth of the Missouri, and the flourishing and important town of St. Louis.

Having accomplished this grand object, our Railway continues from near the bend of the Illinois, and at a distance of little more than sixty miles, reaches the banks of the Mississippi.

The whole distance from the Hudson river to the Mississippi, at the junction of the Rock river, is less than one thousand miles. The route extends along one of the best parallels of temperate latitude, and in a great part through the most fertile and valuable portion of our country. A Railway constructed upon this route, would connect in the most advantageous manner, the agricultural, navigating, and commercial interests of the regions bordering on the numerous rivers, canals and lakes with which it communicates, and would extend the production and dissemination of valuable commodities throughout the most distant portions of our country.

In a military, as well as a commercial point of view, the results of such a Railway would surpass the power of calculation. With such ample means for throwing any amount of military force and material, at any time, to almost any point of our frontier, with a rapidity resembling that of an express rider, we should have little occasion to claim the respect of our proudest foes, whether savage or foreign.

The whole extent of the proposed Railway could be constructed for a sum, little, if at all, exceeding that which the state of New-York has expended on her justly celebrated canals; and its cost would be trifling in comparison with its benefits, or even to the increased value which it would give to the lands which border on its route. It would, when completed, be far more beneficial in its effects on the intervening country, and on our national prosperity, than to turn the Mississippi itself in the same course. Free from the inundations, the currents, the rapids, the ice, and the sand bars of that mighty stream, the rich products of its wide spread valley would be driven to the shores of the Atlantic, with far greater speed than if wafted by the wings of the wind; and the rapid return of commercial equivalents, would spread life and prosperity over the face of the finest and fairest portion of the habitable world.

Appendix.

The distances are as follows: Miles.

From the Hudson river across the Gennessee, &c. to French creek, a branch of the Alleghany river,	400
From French creek to the Maumee river at Fort Defiance,	260
From the Maumee to the Illinois river, at the head of steamboat navigation,	270
From the Illinois river to the Mississippi river,	63
Whole distance,	993

The cost of canals, with the knowledge which our experience in constructing them has afforded, is said to average about seventeen thousand dollars per mile.

The cost of Railways, as appears by the results of some experience, various and careful estimates by skilful engineers, and by extensive contracts already entered upon, may be stated as follows:

A single Railway, or one set of tracks, with suitable turn-outs, will cost from seven to eight thousand dollars per mile.

A single Railway and turn-outs, graded sufficiently wide for two sets of tracks, will cost from ten to eleven thousand dollars per mile.

A double Railway, with two complete sets of tracks, will cost from fourteen to fifteen thousand dollars per mile. The tracks in all cases plated with wrought iron.

A Railway of the first description, extending from the Hudson to the Mississippi river, would cost $8,000,000. If of the second kind $11,000,000—and if constructed with doubly tracks throughout, would cost fifteen millions of dollars.

The largest sum is but little more than half the annual amount of the national income. With the public voice in its favour, it would not exceed the means, nor the enterprize of half a dozen of our most wealthy and respectable citizens. It does not exceed half the amount paid in a single year by the consumers of wines and spirits in our country; and, in time of war, would not pay half the expenses of a single campaign.

Appendix.

The actual average cost of transportation on a Railway does not exceed one dollar per ton, per 100 miles, exclusive of the tolls.

With this Railway in operation, merchandize could be conveyed from Philadelphia, or New-York, to the Illinois or Mississippi in a week ; and in two days more, to St. Louis, Green Bay, or the Falls of St. Anthony. Passengers and mails could be transported with still greater rapidity.

INDIAN POPULATION.

From a statement on this subject, it appears that the whole Indian Population in the United States amounts to three hundred and sixteen thousand. Of this number,

20,000	are Choctaws,	4,000	are Menomonies,
20,000	Creeks,	4,500	Crowes,
20,000	Snakes,	4,000	Arripahas,
15,000	Cherokees,	4,000	Seminoles,
15,000	Black Feet,	3,600	Chickasaws,
12,000	Chippewas,	3,000	Crees,
15,000	Sioux,	4,000	Ottawas,
12,000	Pawnees,	3,000	Algonquins,
8,000	Assinaboins,	41,600	in thirty-six small tribes.
6,500	Pottawatamies,		
5,800	Winebagoes,	80,000	west of the Rocky Mountains.
6,800	Sacs,		
5,000	Osages,		

TO THE READER.

The GUIDE FOR EMIGRANTS has been delayed by unavoidable reasons much beyond its contemplated time of publication; but it is hoped that, by the insertion of new and additional matter, its value as a *Guide* is enhanced.

A separate work that shall contain particular information of the colleges and schools, with the public and private efforts to promote education in the new States, and embrace a sketch of the early history and present condition of the religious denominations in Illinois, and the adjacent parts, with an account of the commencement of Bible, Sunday school, tract, and other benevolent operations, including biographical sketches of those who have been pioneers in the cause of truth and righteousness, but who have been called to their reward, is in contemplation.

The distance of the author from the place of publication, put it wholly out of his power to correct the proof sheets. It is hoped, however, that no material errors will have occurred.

J. M. P.

INDEX.

	Page
Introduction,	3

PART FIRST.

General, Geographical and Statistical View of the Valley of the Mississippi,	9
SECTION I.—Boundaries,	ib.
Extent,	10
Population,	11
Physical Features,	14
SECT. II.—Rivers,	15
Missouri River,	16
Mississippi River,	23
Climate,	37
Animals,	48
Observations on Lower Valley,	50
Manners and Customs,	69

PART SECOND.

General and Particular Views of the States of Illinois, Missouri, Indiana, and the adjacent States,	85
SECTION I.—Boundaries,	ib.
SECT. II.—Situation, Boundaries, and Extent of Illinois,	89
Face of the Country, and Soil,	90
Inundated Lands,	92
River and Creek Bottoms,	95
Level Prairies,	105
Rolling Prairies,	107
Barrens,	118
Timber, and Timbered Uplands,	120
Knobs, Bluffs, Ravines, and Sink-holes,	128
Stony Ground,	130

Index.

	Page
Productions,	131
Lead Manufactured,	133
Coal, Soda, &c.	135—138
Vegetable Productions,	ib.
Animals,	161
Location, Method of Farming, Building, &c.	175
Expenses of preparing Farms,	183
Cost of Buildings,	188
Manufactures,	190
Salt,	191
Steam Mills,	194
Castor Oil,	197
Cotton Spinners,	199
Climate, Diseases, &c.	200
Advice to Emigrants respecting Health,	213
Comparisons of Health between St. Louis and other Cities,	338, 239
Education,	243
Public Lands,	257
Religion and Religious Societies,	258
History of Illinois,	261
SECT. III.—Statistics of Counties, Towns, &c.	281
INDIANA,	322
Census of Indiana,	323
Religious Denominations,	326
OHIO,	327
Census of Ohio,	328

APPENDIX.

Atlantic and Michigan Railway,	329
Indian Population,	333
TO THE READER,	334

MID-AMERICAN FRONTIER

An Arno Press Collection

Andreas, A[lfred] T[heodore]. **History of Chicago.** 3 volumes. 1884-1886

Andrews, C[hristopher] C[olumbus]. **Minnesota and Dacotah.** 1857

Atwater, Caleb. **Remarks Made on a Tour to Prairie du Chien:** Thence to Washington City, in 1829. 1831

Beck, Lewis C[aleb]. **A Gazetteer of the States of Illinois and Missouri.** 1823

Beckwith, Hiram W[illiams]. **The Illinois and Indiana Indians.** 1884

Blois, John T. **Gazetteer of the State of Michigan,** in Three Parts. 1838

Brown, Jesse and A. M. Willard. **The Black Hills Trails.** 1924

Brunson, Alfred. **A Western Pioneer: Or, Incidents of the Life and Times of Rev. Alfred Brunson.** 2 volumes in one. 1872

Burnet, Jacob. **Notes on the Early Settlement of the North-Western Territory.** 1847

Cass, Lewis. **Considerations on the Present State of the Indians,** and their Removal to the West of the Mississippi. 1828

Coggeshall, William T[urner]. **The Poets and Poetry of the West.** 1860

Darby, John F[letcher]. **Personal Recollections of Many Prominent People Whom I Have Known.** 1880

Eastman, Mary. **Dahcotah:** Or, Life and Legends of the Sioux Around Fort Snelling. 1849

Ebbutt, Percy G. **Emigrant Life in Kansas.** 1886

Edwards, Ninian W[irt]. **History of Illinois, From 1778 to 1833:** And Life and Times of Ninian Edwards. 1870

Ellsworth, Henry William. **Valley of the Upper Wabash, Indiana.** 1838

Esarey, Logan, ed. **Messages and Letters of William Henry Harrison.** 2 volumes. 1922

Flower, George. **The Errors of Emigrants.** [1841]

Hall, Baynard Rush (Robert Carlton, pseud.). **The New Purchase:** Or Seven and a Half Years in the Far West. 2 volumes in one. 1843

Haynes, Fred[erick] Emory. **James Baird Weaver.** 1919

Heilbron, Bertha L., ed. **With Pen and Pencil on the Frontier in 1851:** The Diary and Sketches of Frank Blackwell Mayer. 1932

Hinsdale, B[urke] A[aron]. **The Old Northwest:** The Beginnings of Our Colonial System. [1899]

Johnson, Harrison. **Johnson's History of Nebraska.** 1880

Lapham, I[ncrease] A[llen]. **Wisconsin: Its Geography and Topography, History, Geology, and Mineralogy.** 1846

Mansfield, Edward D. **Memoirs of the Life and Services of Daniel Drake.** 1855

Marshall, Thomas Maitland, ed. **The Life and Papers of Frederick Bates.** 2 volumes in one. 1926

McConnel, J[ohn] L[udlum.] **Western Characters: Or, Types of Border Life in the Western States.** 1853

Miller, Benjamin S. **Ranch Life in Southern Kansas and the Indian Territory.** 1896

Neill, Edward Duffield. **The History of Minnesota.** 1858

Parker, Nathan H[owe]. **The Minnesota Handbook, For 1856-7.** 1857

Peck, J[ohn] M[ason]. **A Guide for Emigrants.** 1831

Pelzer, Louis. **Marches of the Dragoons in the Mississippi Valley.** 1917

Perkins, William Rufus and Barthinius L. Wick. **History of the Amana Society.** 1891

Rister, Carl Coke. **Land Hunger: David L. Payne and the Oklahoma Boomers.** 1942

Schoolcraft, Henry R[owe]. **Personal Memoirs of a Residence of Thirty Years With the Indian Tribes on the American Frontiers.** 1851

Smalley, Eugene V. **History of the Northern Pacific Railroad.** 1883

[Smith, William Rudolph]. **Observations on the Wisconsin Territory.** 1838

Steele, [Eliza R.] **A Summer Journey in the West.** 1841

Streeter, Floyd Benjamin. **The Kaw: The Heart of a Nation.** 1941

[Switzler, William F.] **Switzler's Illustrated History of Missouri, From 1541 to 1877.** 1879

Tallent, Annie D. **The Black Hills.** 1899

Thwaites, Reuben Gold. **On the Storied Ohio.** 1903

Todd, Charles S[tewart] and Benjamin Drake. **Sketches of the Civil and Military Services of William Henry Harrison.** 1840

Wetmore, Alphonso, compiler. **Gazetteer of the State of Missouri.** 1837

Wilder, D[aniel] W[ebster]. **The Annals of Kansas.** 1886

Woollen, William Wesley. **Biographical and Historical Sketches of Early Indiana.** 1883

Wright, Robert M[arr]. **Dodge City.** 1913